FUTURE WARFARE
Anthology

Revised Edition

MAJOR GENERAL
ROBERT H. SCALES, JR.

U.S. ARMY WAR COLLEGE
CARLISLE BARRACKS, PENNSYLVANIA

*****

The views expressed within this publication are those of the authors and do not necessarily reflect the official policy or position of the Department of the Army, the Department of Defense, or the U.S. Government. This report is cleared for public release; distribution is unlimited.

*****

ISBN 1-58487-026-5

CONTENTS

FOREWORD

This Revised Anthology is about the future of military operations in the opening decades of the 21st Century. Its purpose is not to predict the future, but to speculate on the conduct of military operations as an instrument of national policy in a world absent massive thermonuclear and conventional superpower confrontation characteristic of the Cold War. Also absent are indirect constraints imposed by that confrontation on virtually all political-military relationships, not solely those between superpower principals.

It is likely not possible to predict the future. Its uncertainties increase the number of assumptions that need to be made and taken as fact in order to think ahead. So, all futures investigations are really speculation.

Further, looking ahead, it is necessary to accommodate the past. For the present is the leading edge of the past, as well as the line of departure to the future. With us are legacies of the past; we struggle with them daily in problems of the present. Dialectically, accommodating the past inhibits free thinking about the future; but ignoring, or assuming away the past, foredooms thinking about the future to the trash bin of non-credibility.

This foreword is not to critique General Bob Scales' essays. It is rather to illuminate perceptions about past and present to help evaluate the intellectual strength and relevance of speculations about the future.

What's in the baggage? What legacies need be accommodated? Our military heritage reflects three first order legacies: Napoleon, the Industrial Revolution, and Modern Technology. Our Napoleonic heritage, observations from Jomini and Clausewitz, amended by our own unique post-Napoleonic experience, provided a set of military concepts embracing mass conscript military forces in time of emergency. Forces whose primary modus would be destruction of enemy armed forces and infrastructures, largely by overwhelming numbers—of soldiers, of units, of weapons systems.

Secondly, the systemic processes of the Industrial Revolution have reinforced and facilitated our convictions about mass armies and the nation in arms, and provided the material means for the ultimate battle—annihilation and unconditional surrender.

Thirdly, Modern Technology enabled these concepts, beginning with rifled shoulder weapons in the 19th Century, advancing to thermo-nuclear weapons aboard intercontinental ballistic missiles in the 20th Century.

Realities of post-World War II Soviet conventional power, overlain with thermo-nuclear weapons, made apparent that no longer could we plan to win by mass forces and fire power—numbers alone, even with the aid of allies, were insufficient. Then thermo-nuclear weapons aboard intercontinental ballistic missiles extended the battle of annihilation to a potential Armageddon, from which there would be few survivors, and no winners. Thus the concept of Limited War—something short of Armageddon—emerged during Korea and Vietnam.

Limited War raised inevitable questions: what political goals are sought by the use of arms; what does it mean to win; how is winning to be accomplished; what price are we willing to pay? Political collapse of the Soviet Union, an end to the Cold War, ensuing uncertainties about Russian political and military futures, and the growth of militarization of conflict (with modern weapons) in the Third World, especially in the Middle East—all made the suite of Limited War questions more acute. For, absent Cold War superpower confrontation, there were far fewer political constraints bearing on Limited War confrontations. This was a clear call to revisit primary national political-military policies in a vastly changed world.

It was Secretary of War John C. Calhoun who, circa 1818, laid down the basic underpinnings of a military policy whose implementing processes and structures provide most of the inhibiting legacies confronting us as we speculate about the future from the vantage point of the present. Secretary Calhoun's policy saw the Navy as our first line of defense. There would be a very small regular Army, expanded by volunteer militia when required. Conscripts replaced volunteer militia in the Root reforms of the early 20th Century; and structurally, forces were denominated into regulars, National Guard and Reserves; nonetheless the Calhoun "Expansible Army" idea, now the Mobilization System, survives. Present and recent past experience suggests that most processes of the Calhoun system are anachronisms—Second Wave systems in a Third Wave World. In particular: the individual replacement system; Service and Joint logistics systems; the Defense Department materiel research, development and acquisition system; command and control systems that are now overwhelmed by burgeoning information technology; and the continuing search for relevant strategic and operational level doctrine.

Meantime the national security policy of the United States has changed. Required by the National Defense Reform Act of 1986, there is now an annual published statement of national security policy by the incumbent administration. The current statement, circa 1999, sets forth an interventionist policy. Secretary Calhoun's policy was one of protection of the United States from foreign aggression. The 1999 policy statement sees the United States as the keeper of world order, peace, health, stability, and a host of other conditions whose relationship to U.S. national security interests, vital or not, is in most cases obscure, and in too many cases nonexistent.

Most of General Bob Scales' essays are attempts to define military operational concepts that might be employed to execute such an engagement strategy. All the Limited War questions cited above are obviously relevant: what are the political goals, what does it mean to win; how is winning to be accomplished; what price are we willing to pay?

These are tough questions; there are others. For unless we are willing to address ourselves to fundamental changes required in obviously dysfunctional processes of the old mobilization system, is anything like what General Scales suggests even possible? Among many examples, just one: if we are unwilling to look for effective alternatives to the individual replacement system, alternatives which will field effective units, then is it even possible to consider the operational concepts suggested within these essays? The effectiveness of units is driven largely by budget. Combatant forces are ever overstructured and understrength. If we are unwilling to provide enough end-strength (budget) to fill all the structure, then is it even reasonable to speculate on full-up units, well-trained, ready to deploy quickly, without providing fill-up personnel and equipment, and adequate time for training units to effectiveness?

Finally, one ultimate tough question. Is it an appropriate policy for the United States to undertake to regulate world affairs? Meddle in other nations' business? Keep everyone in every nation quiet, stable, happy, prosperous, healthy? If that is considered an appropriate role for the United States, then do we have, and are we willing to sacrifice ourselves in order to expend on others, the resources—requisite time, energy, money? But most importantly, can we find the wisdom to comprehend problems we are likely to encounter, the intellectual power to know for certain what to do, and the leadership capability to literally save the world from itself?

DONN A. STARRY,
General, USA, Retired
Cavalry Hill, Fairfax Station, Virginia

August 2000

PROLOGUE

As I complete my third year as the Commandant of the Army War College, it is a great pleasure to introduce this new version of *Future Warfare*. The first *Future Warfare Anthology*, published in May 1999, received much greater distribution than anyone expected. Now in its second printing, it continues to be in great demand among readers both at home and abroad. *Future Warfare* has also proven to be popular among the Internet users who surf our homepage. Because of easy Internet access, it has been translated into two versions of Chinese and published as a text in both Taiwan and the People's Republic of China.

This revised edition republishes the complete content that appeared within the 1999 edition. Additionally, six new chapters have been developed during this past year and, subsequently, are included within this new edition. I am also grateful to General (R) Donn A. Starry for graciously consenting to write a new Foreword for this revised edition.

Each essay was developed and tailored for a specific reading audience. The collection presents a heuristic argument that has been refined after many wargames, simulations, symposia and extensive overseas travel, dialogue and study. The consistent thesis that pervades all of the articles, however, is simply that ten years after the end of the Cold War, we are beginning to see the faint outlines of an emerging and entirely new transformation of warfare. It is my hope that this new book will contribute some insights into the ongoing and healthy "battle of ideas" within our national security community. The conclusions from this debate will have a lasting impact upon how our military forces will be shaped to accommodate the new realities of precision age warfare.

ROBERT H. SCALES, JR.
Major General, U.S.A.
Commandant
U.S. Army War College

July 28, 2000

REVISED ACKNOWLEDGEMENTS

This revised anthology assembles a collection of essays that have been developed and published over a period of almost four years. The chapters are presented in the same sequence that would be used during a staff briefing. Each essay represents a reflection of my evolving thoughts regarding future warfare and the urgent need to explore the development of a new generation of military capabilities.

The thesis within each article was tailored for a specific reading audience, but, in a broader sense, each message also represents my attempt to make a professional contribution to our national defense debate. During the next five years, without question, the emerging conclusions from this "battle of ideas" will shape the formulation of U.S. National Security Strategy for the next two decades. These maturing concepts, moreover, will define the research and developmental boundaries that will create the next generation of defense capabilities.

To be sure, there is a holistic pattern of thought that has stimulated and refined the overall content within each essay. We must develop a long-range vision of America's Army beyond 2010 that will communicate both a realistic outline of future warfare and the broad organizational concepts that will underscore future capabilities. I believe the next decade will find the Army emerging as the most important member of future Joint Task Forces because the U.S. will not be able to collapse an opponent's national will to fight without orchestrating both lethal firepower and agile ground maneuver. Without question, there will be a dramatic increase in future landpower responsibilities because of the *Way* we will commit our military *Means* to achieve our political *Ends*.

Before you begin reading this book, please permit me to thank the following publishing sources because they have willingly granted their permission to reprint the essays that appear within this revised anthology:

- *Strategic Review Journal*

- *The Armed Forces Journal International*

- Center For Strategic and International Studies

- *Parameters*

- *The Army RD&A Journal*

- *Newsday* Daily Newspaper

- *Defence Systems International*

- *National Security Studies Quarterly*

- *Joint Forces Quarterly*

- *Jane's Defence Weekly*

Furthermore, I am indebted to many colleagues who have shared my professional interests and helped me refine the acuity of my intellectual investigations. It is not feasible to list the names of these individuals within this brief space but my circle of "fellow travelers" literally extends around the world. I do, however, want to acknowledge the faculty and staff from the Strategic Studies Institute, U.S. Army War College. Their assistance helped me transform the idea for this revised anthology into a published reality.

Robert H. Scales, Jr.
Major General, U.S.A.
July 2000

INTRODUCTION

TO THE FIRST EDITION

We stand at the brink of a new century as well as a new millennium. The pace of technological change is steadily accelerating, while the strategic environment remains opaque and uncertain. Once again the United States is between major wars. Yet, the current period is not the first time the American military have confronted an inter-war period. Between 1919 and 1941 the services developed a wide range of capabilities from carrier aviation and amphibious warfare to combined arms tactics that stood the country well in the terrible conflict that followed the bombing of Pearl Harbor. Similarly, in the inter-war periods between 1953 and 1965, and 1973 and 1991, the American military confronted a wide disparity of challenges. Again, the development of airmobile and then air-land battle underlined the importance of peacetime innovation to battlefield performance.

But unlike these earlier inter-war periods, the U.S. military faces no clear threats at present. Thus, the problems of innovation and adaptation that have beset military organizations over the past two centuries present even greater uncertainties and ambiguities. Unlike the American military of the 1930s which confronted threats in the Pacific as well as in Europe against which the services could design solid concepts of operation, today's armed forces do not know against whom they will fight, when they will fight, and even where they will fight.

Throughout U.S. history the American military services have had an unfortunate penchant for not being ready for the next war. Part of the problem has had to do with factors beyond their control: the American polity has been notoriously slow to respond to the challenges posed by dangerous enemies. On the other hand, American military institutions have been surprisingly optimistic in weighing their preparedness as they embarked on the nation's wars. The first battles involving American military forces hardly give reason for optimism. The initial defeats in the War of 1812, Bull Run, Belleau Woods, Savo Island, Kasserine Pass, Task Force Smith, and Landing Zone Albany hardly suggest unalloyed success by America's military in preparing for the next war. Admittedly, in each of its major wars the United States did enjoy the luxury of time to repair the deficiencies that showed up so glaringly in the country's first battles. Unfortunately, in the twenty-first century the United States may not have that luxury of time.

The Gulf War does stand out as an anomaly in America's wars. In that conflict, service leaders were profoundly pessimistic about the losses their forces might suffer were war to occur. In the end, the armed forces of the United States smashed the Iraqis in a *blitzkrieg* campaign, the ground portion of which lasted barely 100 hours. But the very ease of that victory may carry with it dangerous seeds. The current belief that technology alone and the capabilities of distant strike will allow American military forces to fight simple, decisive campaigns with few casualties flies in the face of 3,000 years of accumulated military history. Such idle hopes are the direct result of the "victory disease" that broke out in the immediate aftermath of the Gulf War. If the American military are to innovate in an intelligent and effective fashion, they cannot afford to believe their own press releases from that conflict.

Military institutions have always had considerable problems in adapting and innovating during inter-war periods, particularly during periods of technological change. The catastrophe of the First World War is a particularly good example. It took three long years of interminable slaughter before Europe's armies began to understand and adapt to the complexities of combined-arms warfare. Even then, the operational solutions took another twenty years of peacetime innovation to work out. Unfortunately for everyone, it was the Germans who worked out the equation of tactics, doctrinal change, and technology to its fullest in the operational successes of *blitzkrieg* war that won such devastating victories between 1939 and 1941.

The requirements for successful innovation, as well as the ingredients for unsuccessful innovation, have begun to emerge from the work of military historians over the past several decades. Successful innovation in times of rapid technological change possesses a number of characteristics, the least important of which is technology. The German *Blitzkrieg* resulted from a sophisticated historically based analysis of what had happened on the battlefields of 1918, a solidly grounded system of professionalism that judged officers on the basis of their intellectual attainment as well as their tactical proficiency, and a careful, ruthlessly honest analysis of what was really happening in exercises and combat. Technology was no more than an enabler that allowed the Germans to realize the potential of successful innovation in combined arms. And it is well to remember that French artillery and armored fighting vehicles were superior to those possessed by the Wehrmacht in May 1940. It was the tactical and doctrinal concepts that the French got wrong, and the result was military catastrophe. But it was not the Germans alone who successfully innovated in the inter-war period. The American military in most respects equaled the Germans and in some respects outshone their future opponents in their willingness to examine doctrinal concepts in the harsh light of actual capabilities.

Unfortunately, there is an emerging belief in the current American defense community that capabilities and platforms represent the *essential* component in how the United States needs to design its forces for war in the next century. To put it bluntly, this approach, no matter how much easier it may make defense planning, will not do. Capabilities, no matter how impressive to the engineer or technologist, may prove irrelevant in the next war. In fact, they may prove worse than irrelevant, because technological capabilities that are irrelevant to the war at hand will have involved the expenditure of sums better spent on other systems and capabilities. As with so much of the art of war, the best may be the enemy of the good. In the end technology is no more than an enabler—helpful in extending coherent, intelligent concepts of operations, but useless in forces without training or intellectual preparation. Vision and serious thinking about the future of war in the next century are the crucial components to insure vibrant military innovation in the next century.

Whatever approaches the American military take to innovation, war will occur. And it will provide a harsh audit. Almost certainly the next war will take the United States by surprise. U.S. military institutions may well have prepared for some other form of warfare, in some other location. To paraphrase Omar Bradley: it may well be the wrong war, in the wrong place, at the wrong time. But there it will be, and the American military will have to fight that conflict on its terms rather than their own. Unfortunately, military history is replete with examples of military institutions that have refused to adapt to the real conditions of war, but rather have attempted to impose their own paradigm—no matter how irrelevant or illsuited to the actual conditions.

If we cannot predict where the next war will occur or what form it will take, there are some things for which the American military can prepare as they enter the next millennium. Obviously, the services have to prepare the physical condition and training of soldiers, marines, sailors, and airmen. But equally important, they must prepare the minds of the next generation of military leaders to handle the challenges of the battlefield. And that mental preparation will be more important than all the technological wizardry U.S. forces can bring to bear in combat. Most important in that intellectual preparation must be a recognition of what will not change: the fundamental nature of war, the fact that fog, friction, ambiguity, and uncertainty will dominate the battlefields of the future just as they have those of the past.

There are at present many who are arguing that technology offers America's military forces an easy route to solving the intractable tactical and operational problems that will be raised by war in the next century. They believe that technology, computers, and other information systems will allow the United States a complete transparency over not only the enemy's forces but his intentions as well. The problem with such views is that America's opponents in the next war are already at work studying how the U.S. military works. As the services discovered in the Vietnam War, military organizations are human and therefore adaptive and creative, even though they may not possess sophisticated technology. They may also have the motivation of religion or ideology to back up their capacity to adapt to the battlefield. Nevertheless, those who argue for a technological view of future war clearly believe that history is irrelevant and that the new technologies will allow American forces to exist in a frictionless environment, one in which our opponents cannot adapt. However, 3,000 years of history underline that fog, friction, ambiguity, and uncertainty have always formed the underlying typography of war. Furthermore, modern science has underlined that the ambiguities and uncertainties of war only reflect the actual state of the universe. Thus, the view that technology will allow absolute knowledge and predictability is one that requires a dismissal understanding of not only history, but science as well.

When the next war occurs, the United States may well face opponents who will have prepared themselves to fight on their home ground. Wars in the next century will not look like the Gulf War, where an inept and unmotivated opponent collapsed almost as soon as the fighting began. Americans should not forget what the North Koreans, the Chinese, and the North Vietnamese were able to do against technologically superior American forces in the 1950s and 1960s. The ambiguous nature, however, of future challenges (the who, what, and where of the equation) demands serious intellectual preparation for war. As Sir Michael Howard has suggested on a number of occasions, war is not only the most physically demanding of professions, it is also the most intellectually demanding of professions. To make the next century "an American Century," U.S. military organizations must engage in serious debate. They must examine the past with something more than idle curiosity. They must understand that technology is only an enabler. And they must tie the world of conceptualization and technology to a solid understanding of the fundamental nature of war and the harsh reality of muddy boots.

Major General Robert Scales has been a willing participant in this debate. He has been one of the few to stand up and question the easy assumptions that characterize so much of what passes for thinking at the present moment. The articles that this book has brought together represent the work of a scholar-soldier who has devoted his life to thinking long and hard about the fundamental business of his profession, the profession of arms. It is a book that army, marines, air force, and naval officers must read. And if they do not agree with everything that General Scales suggests, at least they will begin the process of debate within their own minds. And that is where those who wish to think seriously about preparing for war in the next century must begin.

Williamson Murray
Harold K. Johnson Professor
 of Military History
U.S. Army Military History Institute
Carlisle Barracks, Pennsylvania

PREFACE

TO THE FIRST EDITION

Between the Fall of 1995 and the Summer of 1997, I led a remarkable organization charged by the Army Chief of Staff to delve into the distant future in order to postulate the course of warfare beyond the year 2010. The Army After Next (AAN) investigation has stimulated a rich intellectual debate within the defense community. What follows is a collection of essays and articles either written by me or co-authored with a small band of trusted colleagues who sought to meet the intent of the Army leadership.

The AAN project remains controversial today due in part because it differs considerably in scope, period, methodology and focus from similar future gazing efforts by the Army and other services during the past few years. Controversy began with the time period of our observation. We chose a far more distant perch, the years 2020-2025, so as to move comfortably beyond the acrimony usually associated with debates over existing or near term programs and budgets. We did not anticipate that a real revolution in military affairs could be even a remote possibility in less than half a generation. Also, with few exceptions, we felt that for at least the next decade the nation would be able to achieve its security goals with the materiel and structures on hand today. Some time after 2010, however, the huge mountain of Cold War equipment accumulated during the past quarter century will begin to wear out and need replacement or refurbishment. Thus a focus comfortably beyond 2010 would give us the perspective necessary to forecast what new structures and materiel the Army will need "next."

Initially, AAN studies and gaming focused on the strategic level of war. This proved to be an enormous cultural shift for a service which takes great pride in having brought about a renaissance in the art of war at the operational level with the development of Airland Battle doctrine during the waning days of the Cold War. But the secure strategic anchors of the Cold War as manifested by the great global war plans had been wrenched from their moorings by the time the Berlin Wall fell. To our minds the Post Cold War Army needed to reset its strategic moorings and derive a clear understanding of its strategic relevance to America's future national policy before it could reasonably be expected to devise a new operational method for fighting on land.

We created some nervousness when we committed ourselves to testing our hypotheses about the future in a rigorous synthetic environment of force-on-force, free play war games. These were enormously elaborate and complex affairs conducted at the Army War College and elsewhere that often involved hundreds of players, gamers, and observers as well as some of the most sophisticated gaming and simulations models and facilities available in the world. We made sure that our "virtual" enemy was competent and credible. He was free to engage us using any style of war consistent with his own culture, means and national strategic ends. Often our AAN battle force did not do well against such competent opposition but the experience convinced us that we were pursuing a meaningful course whenever we beat him cleanly and fairly.

Each exercise would be followed by a period of validation and reassessment by a cadre of scientists and operational artists charged with refining our hypotheses and developing a new set of structural and doctrinal parameters for the next yearly gaming cycle. The process was iterative and dialectical. We began the gaming virtually unconstrained. For instance, during the first war game we assumed that in 2020 we would have the capability to deploy a close combat battle force directly from the

Continental United States into a distant theater of war ready to fight. While such a capability fit the requirements of our national strategy, scientists in our group determined that such a capability was neither affordable nor technically practicable by 2020. Therefore, for the next game we were obliged to shorten the operational reach of our force by inserting an intermediate staging base with a jump-off point between the Continental United States and the battle area.

Technical changes demanded doctrinal changes. Adding an intermediate base to our strategic deployment scheme slowed our rate of strategic closure and opened the prospect of exposing our intermediate bases to the enemy's weapons of mass destruction delivered by long-range cruise and ballistic missiles. These realities in turn demanded a substantial change in our postulated warfighting doctrine and caused us to search out other imaginative technical solutions to these new and unforeseen variables in our warfighting equation. Thus, over time and with due deliberation our AAN study group derived a credible strategic environment for a war in the next century. Subsequently, we postulated a concept for fighting the conflict and refined structural and materiel requirements to allow this new style of war to be prosecuted successfully on some future battlefield.

The knowledge gained from four rich years of AAN experimentation allows us now to begin to move from the esoteric to the concrete, from the general to the specific, from strategic to operational and from the distant future to a period closer to the present. Granted, many of our ideas are as yet indistinct. Some will require major technological advances to become wholly feasible. Others will require time and additional gaming before they can be considered mature enough for experimentation in an operational environment. Yet with time to reflect I have come to the conclusion that many of the concepts derived by the AAN effort for the distant future increasingly seem to have remarkable currency today. Some examples may illustrate this point. In the articles that follow we postulate the rise of a "Major Competitor," a nation or nation-like opponent that could well have the means and the will to present a serious strategic challenge in a region of vital interest to the United States some time beyond 2010. However, recent events in the Middle East, the Balkans and elsewhere make a convincing argument that legitimate strategic challenges may not wait until the end of the next decade to mature into a real challenge to our national security interests.

Another insight: Throughout the AAN study process we took as an article of faith that a true revolution in maneuver warfare could not occur until certain leaps ahead in technology were made in military science necessary to operationalize most of our warfighting concepts. However, there is much that we can do now to make the Army's structures and doctrine more receptive to the opportunities offered by technologies already at hand or just over the horizon. Any military revolution that we expect to mature beyond the end of the next decade must set its azimuth firmly in place today or in the near future. It takes half a generation to educate a battalion commander or train a platoon sergeant. At least that long is needed to produce a new weapon, even one derived from today's technology. Taken together, from today's headlines or from insights gained from our intensive and introspective look into the future of warfare, I am convinced that the argument is compelling for us to accelerate our research. We must examine some of the critical areas that demand attention now rather than in the years beyond 2010–especially those areas related to the shape and purpose of our national defense structures and our landpower structures.

If the Army is to remain relevant to the security needs of the nation we must begin now to accelerate the speed with which we can project legitimate, powerful and balanced forces to threatened regions overseas. There are two near term alternatives for achieving this goal. First, we can continue to maintain and exploit overseas bases currently in our possession. Bases, particularly those within or close to areas whose stability is vital to our national interests, offer a launch platform as well as an observation post very close to a potential theater of war. Second, we can reduce the time it takes for units stationed in the U.S. and overseas to arrive on the scene of conflict prepared to fight. Experience in recent wars tells us that maximum strategic speed can best be achieved by projecting units organized into the smallest self-contained entities of all arms capable of sustained combat. Today we possess units that can arrive quickly but have very little capacity to fight sustained combat against significant opposition. Or, we can project units capable of sustained combat but which cannot arrive quickly enough to prevent an enemy force from achieving his initial wartime operational objectives.

We must commit ourselves to repackaging our combat forces into the smallest discrete entities of all arms capable of sustained, autonomous operations. Recent experience tells us that we habitually organize our ground and air units into packages of about five thousand. We have learned that anything less becomes unsustainable or leaves out an important combat function and anything much larger becomes too cumbersome and inflexible for rapid projection. We must learn to leverage the information age to permit us to leave behind either in the U.S. or in a forward base overseas much of the impedimenta that slows us down and prevents us from intervening in a theater of war quickly and decisively. During the Gulf War it took us nearly six months to build up a theater of war mainly because we had to bring all of the manpower and materiel to construct a structural analog of one of our stateside logistical and support facilities. For that reason and others an American armored division weighted over a hundred thousand tons and the materiel to keep it in the field for the length of a campaign weighed almost as much. We transported, mainly by sea, over six hundred thousand tons of ammunition to the Gulf and brought most of it back unexpended. Likewise, we transported tens of thousands of shipping containers into the theater and had to open most of them on the docks to find out what was in them.

The image of the air campaign is one of power projected quickly and efficiently into the Gulf. In fact, however, air power was just as constrained by the realities of our logistical umbilical cord as that of the ground force. Practically every weapon delivered by air began its journey to Iraq by sea from a U.S. port. Over forty tons of aviation fuel were burned to drop one ton of bombs within the theater.

So a force tailored for strategic projection must be as lean as possible consistent with the need also to possess the combat power to dominate an enemy force with overwhelming lethality and agility. To achieve this goal a strategic force must leave behind those structures that do not contribute directly to success on the battlefield. Today information age technologies allow finance, personnel, intelligence, communications, and some supply functions to be performed outside the immediate confines of the close battle area.

The precision revolution allows much of the munitions train that traditionally accompanies ground units to be shrunk considerably. Air power can provide much of the distant supporting fires a ground force will need to maintain firepower dominance without demanding a mass of munitions to be carried along with the intervening force. But as recent experience has shown, air delivered munitions are heavy, expensive and rare. Plus, our experience has demonstrated dramatically that the more expensive the munitions and the more distant the source of delivery the less responsive the source of firepower will be to soldiers on the ground. Fortunately technology is available today to make precision cheaper, smaller and more available to ground forces. This capability becomes all the more desirable as our future enemies learn to disperse and go to ground in an effort to lessen the destructive effects of precision delivered from the air.

Once in the presence of the enemy these early arriving forces will have to face the reality of close combat on land. As the article "A Sword With Two Edges" contends, the introduction of ground forces into combat does not need to imply that the cost of the operation in terms of human life now becomes prohibitively expensive. First, it must be obvious after recent experience that the time it takes to bring a campaign to closure is, in itself, a cause of friction and a producer of casualties. An air campaign takes time because it is an instrument of attrition and attrition demands a protracted period to kill and destroy enough of the enemy force to break his will and force him to capitulate. A thinking enemy with a will to resist will use the gift of time to his own advantage. Also, air attacks are not free. To be sure, today we are ahead in the technological contest to protect pilots with radar jamming and stealth. But, again, we must expect that given time, ingenuity, and the necessity driven by a will to survive our enemies will be induced to develop the technical and tactical means to prevail under air attack while making the cost of a prolonged air campaign more and more expensive to our side.

Yet the image still exists of the helicopter pilots being dragged through the streets of Mogadishu or, more contemporaneously, the image of the horrific opening scene in "Saving Private Ryan" where the true horror of face-to-face ground combat is driven into the psyche of the movie goer. I am increasingly convinced, however, that the technologies and structures available today, suitably modified, offer the potential for ground forces to interpose themselves into the midst of an enemy's ground force, isolate him and collapse his will very quickly with an absolutely minimal loss of life.

How would such a force differ from forces today? First, the force would be balanced. It would possess the means both to strike the enemy with great precision but also to maneuver throughout the enemy's area of operations with equal competence and precision. Balanced forces are always joint, that is, they possess the flexibility and means to confront the enemy with a variety of capabilities from all dimensions of combat: air, sea, land, and space. Second, the force must have the ability to apply all dimensions nearly simultaneously so as to deny the enemy the opportunity to confront us sequentially, one dimension at a time.

A force balanced between firepower and maneuver prevents an adaptive enemy from optimizing his force to prevail against American firepower alone. Centuries of experience in war tells us that an enemy arrayed to absorb firepower is immediately vulnerable to a force optimized for maneuver. As an enemy scatters and goes to ground he becomes paralyzed, incapable of maneuver and thus a vulnerable target for small mobile forces capable of interposing themselves amongst and between an immobile enemy. Simultaneously, continuous and balanced pressure gives the enemy two unacceptable alternatives. He can attack our forces deposed in his midst and suffer defeat by precision fires or he can remain static only to wither in place or be systematically found, fixed and overwhelmed by decisive and balanced ground and air attack.

The articles that follow make the case for a balanced force in future war. Our thesis is reinforced by Joint Vision 2010 which echoes the nearer term case for a balance between the two active offensive components of joint warfighting, "precision strike" and "dominant maneuver." However, if one looks at what we are doing rather than saying the issue of balance is much in doubt. Today we can strike with precision as evidenced by our performance in the Gulf War and thereafter. But we cannot maneuver with equal precision, or with the speed necessitated by the demands of a greatly expanded and infinitely more lethal battlefield. More troubling is the realization that we most certainly cannot maneuver with the assurance that we have done all that we can to lessen the cost of human life. Thus we are continually faced with two conflicting alternatives: attack by precision from the air and achieve no decision or introduce ground troops to ensure a decision but risk unnecessary casualties. This assertion is all the more disturbing when one looks out into the programmatic future and sees that firepower programs, particularly aircraft and platforms to support aerial combat, dominate our future hardware acquisition programs.

Granted, there is much that we in the Army can do to make our existing landpower forces more suitable to the future conflict environment. We must begin soon to lighten our force. We must repackage our combat forces into more projectable and more tactically mobile entities. We must increase the proportion of our close combat force that maneuvers by air. We must better exploit information technologies so that we will be able to see the enemy about us with greater clarity and immediacy. We must improve our system of battle command and our method for inoculating our leaders to deal with the shock, confusion and complexity of modern close combat so they will be better able to use the instruments within their command.

But if we are to provide our national leaders in the future with the instruments necessary to prosecute our national military strategy we must ultimately refocus our intellectual and fiscal resources in a concerted effort to rebalance our fighting forces. It is important to remember in this high-tech-era that certain timeless principles still govern the course of conflict. The first among these is that war will be ultimately and foremost a test of will. History tells us repeatedly that a military that can only attack by fire alone is a military capable of achieving only fleeting advantage. A balanced force, on the other hand, capable of paralyzing by fire and gaining and holding ground by maneuver, can translate temporary into lasting advantage by collapsing the enemy's will to resist. A damaged enemy with his territory intact will continue to resist. The same enemy ejected from or dislocated within his territory will fall victim to the paralysis that always must precede defeat. Only when paralysis occurs can our side gain the overwhelming decision we seek at minimum cost in life. As the fourth essay in this anthology contends, our future arsenal must include a 21st Century sword with two edges: one side—precision firepower; and the other—equally precise maneuver. Unless we apply both in balance and harmony future wars might well devolve into massive wars of attrition.

Current events only serve to reinforce and add an element of urgency to what we have learned from our AAN studies. These events now tell us that we may not have until 2020 to implement the strategic and operational AAN tenets. In fact, the future is now and we must begin immediately to make today's weapons and structures as suitable as possible to fit our newly emerging image of future warfare.

ROBERT H. SCALES, JR.
Major General, U.S.A.
Commandant
U.S. Army War College

Chapter One

SPEED AND POWER: PRIMAL FORCES IN THE NEW AMERICAN STYLE OF WAR

Major General Robert H. Scales, Jr.

Under the title "Learning From Past Mistakes,"
a condensed version of this essay was published by:
JANE'S DEFENCE WEEKLY
Volume 34, Issue Number 2
12 July 2000

SPEED AND POWER: PRIMAL FORCES
IN THE NEW AMERICAN STYLE OF WAR

The nature of war is changing and the rate of change is more rapid than any similar period of modern history. Evidence of how profoundly contemporary events have affected America's style of war is clearly documented within the historical record of American conflict since the end of the Second World War. For almost forty years we planned for a return to a total war with the Soviets—a war that never came—while we evolved, through bloody practical experience, a new style of limited liability wars fought for ends not necessarily vital to our national interests at the time. Only recently, thanks to our experience in Kosovo, have we just begun to associate our years of experience in limited wars as perhaps the most relevant analog for understanding the nature and character of wars we will continue to fight for generations to come.

Our bloody education began in Korea. We started this war in the European style with division level operations supported by concentrations of air and surface delivered firepower established by norms developed from our war against the Germans. By the winter of 1951, the contours of a future stalemate were already discernable. Our opponent had become an adaptive enemy capable of absorbing doctrinal doses of killing power while remaining effective on the battlefield. Back in the states, the American populace increasingly became unwilling to tolerate unlimited expenditures of life in order to achieve unclear ends. The combination of these two realities compelled military leaders in the field to radically reverse the established doctrinal relationships between fire and maneuver. Subsequently, attacks were lead by infantry platoons supported by hundreds of guns and aircraft whose killing effects were orchestrated by an increasingly complex and cumbersome firepower system that was uniquely American.

> **In The Future, A Thinking, Adaptive Aggressor Will Occupy Quickly, Gain Control Of The Ground To Subdue The Population And Disperse To Avoid Destruction By Fire.**

The lessons of Korea, unfortunately, did not endure thanks to our preoccupation with fighting the big war in Europe. So we were reeducated, often tragically, in Vietnam. In time, the Army shifted away from the wasteful large-scale search and destroy operations to the use of smaller platoon sized units to find and fix the enemy followed by copious doses of air and artillery to finish him. But, as in Korea, the process took too long. Given the gift of time, a dedicated enemy with the will to endure and absorb punishment by fire eventually learned to maneuver at will without the benefit of a firepower advantage.

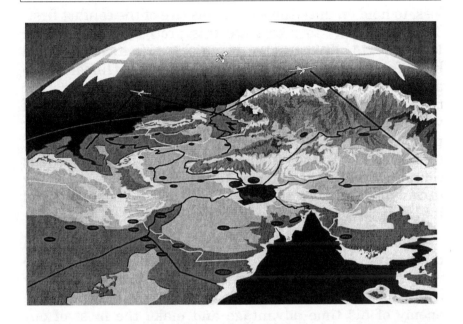

Our successful performance in Just Cause and Desert Storm shows that by the end of the Cold War we had begun to learn the lessons for winning limited liability wars. The first lesson was to win quickly by the application of overwhelming combat power. The object was to collapse the enemy's will to resist before his soldiers became inured to the psychological trauma induced by firepower and before he could learn of our weaknesses and adapt his method of war on the battlefield to offset our firepower advantage.

Kosovo reinforced the need to win quickly by applying overwhelming power in the shortest time. But this conflict also demonstrated that our enemies are beginning to relearn the lessons taught by successful enemies during past wars of limited liability. As we have become more proficient in finding, tracking and striking the enemy, the enemy has also learned how to mitigate the effects of

5

superior firepower by adapting the tenets taught to them by the Chinese, Vietnamese, Afghans, Iraqis and others.

Our potential opponents have learned to gain and use the advantage of time. They will seek to win by avoiding loss, to hold on until the Americans tire of the conflict first. The surest way to accelerate this process, they all have learned, is to kill Americans — quickly. Time can be gained by shifting from a traditional European style of linear war to a non-linear style based upon the control of territory rather than the command of key terrain and critical nodes, all of which are prime targets for destruction from above by precision weaponry. The enemy can stretch out the conflict by going to ground, dispersing, hiding, and occupying complex terrain such as mountains and cities and by deceiving the Americans through the use of camouflage and information deception.

If done correctly, an adaptive enemy can turn a one-sided conflict into a close contest as we saw in Kosovo. So, how do we insure that we will continue to win and win cheaply against such an opponent? We must be able to deprive the enemy of his time advantage and make the most of our firepower advantage by robbing the enemy of his ability to deceive, disperse and go to ground.

The surest way to gain the advantage of time is to arrive within the battle area quickly, armed with overwhelming force. Speed of arrival will allow us to literally catch the enemy in the open before he is able to capture his operational objectives and go to ground in terrain advantageous to the defensive. The paralytic effect of precision strikes will serve to freeze his forces in place and then force him to disperse.

Our past wars have taught us that as an enemy disperses to absorb firepower, he becomes vulnerable to quick destruction in detail by ground forces. Once enemy forces are sufficiently weakened by fire and find themselves unable to mass, friendly maneuver forces must be inserted quickly across the entire span of his operational area to

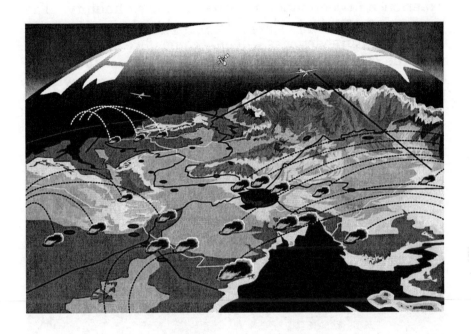

ensure the immediate disintegration of his force and the ultimate collapse of his will to resist. The inter-disposition of forces in the enemy's midst ensures that we control the clock, not him.

Enemy units gone to ground can now be found and fixed by maneuver forces. Exposed, cut off and unable to move or mass, each enemy pocket can be destroyed in detail with minimum loss to the intervening force. As long as we hold the initiative by occupying his territory, time is on our side. We now have the luxury of taking him down using a balanced application of firepower and maneuver. The enemy is faced with a deadly paradox. If he remains

7

dispersed our forces will destroy him at leisure. If he attempts to mass he summons the full wrath of American precision strike. Check and checkmate.

Kosovo serves as just another compelling data point along a remarkably clear continuum of American experience in contemporary wars of limited liability. The lessons are strikingly clear. To win cheaply we must win quickly. Future victories will only come if we are possessed with the speed to arrive quickly and the power to end the conflict decisively by overwhelming the enemy with a balance of precision firepower and maneuver.

**Third Phase:
Strategic Maneuver to Occupy and Culminate . . .**
__Checkmate__

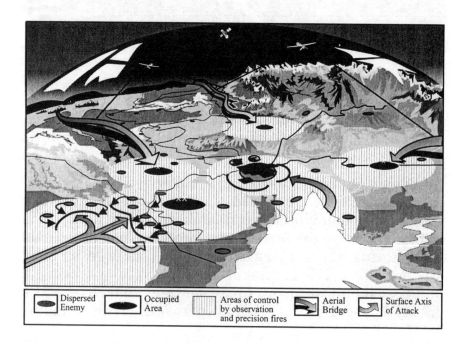

| Dispersed Enemy | Occupied Area | Areas of control by observation and precision fires | Aerial Bridge | Surface Axis of Attack |

Chapter Two

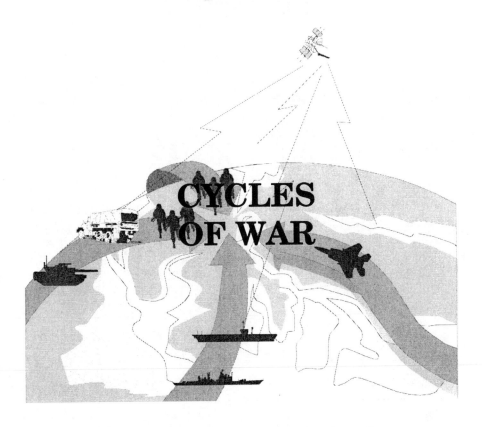

Major General Robert H. Scales, Jr.

Reproduced with Permission Granted by:
July 1997 Issue
ARMED FORCES JOURNAL
INTERNATIONAL
Volume 134, Number 12

CYCLES OF WAR

Speed Of Maneuver Will Be The Essential Ingredient Of An Information-Age Army

The nature of warfare, like other forms of collective, complex human behavior, changes slowly. Cycles of change in warfare are particularly difficult to comprehend and even more difficult to anticipate because, unlike endeavors in finance, medicine, or law, active experience in war is, thankfully, infrequent. Because warfare cannot be practiced often, soldiers are obliged to rely on the laboratory of past experiences to gain vicarious experience in war.

CYCLES AND PATTERNS

Before the advent of the industrial age, study in the laboratory of past wars served soldiers well. Cycles of change were centuries long, and factors that generated change, such as demographics, politics, and relative power among contenders, while not necessarily predictable, were at least constant and familiar enough to give soldiers confidence that data derived from past campaigns would remain relevant and useful as signposts into the future. Since the beginning of the Industrial age, technological warfare—the applied science of killing—has eclipsed all other dynamics of change. For many, this magnitude and newness of science threatens the reliability of precedent as a useful mechanism for predicting the future course of war.

To be sure, the frenetic pace of technological change in the modern world has served to compress the interval and stretch the amplitude of the cycles of change. Nonetheless, identifiable cycles remain. If our historical laboratory serves us, we should be able to search the recent past to identify new cycles driven principally by technology. Should we find a common pattern in technological cycles, and if we

11

CHANGES IN THE ART OF WAR FOLLOW TECHNOLOGY DRIVEN CYCLES

2nd Wave Industrial Age — Third Wave Information Age

	1865	1917	1961	1991	2010
	Defense	Offensive	Defense	Mental — Physical Offensive	

	Speed	Killing Zone	Speed	Killing Zone	Speed	Killing Zone	Speed	Killing Zone	Speed	Killing Zone
	2.5 km/hr	1.0 km	20 km/hr	15 km	30 km/hr	250 km	40 km/hr	?	200 km/hr	?

American Civil War — Gulf War — War in 2020

• Firepower Dominance	• Maneuver Dominance	• Precision Firepower Dominance	• Information Enables Precision Maneuver
• Forces tied to Railhead	• Motorization, Wireless, Airpower	• Early Warning, Tracking	• Platforms Accelerate Speed
• Exhaustion through Attrition	• Strike COG	• Attack to Operational Depth	• Global Maneuver
• Symmetric Forces	• Asymmetric Forces	• Symmetric Forces	• Asymmetric Forces

accept the premise that technology will continue to drive future change, then we should be able to use the recent past to fix the central axis aligning those cycles and project it into the future.

Technology began to dominate patterns of change with the rise of industrial production and the appearance of precision warmaking machinery like rifled weapons in the mid-19th century. The small bore repeating rifle, the machine gun, and quick-firing field artillery extended the deadly zone, or the distance that soldiers had to cross to turn a defender out of his position, from 150 meters in Napoleon's day to a thousand meters or more by the end of the American Civil War. As the deadly zone increased by nearly a factor of 10, the risks of crossing it were further multiplied by the lethality induced through the precision and volume from the massive proliferation of repeating arms. Thus, technology favored the defender. Images of the terrible slaughter of World War I remain as testimony to the cost in blood exacted by an operational method that relied principally on killing effect to achieve decisive results.

Before the slaughter ended, military professionals on both sides of no-man's land sought to solve the tactical and operational dilemmas imposed by dominance of firepower on the battlefield. The tactical problem simply was to cross the killing zone alive. The operational problem was to make a successful crossing militarily decisive. Once across, a force had to reach deep, concentrate, and strike to dislocate and eventually disintegrate the order and cohesion of an opposing force.

The conceptual solution came first to the Germans in 1918, and it was deceptively simple: short, highly intense doses of firepower to prepare the assault; small units to exploit the shock effect of firepower in order to infiltrate and bypass centers of resistance; and operational formations to move through exposed points of weakness to push deep into the enemy's rear. While the Germans had the method, they lacked the means to translate theory into effective action. After the war, the development of the internal combustion engine provided the means. The graft of practical science to an innovation born in war turned the cycle of war a second time and restored dominance to the offensive. Motorized armored vehicles allowed soldiers to cross the deadly zone protected and at enormously greater speed. Large units could now dash great distances into the enemy's rear to strike at his brain and avoid his powerful extremities. The object of Blitzkrieg became the collapse of an enemy's will to resist. Victory was gained through psychological paralysis induced by movement, rather than through butchery induced by massive application of firepower.

After World War II, the Western Powers faced another tactical and operational dilemma. The problem now was to halt a Soviet-style blitzkrieg across the Northern German Plain. Tactical forces needed defensive killing power to absorb the initial Soviet armored shock and hold their defensive positions. The operational problem was to strike deep with long-range firepower in order to slow the rate of arrival from follow-on armored forces at the front line. Billions of dollars and the collective genius of a generation of brilliant minds succeeded in developing a remarkable set of technologies capable of stopping a mechanized offensive with precise, long-range killing power. Microchip technology provided the tools necessary to extend the killing zone and made targets easier to find, track, and kill.

Signs foretelling how the defensive's return to dominance might turn the cycles of war a third time began to appear as early as the closing days in Vietnam. A few laser-guided bombs destroyed targets that had previously required hundreds of unguided dumb bombs. In World War II, an average of 18 rounds was needed to kill a tank at a range of 800 yards. During the 1973 Arab-Israeli War, the average was two rounds at 1,200 yards, and by Desert Storm one round at 2,400 yards.

The ability to see and strike deep using ground and aerial platforms served to expand the battlefield by orders of magnitude. What was once a theater area for a field army now became the area of operations for a division or a corps. Just as an army moving at two miles per hour could not cross a killing zone dominated by long-range, rapid-firing, rifled weapons in 1914, the precision revolution made it prohibitively expensive for an army moving at seven times that speed to cross an infinitely more lethal space a hundred times as large. Thus, in a conflict involving two roughly equal—or symmetrical—forces, evidence seems to show convincingly that the advantage goes to the defender.

Today, seven years after the prospect of a Soviet blitzkrieg has crumbled with the same finality as the fall of the Berlin Wall, we seem strangely content to remain frozen in the third cycle. As the post-industrial age begins to give way to the information age, we still find comfort in a vision of future warfare that continues to emphasize the capacity to kill with greater and greater efficiency.

THERE IS NO SILVER BULLET

Arguments against a firepower-centered approach to warfare have been with us since the earliest days of the industrial age. War is a deadly business. Yet the object of war is not to kill the enemy so much as it is to break his will to resist. No matter how efficient and precise a firepower system might be, victory is rarely defined by killing everyone on the other side. The extension of influence or control by force is much more powerful and palatable than genocide through firepower. Therefore, our object in applying firepower must be to exploit its substantial paralytic effects to gain advantage.

Unfortunately, recent experiments in the laboratory of real war substantiates the view that the paralytic effects of firepower erode quickly over time. Soldiers become inured to hardships and danger. Firepower that might break an enemy formation early in a conflict eventually becomes merely a nuisance once soldiers accustom themselves to firepower's pyrotechnic drama and devise effective means to deflect, deceive, dissipate, and protect themselves from firepower's killing effects.

To win quickly and decisively at low cost in the future, we must have the means to conduct the battle quickly and to end it cleanly, preferably at the moment when the paralytic effect of firepower is greatest. To delay beyond that moment only increases the killing and makes the enemy more effective by stiffening his will to resist and by allowing him to reconstitute. Decision is best guaranteed through maneuver of forces on the ground. Psychological collapse—the breaking of an enemy's will to resist—comes when an opponent finds himself challenged and blocked wherever he turns. He admits defeat when further pursuit of his political objective is not worth the cost or when his centers of gravity are threatened, controlled, or occupied and he has no remaining options for restoring them.

LETHALITY AND MANEUVERABILTY

To avoid the horrors of protracted firepower-attrition warfare in the future, we must be sure to maintain a necessary but delicate symbiosis between the ability to kill and the ability to maneuver. Easier said than done if one assumes that we still dwell in the third cycle of warfare, a period that favors the defender.

As we gaze into the distant future and face the prospect of a competent enemy with both the will to fight and the means to develop or purchase his own systems of precision firepower, the prospects of winning a third-cycle conflict become even more sobering. Possessed with the intrinsic power of the defensive and most likely defending on familiar terrain, such a foe would not necessarily have to defeat us tactically to win the conflict. He would most probably bow to our overwhelming superiority in the air and at sea and concede both. He would not have to seek victory so much as the avoidance of defeat. He would only need to preserve his ground force in the face of superior firepower long enough to create stalemate and cause enough casualties for the Americans to tire of the contest first. Again, an enemy possessed with a will to fight at the beginning of a conflict is likely only to grow stronger over time without direct intercession and eventual domination on the ground.

RESTORING THE OFFENSIVE

The restoration of the offensive as the dominant form of war will come with the appearance of a fourth cycle of warfare, a cycle defined more by the new revolution in information rather than the stale remnants of the machine age. Imagine a maneuver force possessing the ability to see with unprecedented clarity, to anticipate with unparalleled sureness, to accelerate the pace of movement with unequaled velocity, and to maintain an unrelenting operational tempo. Such a force would be able to traverse the killing ground, however expansive and lethal, relatively untouched, and decide the campaign with a violent and

16

debilitating movement that ends quickly with minimum loss of life to all sides.

The fourth cycle of war will seek to exploit the information age in order to increase the velocity of maneuver. Speed must be the essential ingredient of a future landpower force. Speed will be achieved by creating a force unburdened by the logistical yoke that has long been the principal impediment to agility and speed.

The secret of the dominance of the offensive in the second cycle was not to be found in the tanks, personnel carriers, and self-propelled artillery of blitzkrieg armies. The secret lay, instead, in the ability of a portion of the maneuver force—in the case of the Wehrmacht, just 10 of 117 divisions—to break free of the railhead long enough to reach deep into an enemy's rear with enough sustaining strength to collapse his psychological center of gravity and hold it down long enough for following forces to solidify the victory.

Today the railhead has been replaced by an equally cumbersome and constrictive logistical umbilical cord. Like the Germans in 1940, we must develop the means to break a portion of our force free to achieve the same objective. The information revolution promises to give us the means. Information technologies will allow us to deposit outside the close combat zone all but those forces necessary to move, observe, and kill. Detailed knowledge of the enemy's strength will free us from our traditional fixation on stockpiling and "worst casing" so that we will be able to carry with us into the close combat zone only what we need when we need it. In effect, we will know enough to know what to leave behind.

The information revolution should allow us to track the individual elements of a force with exquisite clarity and detail. But knowledge of the enemy, alone, is not enough. We must possess the means to act on what we know and action is dependent, again, on speed. The combination of knowledge and speed of movement will allow a future battleforce to anticipate enemy movement and turn costly force-on-force engagements of past wars into surer and less costly engagements by choice.

That combination will allow a battleforce to maintain an unrelenting tempo. In the chess game of operational planning, superior battlefield awareness will enable us to stay four or five moves ahead of an opponent. Speed will allow battleforces to shift quickly about the battlefield to check, block and, when conditions are optimal, strike in a ratio of friendly action to enemy reaction of, again, perhaps four or five to one. Thus, the object of a maneuver force of this type will not be to kill so much as to paralyze, to exploit the ability to maintain a constant advantage of position in order to close an enemy's options, wear him down, and eventually collapse his will. Speed of maneuver offers the essential finishing function that balances our prodigious ability to kill.

The imperative for speed in this new form of warfare begins at home ports, airfields, and installations. A highly lethal force, shorn of its Cold War impedimenta, will be able to project itself from the homeland or from strategic points overseas in days rather than weeks or months and arrive in the operational theater ready to fight. The ability to get into a theater "firstest with the mostest" reduces risk to forces first to arrive and prevents the enemy from setting himself into an advantageous defensive position.

Early arrival will change the elemental patterns of war at the theater level. Such a campaign will allow near-simultaneous rather than sequential applications of both killing power and maneuver. Strategic speed will allow a theater war to take the form of a *coup de main*. The bloody, set-piece, sequential campaigns of the industrial age will give way to sharp, intense acts of strategic preemption.

A landpower force optimized to capture the benefits of the information age would take on physical characteristics distinctly different from industrial age armies. First, such a force would be able to divide itself into two functional groupments: the first, essentially sustaining in character,

18

might be removed from the combat zone entirely, relying on sure communications and rapid aerial logistics to deliver the goods and services of war to the combat zone in just the proper quantities just when needed.

The combat force would become the second major group. It must be compact, possessing just the people and gear necessary to sense, track, move, and kill. Many essential combat functions necessary in contemporary armies would displace from the ground upward into the exosphere and space. This "space-to-surface continuum" between the close combat force and the information structures that sustain it from above would, in fact, form the central nexus of an information-age maneuver force. In effect, space becomes the new high ground. When all the services occupy vertically oriented battlespace, the character of multi-service missions changes from the segregated land, sea, and air operations to a new approach which will be characterized by total interdependence throughout this surface-to-space continuum.

UNPRECEDENTED BATTLESPACE AWARENESS

The ability to see the battlefield and to know the enemy, combined with the speed to exploit these advantages, will fundamentally change the dynamics of fire and maneuver. A commander able to observe enemy movement with fine granularity would be able, with confidence, to divide his own forces into comparably fine increments and position each precisely enough to control and dominate each discrete bit of enemy combat power. The ability to employ many small units at once would allow a commander to cover a large operational area with discrete combat elements. A sports analogy is appropriate: a basketball team with superior speed, agility, and understanding of the opposition would be more effective playing man-to-man rather than zone.

A commander with the dual advantage of speed and killing power will dominate the battlefield. Superior killing

19

power allows incapacitation of an enemy force, a necessary capability, but by itself intrinsically indecisive. Superior mobility allows exploitation of the temporary advantage gained by the stunning effect of killing power.

If these two essential elements of combat power are orchestrated with skill so that they are applied in harmony, an unfettered battleforce would be able to strike multiple vital points simultaneously or in a sequence of our choosing. In a very short time, perhaps only hours, such a force would be able to inflict a rapid sequence of local tactical disasters. The cumulative effect of these closely spaced events would serve to dislocate and confuse an enemy to the point that his warfighting structures quickly disintegrate. This confusion, dislocation, and disintegration will combine to produce an unequivocal military decision with minimum cost to both sides.

EXPERIMENTATION AND INNOVATION

The image of a landpower force to accomplish such deeds is purely conceptual today. But certain realities have begun to appear dimly through the veil of the future. First, at a time when American arms will most likely be called on to win an offensive campaign cheaply, the third cycle seems to tell us that the advantage goes to the defender. The offensive cannot be restored by firepower alone, because firepower cannot provide the essential decisive function necessary to end a campaign quickly on our terms at minimum cost. Second, even when preceded by overwhelming doses of precision firepower, a maneuvering force cannot hope to succeed against a determined, thinking enemy if its speed of movement cannot exceed the 20-kilometer-per-hour pace of a third-cycle force. An information-age army must move at 10 times that velocity. Finally, as in past cycles, technology promises a way out of this dilemma. The information revolution will give land forces both the mental agility and matching physical speed to restore the essential balance between firepower and maneuver on a future battlefield.

Henry Ford never met Heinz Guderian, the German general commonly held most responsible for exploiting Ford's invention to gain victory on the battlefield. Likewise, history will eventually produce the warrior who will capitalize on the opportunities offered by Bill Gates and the revolution most often associated with his name. The name and nationality of the warrior who someday will proclaim himself the Guderian of the information age has yet to be recognized. But one fact is certain: the information revolution will continue to alter our world at an ever-increasing pace whether we choose to engage ourselves in it or not.

We cannot remain fixed on the third cycle of warfare for much longer. Already, competing nations are striving to chip away at America's dominance in precision fires. Sooner or later someone will find a way to match or counter our firepower advantage. The result may well be equilibrium on the battlefield that might lead to stalemate or eventual defeat.

Imperatives for innovation and change are overdue. We need to begin now to forge a new marriage between battlefield knowledge and unprecedented landpower speed. We must do no less than draw the outline for a new army whose structure is predicated on the premise that the machine age is past and the age of information has just begun.

Chapter Three

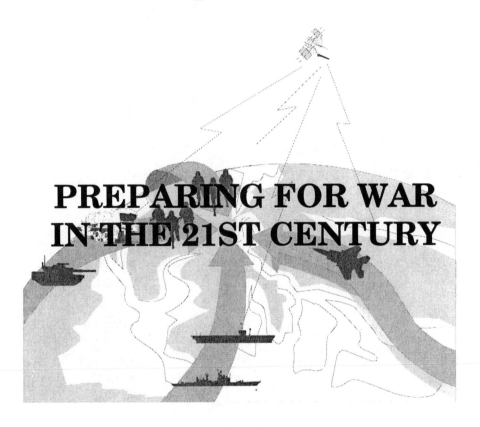

PREPARING FOR WAR IN THE 21ST CENTURY

Major General Robert H. Scales, Jr.
Lieutenant General Paul K. Van Riper, USMC

Reproduced with Permission Granted by:
Summer 1997 Issue
STRATEGIC REVIEW
Volume 25, Number 3

PREPARING FOR WAR
IN THE 21st CENTURY

IN BRIEF

Recurring proposals to substitute advanced technology for conventional military capabilities, epitomized by the New Look of the 1950s, reflect a peculiarly American faith in science's ability to engineer simple solutions to complex human problems. But as Vietnam proved, technological superiority does not automatically guarantee success of arms. Unpredictability constitutes the enduring nature of war. Thus, success in war requires the rejection of over-reliance on any single capability. America's next war, like those that have preceded it, almost certainly will be won—or lost—on land.

The U.S. government has now embarked on its third major reassessment of current and future military requirements since the end of the Cold War. Given the leadtime involved in making any significant change in the nation's defense posture, the results of this review are likely to influence American military capabilities well into the next century. All the more reason to insist that any such reexamination of America's military requirements should reflect a clear understanding of the likely character of future war. Thus we are troubled by recent claims that technological supremacy will allow the United States in the future to abjure the use of ground combat forces in favor of delivering advanced precision weaponry from platforms remote from conflict areas.

This is not the first time we have been lured by promises of high-tech, bloodless victory. In the early 1950s, similar promises produced the New Look, a strategy proposing to rely on strategic nuclear weapons as an alternative to conventional warfare. Describing the origins of the New

Look, one observer noted "the American yearning for some simple, single solution to all the bothersome and frustrating complexities of living in a world of perennial conflict."[1] Then, as today, optimists insisted that technological change had rendered conventional warfare obsolete. Events in Southeast Asia and elsewhere soon disabused them. But the resulting damage to conventional military capabilities persisted long after the United States had abandoned the New Look.

What overconfidence in nuclear weapons produced then, overconfidence in the microchip threatens to reproduce today. Recurring proposals to substitute advanced technology for conventional military capabilities reflect a peculiarly American faith in science's ability to engineer simple solutions to complex human problems. They also gratify both economic and political interests. That remains true even though the practical military impact of technological supremacy over the past half-century has been equivocal at best. Such supremacy could not prevent the Netherlands' defeat in Indonesia, France's defeats in Indochina and Algeria, America's defeat in Vietnam, the Soviet Union's defeat in Afghanistan, or Russia's more recent defeat in Chechnya. All these episodes confirm that technological superiority does not automatically guarantee victory on the battlefield, still less at the negotiating table.

Nonetheless, belief in the possibility of a technological "fix" for the challenges of war has shown astonishing persistence. In addition to its impact on force postures, it has significantly affected even how Americans define military success. That influence peaked during Vietnam, in which reliance on body counts and other quantitative "indicators" virtually replaced strategic reasoning. And while defeat in Vietnam temporarily discredited such mechanistic thinking, some still insist that a technological solution for war is "out there somewhere," if only we could discover it.

In an important sense, therefore, U.S. military policy remains imprisoned in an unresolved dialectic between history and technology, between those for whom the past is prologue and those for whom it is irrelevant. Today's debate about the preferred structure of American military forces thus in the end is a debate about the future of war itself. The debate goes far beyond which weapons to buy or whether to favor this or that capability. At its heart, rarely considered and even less often articulated, are fundamentally incompatible views about the nature of war, about what conditions produce victory and defeat—indeed, how one should define these concepts—and ultimately, about the purpose for which we maintain military forces in the first place.

For those placing unbridled faith in technology, war is a predictable, if disorderly, phenomenon, defeat a matter of simple cost/benefit analysis, and the effectiveness of any military capability a finite calculus of targets destroyed and casualties inflicted. History paints a very different picture. Real war is an inherently uncertain enterprise in which chance, friction, and the limitations of the human mind under stress profoundly limit our ability to predict outcomes; in which defeat to have any meaning must be inflicted above all in the *minds* of the defeated; and in which the ultimate purpose of military power is to assure that a trial at arms, should it occur, delivers an unambiguous political verdict.

Such a view of war does not discount the importance of technology. But it recognizes that technology is only one of many influences on the conduct and outcome of military operations, an influence mediated by the nature, scope, and locale of the conflict, the character and objectives of the combatants, the attitudes of local, domestic, and international publics, and above all, the political issues in dispute. Acknowledging war's inherent unpredictability, it rejects over-reliance on any single capability, seeks maximum force versatility, and requires that military operations conform to the peculiar conditions and demands of the conflict itself.

America's military forces in the 21st century must exploit every advantage our technological genius can supply. But as we will argue in this article, the central ingredients of military victory or defeat will continue to reflect the enduring nature of war at least as much as the transient means used to prosecute it. And in the end, America's next war, like those that have preceded it, almost certainly will be won—or lost—on land.

The Geopolitics of Future War

From a geopolitical perspective, the world in which that war might erupt may be indefinite, but it is not indecipherable. On the contrary, it promises to look much like that of the late 19th century. As in that era, the principal engines of economic progress will continue to be the wealthy nations of Western Europe, North America, and the Asian rim. Political relations among these First World nations are, if anything, more stable than those which prevailed among the major powers after the Congress of Vienna, which inaugurated modern history's longest period of sustained great power peace. Healthy democracies, economic interdependence, cultural affinities, and the shared memory of two appalling world wars have created a community of interest that makes war among the developed democracies nearly unthinkable.

Unlike the major powers for 130 years after Napoleon, however, today's developed nations do not dominate the remainder of the world. Instead, they confront both developing states—some of which, like Russia, balance precariously between aspirations to join the developed world and the threat of political, economic, and demographic collapse—and Third World societies mired in economic and demographic misery. Nations in both groups tend to organize on different principles and operate on different premises from those of the developed democracies,

28

and it is in relations within and among them that future military challenges are most likely to arise.

While some developing nations are poised economically to enter the developed world, neither political freedom nor respect for law, two of history's most reliable inhibitors of aggression, necessarily have accompanied their economic growth. Some like China continue to pursue irredentist claims against the territory of their neighbors. Others like Iran assert religious suzerainty over entire regions. All seek access to the raw resources that fuel development. And most continue to see war as a legitimate way of achieving their objectives. For many of these states, acquiring territory remains a basic impulse, for prestige if for no other reason. Armed aggression may not be their only or even their preferred means. But especially among states with authoritarian governments, the conquest of land remains a legitimate ambition, and given their own economic and strategic interests, the developed democracies cannot remain unaffected.

In the meantime, vast portions of the world are economically either stagnant or retrogressing. While the proximate causes may be violent, venal, or otherwise misguided governments, the fundamental problems are structural. Many developing world societies remain economically dependent on subsistence agriculture and simple mineral extraction. In the meantime, the introduction of modern medicine has only accelerated a demographic explosion straining both their economic and political arrangements.

Among these societies, war tends to revert to its most primitive character. Driven by ethnic or tribal rivalries—themselves often a function of differential population growth—civil warfare will fester. Populous states will launch calculated invasions of less-crowded neighbors. Hordes of refugees will spill across borders provoking violence. And while war in the Third World may be waged with relatively unsophisticated forces, it frequently will drag on beyond any apparent strategic purpose, in part because it is aimed deliberately at depopulation. Finally, as recent events in Rwanda, Burundi, and Zaire illustrate, it often will manifest war's worst excesses—intentional starvation, extreme brutality, and mass slaughter.

In these unhappy struggles, the developed democracies typically will seek reasons not to intervene. But as we have seen already, media-generated public revulsion may compel intervention. The visual horrors of genocide may be intolerable. Humanitarian efforts may backfire, as they did in Somalia. Or the collapse of Third World societies whether through internal dynamics or external invasion may threaten to destabilize an economically vital region to the point where nonintervention is imprudent.

Finally, we will continue to confront military challenges from nongovernmental groups which fall neatly into none of these categories, but whose military capabilities and political, ideological, or economic objectives make them impervious to restraint by the civil police power. Such groups are far from a historical novelty, but their potential access to sophisticated military technology is unprecedented. They will remain among the most difficult military problems confronting us.

The Siren Call of Technology

While the military challenges outlined in this appraisal vary in origin, kind, and degree of threat to U.S. interests, all have one thing in common: In each case, strategic success ultimately will require the direct control of land, people, and resources. In confrontations with developing states, war is likely to be about the control of territory. In Third World episodes, it is likely to be about the control of populations. And suppressing terrorist and other nongovernmental challengers will require depriving them of political, psychological, and material support.

30

In none of these cases is technology alone likely to be decisive, and in many cases the very nature of the contest will restrict its use. Notwithstanding, some visionaries insist that emerging technologies will utterly transform the nature of war, permitting the defeat of future adversaries from a distance with no need to risk precious lives in the maelstrom of land combat. Such predictions ignore both war's inherent uncertainty and what we have learned about military victory and defeat in our own time.

Soldiers and Marines intuitively recognize the limits of prediction, and increasingly, even physical scientists share that recognition. From quantum physics to meteorology, science has become aware that "nonlinear" interactions pervade the natural world. We call such interactions "chaotic," and where they predominate, confident prediction is impossible. If that is true even of the apparent regularities of nature, how much more true must it be of war? As Clausewitz noted long ago, "No other human activity is so continuously or universally bound up with chance."[2] Indeed, Clausewitz remains relevant today largely because his work is "suffused with the under-standing that every war is inherently a nonlinear phenomenon, the conduct of which changes its character in ways that cannot be analytically predicted."[3]

The Enduring Character of War

Recognizing that, observers as far back as Thucydides have insisted that war can be perceived accurately only through the lens of history. To be useful, military theory must be grounded in the known realities of the past, not because the past repeats itself in specific ways, but rather because it reveals aspects of war which are timeless.

One such enduring feature is the invariable subordination of war to politics. "War is not a mere act of policy," Clausewitz asserted, "but a true political instrument, a continuation of political activity by other means. . . . War should never be thought of as something

31

autonomous, but always as an instrument of policy."[4] In one way or another, political considerations always condition military operations. Allied commanders rediscovered that enduring reality at the very outset of the Gulf War air campaign, when two bombs aimed at a secret police communications bunker in the heart of Baghdad destroyed not only the bunker, but also 200-odd civilians sheltering inside it. Political reaction to CNN's telecast the following morning resulted in the abrupt curtailment of all attacks on the downtown Baghdad area.[5] In the process, it also removed any possibility of destroying the political infrastructure of Saddam Hussein's tyrannical regime.

As this incident confirmed, war in practice is hostage to political concerns that routinely preclude the unconstrained employment of military means. Such concerns tend to be highly situational, hence unpredictable. For that reason alone, the mere possession of advanced technology is no guarantee of its practical utility.

The second and most pervasive of war's enduring characteristics is what Clausewitz called "friction." "Everything in war is very simple," he observed, "but the simplest thing is difficult. The difficulties accumulate and end by producing a kind of friction that is inconceivable unless one has experienced war."[6] In battle, danger, confusion, fear, fatigue, and discomfort combine with a hostile physical environment to curtail the effective performance of both men and machines. Moreover, as battlefields enlarge, formations disperse, and operations accelerate, these stresses increase, even as familiar sources of physical and psychological support—proximity to other units, lulls in activity, and the comfort of known ground—continue to evaporate. Hence the laboratory at best is an imperfect predictor of battlefield effectiveness; and even where the employment of advanced technology is politically unconstrained, it is far from a military panacea.

The stresses of battle, finally, merely are compounded for leaders, who must make crucial decisions with little time for reflection and in a welter of typically ambiguous information. "In the dreadful presence of suffering and danger," Clausewitz reminds us, "emotion can easily overwhelm intellectual conviction, and in this psychological fog it is . . . hard to form clear and complete insights."[7] Hence the profound danger of claims like those of certain Washington consultants who recently asserted, "What the [Military Technical Revolution] promises, more than precision attacks and laser beams, is . . . to imbue the information loop with near-perfect clarity. . . ."[8]

Such arguments verge on the theological, having neither scientific nor historical foundation. On the contrary, as one observer has noted,

> Much of the particular information which any individual possesses can be used only to the extent to which he himself can use it in his own decisions. Nobody can communicate to another all he knows, because much of the information he can make use of, he himself will elicit only in the process of making plans of action.[9]

Similarly in war, there simply are too many critical pieces of information inaccessible to sensors and beyond the power of computers.

In an information-rich environment in which what matters remains buried in noise, individuals at every level are limited in both what they can absorb and what they can pass along. And the more oppressed by danger and fatigue, the more vulnerable they become to both inadvertent misunderstanding and deliberate deception.

It is above all the interactive—indeed, antagonistic— quality of war that makes it unpredictable. "War is not waged against an abstract enemy," Clausewitz points out, "but against a real one."[10] America's adversaries in the next century will have options no matter what our technological advantages. Political limitation, friction, and fog are not artifacts of history, but rather conditions imbedded in the very fabric of war. To suppose that technology could

33

eliminate them from the battlefield thus flies in the face of the natural world *as it is*.

Instead, 2,500 years of history confirm that ambiguity, miscalculation, incompetence, and above all chance will continue to dominate the conduct of war. In the end, the incalculables of determination, morale, fighting skill, and leadership far more than technology will determine who wins and who loses.

Distant Punishment vs. Physical Domination

Acknowledging war's inherent uncertainty by no means argues for ignoring technology. On the contrary, advanced information and munitions technologies already have had a significant influence on Army and Marine Corps doctrine. Some believe they may radically alter the relationship between maneuver and firepower, just as the tank and airplane did from 1918 to 1939. And every modern armed force must cope with increasing battlefield transparency, munitions lethality, information overload, and logistical vulnerability.

Our objection is not to technology itself, but rather to claims that it will permit the achievement of victory by distant punishment alone, with no need to exert direct and continuing influence over the land, people, and resources which are war's ultimate stakes. In addition to what history reveals about the inherent nature of war, our own military experience in this century argues the contrary.

That experience repeatedly has confirmed that distant punishment unexploited by the physical domination of ground is a wasting asset. From Verdun to Cassino, the Iron Triangle to Al Busayyah, firepower alone, even when delivered on a massive scale, rarely has proved capable of ejecting determined troops from the ground they occupy. Even massive bombing in the Gulf War, for all its destructive and demoralizing effect on the Iraqi Army, could not by itself induce that army's withdrawal from Kuwait.

What is true of firepower delivered against troops in the field may be even truer of firepower delivered directly against an opponent's civil infrastructure. In fact, the evidence suggests that such efforts readily backfire, particularly when directed against opponents whose leaders can manipulate their publics' interpretation of events. We also must be concerned with the reactions of our own citizens as they watch modern weapons impacting among apparently defenseless populations, a problem likely to intensify as the developing states which represent the most probable loci of future high-intensity conflict continue to urbanize.

Some argue that the increased precision of emerging munitions will limit collateral damage, making less likely both psychological stiffening on an enemy's part and psychological revulsion on our own. But precision means one thing applied to military forces in the field, quite another applied to heavily populated urban areas. Indeed, fear of media reaction to the scenes of carnage even among military targets along Kuwait's "Highway of Death" in part explains the Bush Administration's decision to end hostilities in the Gulf War after 100 hours, though all the objectives of the ground offensive had yet to be achieved.[11]

There certainly have been a few cases in which the limited use of distant firepower alone produced strategic results. Air attacks against Libya in 1986, for example, seem effectively to have diminished Muamar Gaddafi's eagerness openly to challenge the United States. In such cases, in which objectives are limited or merely demonstrative, distant punishment may well curb hostile behavior. But it is unlikely in any permanent way to resolve the underlying issue, as the history of the 1965-68 air campaign against North Vietnam underlines. Rather, every such application of distant firepower risks the embarrassing possibility that the recipient simply will ignore the attack, forcing the attacker to choose between escalation or impotence.

35

In short, over-reliance on distant punishment ignores the psychology of an opponent's will to resist. There is an enormous difference between enduring distant attack, which however unpleasant must eventually end, and enduring the physical presence of a conquering army with all of its political and sociological implications. We should not lose sight of the difference between a Kuwait liberated by ground forces and an Iraq still truculent and combative, however ravaged by air attack.

The fundamental limitation of distant punishment is that it commits without resolving. Notwithstanding, its ease of use and apparent low risk make it deceptively attractive in cases where U.S. strategic interests are limited or ambiguous. Some even have urged redesigning American military forces specifically for intervention in such cases.[12] Such proposals are a gilt-edged invitation to back into war, and ignore everything we have learned so painfully over the past half-century about the incremental use of force.

Ground Forces and Future War

If resolution and durability are among the most important and irreplaceable contributions of land forces to victory in war and deterrence in peace, they are by no means the only ones. In the geopolitical environment forecast earlier, strategic success will place a premium on military versatility. Even the United States cannot afford to maintain capabilities tailored discretely to every potential military challenge, nor will any single capability accommodate all such challenges. Instead, American military forces must be capable of rapid adaptation to a broad and constantly varying range of strategic tasks and conditions.

Ground forces remain the indispensable foundation of that strategic versatility. Air and naval capabilities complement but can never replace the ability to deploy ground forces tailored to the peculiar conditions and objectives of a given conflict. To say that in no way

36

deprecates their importance. No American commander today would consider launching ground combat operations without command of the air and space, nor littoral operations without command of the sea. Moreover, as the United States continues to shift from a forward deployed to an expeditionary force posture, dependence on both aerospace and naval capabilities will increase merely to ensure ground forces reach the theater of operations rapidly and safely. Hence, to insist that future U.S. military operations will inherently be joint is not just rhetoric but rather frank acknowledgment of strategic and operational imperatives. But only in unusual conditions will air, sea, or space operations alone produce decisive strategic results. In almost every circumstance, the effective integration of all components will be required.

Moreover, U.S. military forces exist to deter as well as fight. Even after a half century of practice, our understanding of the dynamics of deterrence remains imperfect, but we have learned that a key requirement is making a deterrent threat credible. One of the central arguments for relying upon the threat of distant punishment is that its presumed low risk enhances that credibility. As we have seen, however, situations in which distant punishment alone is likely to be effective are precisely those in which the issues in dispute are least fundamental. The greater the stakes, the less likely that distant attack alone will produce a favorable strategic result. It follows that the greater the stakes, the less likely that the threat of such attack alone will deter.

Instead, reconciling credibility with effectiveness requires operational seamlessness. Deterrence is most likely to succeed when complementary capabilities reinforce each other, and when all contribute in a credible way to the assurance of victory should deterrence fail. That emerging precision attack systems promise more effectively to kill people and break things is not at issue. The challenge will be to translate those essentially tactical effects into strategic results. And the principal mechanism of that translation will remain an unrivaled land combat capability.

There is one additional reason why emerging technologies must be designed to enhance rather than replace land power. Whether to deter or fight, the U.S. probably will confront future adversaries as a member of an alliance. We have nearly a century of experience with alliances. And if one lesson can be drawn from that experience, it is that presence on the ground is an irreducible bonafide of alliance commitment, especially for the nation claiming leadership of that alliance.

Central to alliance commitment is the requirement to share risk. Thus, Sir Basil Liddell Hart's effort in the 1930s to restrict the continental role of British ground forces not only diminished deterrence, but also led to doctrinal and material stagnation for which the British paid a heavy price when deterrence failed.[13] More recently, repeated U.S. efforts to "rationalize" America's NATO contributions by substituting air for ground forces in return for greater European ground force contributions invariably foundered over the principle of shared risk.

The reality is that ground combat forces represent the strongest evidence of alliance commitment. That, and the fact that their deployment alone conveys an intention to remain engaged for the duration, makes them the irreplaceable adhesive of any military coalition.

War: A Contest of Wills, Not Machines

Any sustained period of peace challenges military institutions. It requires holding on to the immutable and terrifying realities of war in a climate of peacetime pursuits and ease, because only by an understanding of what war has been can we hope to glimpse what it will be. To prepare for the future, we must keep our grip on the past.

America's performance in its first battles rarely has been impressive.[14] The Gulf War broke the mold. For once,

America took the field with a team that was ready to play. And the result was the shortest, most successful, and in American lives least expensive, military campaign in modern history.

But the military forces which won that war had been built to fight another, and in that fact there is a stern warning for today's planners. In an uncertain world, we dare not base force requirements on preconceived assumptions about whom we might fight in the next century or how. Instead, American military forces must be able to fight and win on any battlefield, under any conditions, and with whatever means the nature of the contest requires. And to do that, America will need robust, well-equipped, and sustainable land combat capabilities as far ahead as we can foresee.

Innovative application of emerging technology will enhance those capabilities. But in the end, war is a contest of human wills, not machines, in which means must be subordinated to ends if the results are to justify the costs. In the world we confront, those ends are likely to be more complicated, and the circumstances in which they must be pursued less predictable, than ever before in our history. A military posture that evades rather than accommodates that reality is doomed to expensive irrelevance.

NOTES

1. Warner R. Schilling, et al., *Strategy, Politics, and Defense Budgets* (New York: 1962), p. 386.

2. Carl von Clausewitz, *On War,* edited and translated by Michael Howard and Peter Paret (Princeton: 1976), p. 83.

3. Alan Beyerchen, "Clausewitz, Nonlinearity, and the Unpredictability of War," *International Security*, Winter 1992/1993, p. 61.

4. Clausewitz, *On War*, pp. 87-88.

5. Williamson Murray, *Air War in the Persian Gulf* (Baltimore, MD: 1995), pp. 190-192.

6. Clausewitz, *On War*, p. 119.

7. Clausewitz, *On War*, p. 108.

8. Michael I. Mazarr, et al., "The Military Technical Revolution: A Structural Framework," Center for Strategic and International Studies, March 1993, p. 38.

9. Friedrich Von Hayek, *The Fatal Conceit: The Errors of Socialism*, in W.W. Bartley III, ed., *The Collected Works of F.A. Hayek*, Vol. I (Chicago: 1988), p. 7.

10. Clausewitz, *On War*, p. 161.

11. Col. (Ret.) Richard M. Swain, "Reflections on The Revisionist Critique," *Army*, August 1996, p. 28.

12. Edward N. Luttwak, "A Post-Heroic Military Policy," *Foreign Affairs*, July/August 1996.

13. Williamson Murray, *The Change in the European Balance of Power, 1938-1939* (Princeton, NJ: Princeton University Press, 1984), pp. 86-91.

14. Charles E. Heller and William A. Stofft, *America's First Battles, 1776-1965* (Lawrence, KS: 1986).

Chapter Four

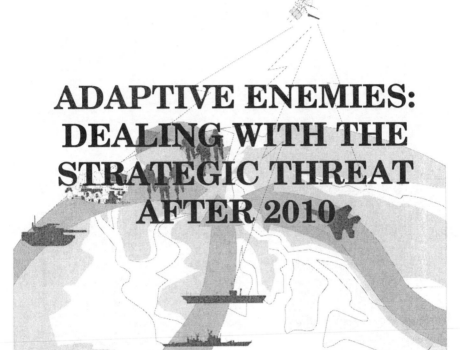

ADAPTIVE ENEMIES: DEALING WITH THE STRATEGIC THREAT AFTER 2010

Major General Robert H. Scales, Jr.

Reproduced with Permission Granted by:
Winter 1999 Issue
STRATEGIC REVIEW
Volume 27, Number 1

ADAPTIVE ENEMIES:
DEALING WITH THE STRATEGIC THREAT
AFTER 2010

IN BRIEF

The history of warfare reminds us that every dominant military advantage eventually yields to a countervailing response. For more than 50 years, the United States has derived its current military superiority from a remarkable ability to translate technological innovation and industrial capacity into effective battlefield advantages. This military dominance has become increasingly manifest by the precise application of explosive killing power. It is only a matter of time, unfortunately, before a creative opponent will develop a method of war that will attempt to defeat our preoccupation with the science of war and the application of precision firepower.

The history of warfare suggests a martial corollary to Newton's fundamental law of physics: every successful technical or tactical innovation that provides a dominant military advantage eventually yields to a countervailing response that shifts the advantage to the opposing force. America's military dominance has been on display for more than 50 years. It has become the standard emulated by most Western nations. The United States has derived its current military superiority from a remarkable ability to translate industrial capacity and technological know-how into effective battlefield advantages—advantages that have become increasingly manifest by the precise application of explosive killing power. But half a century is a long time for a method of war to have been practiced without the

43

appearance of countervailing, competitive methods that will represent a real challenge—something far more dangerous and effective than the Pentagon's current buzzwords, "asymmetric warfare." Inevitably a creative opponent will develop a method of war that will attempt to defeat our preoccupation with precision firepower.

The Established Cycle

The evolving sequence from dominance through challenge and adaptive response has been a hallmark of the Western way of war. In combat, as well as peacetime, Western militaries have proven to be "complex adaptive systems." In other words, unlike the static and stylized forms of combat that characterized much of the way empires and other cultures have waged war throughout history, Western military organizations have consistently adapted and innovated during both peacetime and war. This pattern of successful adaptation reaches back to the very dawn of Western warfare. The Spartans went to sea to beat the Athenians. To counter the genius of Hannibal, the Romans developed the guile of Fabius and the determination of Scipio. The longbowmen of Edward III found their match in the tenacity and patience of du Gueschin's band of Medieval irregulars. Washington developed a body of Continentals to threaten the long service professionals of Great Britain. Moreover, the American militia fundamentally altered the political context within which war among Europeans occurred. The British utilized the strengths of Wellington's ancient regime army with the cold hard cash produced by the Industrial Revolution to defeat the legions of Napoleon. In 1918, Allied armies, after heavy defeats in the spring, utilized not only enemy tactics, but new technology to break the German Army in the field. Furthermore, Americans should not forget that armies forged in the image of Maoist China successfully held off and at times defeated the firepower armies of the West during the Korean and Vietnam Wars.

This process carries an important warning for the U.S. military as the United States embarks on a new century. Military organizations, particularly skilled and motivated ones, will adapt and learn on the battlefield. In fact, the ability to adapt swiftly is an essential component of military effectiveness—and as one side changes and adapts, so too eventually will the other.

Every Age Has Its Own Kind of War

The great difficulty that confronts the U.S. military as it enters a new century is that, for the most part, the services still retain a mental and physical attachment to the combat conceptions that had their origins through innovations occurring in the 1920s and 1930s and served so well during the Cold War. The apparent utility of these methods of war during some of the post-Cold War skirmishes has only served to reinforce this attachment. The U.S. vision has been further clouded by a characteristic Western arrogance that presumes that, to be a challenge, non-Western militaries must mimic the Western way of war. As a result, the movement within the non-Western world to discover methods to counter the Western fixation on firepower has remained shrouded in the shadows of unfamiliar military cultures. Thus, U.S. military analysts have missed much of the recent discourse and experimentation occurring outside of the West due to the cultural schism that divides the world's advanced industrial democracies from the other four-fifths of the planet.

Since 1918 the foundation of the twentieth century Western way of war has rested on the perfection of accurate, predictive firepower. The assumption has been that the explosive power of modern munitions, if delivered with great precision at decisive points in a timely fashion, will create sufficient physical and psychological damage to collapse an enemy's will to resist. The collapse of the enemy's will on the battlefield such as the German Army on the Western Front in 1918 or the French Army in 1940, or in

45

his homeland as evidenced by the surrender of Japan in 1945, offers a warring state the opportunity to translate dominance on the battlefield into decisive political results.

Truth is, challenges, and effective ones at that, to the Western way of war have been germinating over the past half-century. The Japanese in the Pacific displayed a skillful capacity to adapt to the challenges posed by soldiers and Marines in that theater. Over the course of 1943 and 1944, the Americans had won a series of quick and decisive victories by using the mobility and firepower of their amphibious forces. But the Japanese had observed what the Americans had been doing as well; at the end of 1944 they entirely revamped their approach to defending the islands still guarding the approaches to the Homeland. In February 1945 on the small island of Iwo Jima off the coast of Japan, Lt. Gen. Kuribayashi Tadamichi quite literally buried his defending forces and their artillery deep in the natural and man-made caves of Mt. Suribachi. Moreover, he ordered his subordinates not to launch the *banzai,* suicidal charges that had so characterized Japanese defenses before, an approach that had exchanged Japanese bodies for American bullets and shells. When it was over virtually the entire Japanese garrison of 20,000 was dead; but the three attacking Marine divisions had suffered 6,821 dead and nearly 20,000 wounded.

Things were even worse on Okinawa. There the defending Japanese army commander had more troops and more territory to defend. In effect, his defensive plan abandoned the best beaches where the Japanese thought the Americans would attack (and where they did attack), as well as the entire northern two-thirds of the island. But Lt. Gen. Ushijima Mitsuru buried his defending force under a vast array of pillboxes, switch lines, and deep bunkers to carry out an extended defense of the southern portion of Okinawa. Ushijima recognized that his 32d Army could never match American firepower, but he maximized what firepower he had. His objective was to use mortars and artillery in sufficient numbers and with enough deadly effect so as not to cede the firepower advantage completely to the Americans. Fighting their way through deep defensive lines, the Marines and soldiers eventually took the island and completely destroyed the Japanese Tenth Army of 70,000 men (killing 70,000 Japanese civilians as well). But the casualty bill in the island fighting and among the ships forced to stand off Okinawa to support the ground forces in the face of massed Kamikaze attacks were horrendous: 65,631 killed or wounded.

Another effort to redefine and codify an Eastern approach to defeating the Western way of war began in the mountain fastness of Manchuria immediately after the end of the Pacific war. Mao Tse-tung and his marshals developed a body of doctrine adapted from their successful wartime guerrilla campaigns and modified their concepts to fit the demands of a conventional war fought against an enemy superior in technology and materiel.[1] Mao perfected his new way of war against the nationalists during the Chinese Civil War fought between 1946 and 1949. His concepts were simple and centered around three tenets, the first and most important of which was "area control." To be successful Mao's army first needed to survive in the midst of a larger, better-equipped enemy.[2] To ensure survival he divided his army into small units and scattered them across a broad expanse of territory. Controlling and maintaining cohesion among such a disparate and scattered force was and remained his greatest challenge.

Once his force was supportable and stable, Mao proceeded to apply the second tenet, which was to "isolate and compartmentalize" Nationalist forces. The challenge of this phase was to leverage control of the countryside to such a degree that the enemy gradually retreated into urban areas and along major rail and road lines of communications.[3] The final act of the campaign demanded an ability to find the enemy's weakest points in order to collect and mass overwhelming force against each point sequentially, much as one might take apart a string of pearls, one pearl at a time. Mao's new style of conventional

47

war, while effective, demanded an extraordinary degree of discipline and patience to persevere under extreme hardships. It also demanded the ability to transition quickly from an area control force to a force capable of fighting a war of movement.

From China to Korea

Within a year of the end of the Chinese Civil War, the Americans severely tested Mao's methods in Korea. During the early days of the Chinese intervention—beginning in October 1950—the People's Liberation Army (PLA) badly misjudged the killing effect of American artillery and tactical air power. Pushed too quickly into maneuver warfare, the Chinese massed in the open, often in daylight, to expand their control over the northern portions of the Korean Peninsula.[4] They extended their narrow lines of communication farther down the mountainous spine of Korea as they advanced.[5] But they soon found their logistic support exposed to the terrible effects of American air power. The Chinese paid a horrific price for their haste. Their spring 1951 offensive sputtered to a halt as U.S. artillery and aerial firepower slaughtered Chinese soldiers in masses, while air interdiction cut their supply lines and forced a retreat back across the Han.

Brutal experiences led quickly to sober lessons relearned from the Chinese Civil War. As a highly skilled complex adaptive system the Chinese Army quickly adjusted to the actual conditions of this new war. Over the next two years, subsequent Chinese attacks remained limited and controlled. The Chinese high command learned to hold most key logistic facilities north of the Yalu River well out of reach of U.S. air attacks. South of the river the Chinese dispersed and hid their forces while they massed only in the period immediately before launching an attack. Because their forces were so difficult to locate and so easy to transport, mortars became the Chinese weapon of choice. PLA soldiers moved at night and chiseled their front lines of resistance deep into hard, granite mountains. American casualties soon mounted, while the Chinese stabilized their casualties at a rate acceptable to their political leadership. Far more Americans died in combat during this "stability phase" of the war than during the earlier period of fluid warfare. A cost acceptable to the Chinese became too costly to the Americans. The result was an operational and strategic stalemate. To the Chinese, stalemate equaled victory.[6]

From Korea to Vietnam

Over the next two decades the Vietnamese borrowed extensively from the Chinese experience and found creative ways to lessen the killing effect of firepower, first against the French and then against the Americans. The Vietnamese also proved highly skilled in adapting to the new challenges posed by their Western opponents. The Vietminh won the battle of Dien Bien Phu against the French Army in spring 1954; the battle was a straight out conventional confrontation.[7] The Vietminh based their tactical and operational approach on Mao's unconventional methods. Their conduct of the battle was remarkably reminiscent of siege operations conducted by the PLA during the Chinese Civil War. In both cases the secret of success proved to be dispersion and careful preparation of the battlefield. The Vietminh remained scattered in small units whenever possible to offer smaller, and thus less detectable and less lucrative targets, and to allow their troops to live off the land. Fewer supply lines and logistic sites offered even fewer opportunities for interdiction fires.

To win the Chinese and the Vietminh eventually needed to attack. Successful attacks demanded the ability to mass, at least temporarily. The Vietminh needed to exercise great care in massing under the enemy's umbrella of protective firepower. Superior intelligence provided sufficient information to select the right time and place. Their ability to collect and orchestrate the movement of tens of thousands

49

of soldiers at just the right moment allowed attacking forces to collapse the enemy's defenses before French firepower could regain the advantage. This remarkable ability to "maneuver under fire" perfected against the Nationalist Chinese and the French, reached new levels of refinement during the second Indo-China War against the United States.

During the early days of the conflict, impatience as well as ignorance of the enormously more potent U.S. firepower led the Viet Cong (VC) and the North Vietnamese Army (NVA) to push too quickly for a showdown. Nevertheless, there is some evidence to suggest that Giap deliberately sacrificed units in the Ia Drang in 1965 to find out exactly what the American capabilities were. The result, however, was that over the course of 1965 and much of 1966 the VC and NVA suffered terrible casualties. But Giap learned quickly to accommodate his strategic plans to the new realities imposed by American firepower. By 1967, the North Vietnamese had shifted the bulk of their attention to the Marines in I Corps, a region where the NVA was closer to its logistical support and up against U.S. forces that possessed substantially less firepower. Over this period, the North Vietnamese relearned the importance of dispersion and patience. They redistributed their forces to keep their most vulnerable units outside the range of American artillery while they moved their logistic system away from battle areas into sanctuaries relatively safe from aerial detection and strikes.

Thus, the VC and NVA dusted off and applied many of the same methods that had proven useful in previous Asian wars against Western style armies, including the use of submerged bridges, overhead coverings for major facilities, and practically invisible artillery positions. As the Americans developed technologies to find the enemy, the enemy found innovative ways to evade detection. The VC consistently spoofed U.S. aerial and ground based intercept stations with deceptive transmissions; they also built fires and phony roads and deployed elaborate decoys to fool interdicting aircraft.[8] Whenever close combat was necessary, the VC chose to attack soft support bases rather than formidable front-line forces. The enemy continued to refine its doctrine for breaking contact and withdrawing quickly from firefights to lessen the exposure of its troops to American firepower. Increasingly, the VC chose to "hug" American units before attacking in order to remain so closely engaged that U.S. forces could use supporting fires from artillery and aircraft only at considerable risk to themselves. The Tet offensive represented a reversion to earlier tactics, much against Giap's wishes, but the terrible casualties again forced the VC and NVA to return to a more prudent approach. The general results of Giap's indirect approach to the Asian art of war were immediate and dramatic. By early 1969, for example, the ratio of enemy to friendly casualties dropped by half, or two-thirds in some areas, compared to the period before the Tet offensive.[9]

Overconfidence again appeared in the North Vietnamese high command as the South Vietnamese assumed responsibility for the war on the ground. By 1972, the war had lost much of its unconventional nature. Beginning in April 1972 main force North Vietnamese units equipped with effective gun and missile defenses and supported by tanks, artillery, and trucks pushed across the Demilitarized Zone and against several major South Vietnamese cities. Again, U.S. aerial firepower took a terrible toll of enemy forces until Giap's commanders learned how to maintain mechanized formations in the field and to maneuver effectively in spite of American air superiority. When dispersion and patience once again replaced mass and impetuosity, victory was suddenly within the grasp of the North Vietnamese.[10]

To be sure, victory took time. Over the next three years, American firepower continued to generate pyrotechnically impressive displays. But throughout this difficult period, Giap gained ground in the south, and, as long as the resolve of the North Vietnamese leadership remained intact, Giap rightfully recognized that ownership of enemy territory would ultimately guarantee victory. His operational challenge in the south remained unchanged. He needed to reestablish his army's ability to survive and maneuver successfully while under aerial attack; once the doctrine and training were in place to allow this to happen on a broad scale and throughout the combat zone, battlefield success and the ultimate outcome were no longer in question.

From Vietnam to Afghanistan

Half a decade later and half a continent away in Afghanistan, the Soviets learned the same harsh, firsthand lessons of overconfidence when first-world military organizations confront third-world militaries which have the will, tenacity, and skill to remain effective in the field despite complete firepower inferiority. Year after year, the Soviets arrayed themselves for conventional combat and pushed methodically up the Panjir Valley only to be expelled a few months later by a seemingly endless and psychologically debilitating series of methodical and well-placed ambuscades and minor skirmishes. Borrowing a page from the American textbook in Vietnam, the Soviets tried to exploit the firepower, speed, and intimidating potential of armed helicopters. They employed helicopters principally as convoy escorts and to provide fire support. At times, Hind helicopters proved enormously lethal and effective, particularly early in the war, when the Mujahideen were psychologically unprepared. But the Mujahideen eventually borrowed a page from the Vietnamese textbook. They first learned to employ heavy antiaircraft machine guns and later Stinger shoulder-fired missiles to shoot the gunships down in increasing numbers. The result of military frustration and defeat in Afghanistan presaged the collapse of the Soviet Union.

The Middle East

Beginning in 1982, after nearly three decades of failure in open warfare, an alliance of Arab state and non-state actors pushed Israeli mechanized forces out of Beirut. Back streets, tall buildings, and other forms of urban clutter provided the Arabs just enough respite from the firepower intensive methods of the Israelis to wear away Israeli morale both in the field and at home. Unable to bring the full force of their superior maneuverability and shock effect to bear, the Israelis paused just short of their operational objectives. Excessive casualties and the public images of bloody excesses on both sides eventually resulted in an Israeli withdrawal from Beirut. This success in Beirut soon provided Israel's enemies in the region with a new and promising method to offset the Israeli superiority in open mechanized combat. Now a spectrum of low-tech threats, that run the gamut from weapons of mass destruction delivered by crude ballistic missiles, to random acts of terrorism, to children throwing rocks at soldiers, confront an increasingly frustrated Israeli military and public.

One of the more curious ironies of the recent wars in the Middle East has been the fact that Western style militaries have had great success when fighting against non-Western enemies who mimic Western firepower doctrines. The Gulf War is the most recent example of failed efforts by Arab states stretching back through the conflicts in the Middle East to 1948. In 1973 Arab armies enjoyed some measure of success while employing Western methods, but their success was as much due to Israeli overconfidence as to the limited aims the Arabs sought. Even the People's Liberation Army, erstwhile creator and most successful practitioner of a method of war effective against a conventional, firepower-centered system of war, failed when it violated its own recipe by invading Vietnam with conventional and motorized regiments in 1979. In that war, the world watched the extraordinary spectacle of the star pupil teaching a bloody lesson to its former friend and mentor.

Operation Desert Storm

During the Gulf War, despite an extraordinary level of incompetence at the highest level of the Iraqi leadership, the Iraqi Army displayed considerable capacity to adapt on the battlefield. As the American air campaign began to focus on the destruction of the Iraqi ground forces in the Kuwait Theater of Operations (KTO) in early February, the Iraqis almost immediately began to adapt in order to limit their losses.[11] By constructing berms around their tanks and by scattering them widely across the desert, the Iraqis ensured that an aircraft dropping precision guided bombs would only be able, at best, to destroy a single vehicle with each pass. By burning tires next to operational vehicles they spoofed their tormentors into missing the real targets; and finally by using antiaircraft effectively they kept a substantial portion of coalition aircraft at an altitude where they were unable to do substantial damage. The best trained Iraqi units endured several weeks of allied air bombardment with unbroken will and their combat capability essentially intact. The most impressive indication of the Iraqi ability to adapt came in the operational movement of a substantial portion of the Republican Guard during the first hours of Desert Storm. Elements of two divisions shifted from a southeastern defensive orientation to defensive positions facing to the southwest along the Wadi al-Batin. In those positions the Tawakalna Republican Guards Division and the 50th and 37th Armored Brigades would be destroyed by the U.S. VII Corps.[12] Nevertheless, sacrifice by these units provided time for the remainder of the Republican Guard to escape. Significantly, the Republican Guard carried out this movement in terrain and weather conditions ideally suited to interdiction and despite the overwhelming superiority of coalition air power.

The Emergence of Future Threats

Nearly a decade beyond the defeat of the Republican Guard, the United States military has yet to face an enemy capable of doing us serious harm. Yet, if the past is prologue, this vacation from violence must end eventually. It is still too soon to postulate who our significant competitor might be. However, it seems reasonable to anticipate with some degree of certainty that a major military threat to our vital national interest is not likely to arise from the 20 or so developed industrialized democracies. Although warfare among or between mature democratic states is not impossible, such a prospect is highly improbable. Likewise, the huge number of states at the opposite end of the have-and-have-not continuum are not likely to pose a serious military threat either. These "failed states," mostly in the developing world, will certainly continue to call on Western humanitarian and peacekeeping assistance. To be sure, some may seek to do us harm. But the desperate economic condition of these states will simply deny them the means to threaten either our vital national interests or the interests of our allies.

In between these two extremes lies a group of states most likely to become candidates for serious military competition in the next century. Some of these so-called "transitional states," located primarily in Europe, the Middle East and Asia, are already beginning to develop the economic means to generate income to support more sophisticated militaries. While they may expand militarily, a certain number of them will fail to develop a concomitant facility with democratic institutions. Thus, we should anticipate that perhaps by the end of the next decade a few transitional states will be able to procure the military means and build a collective will to challenge Western interests seriously within their respective regions of influence. And should these threatening states be astride or near a region whose continued stability is vital to the interest of a Western nation, we must be prepared to respond by force if necessary.

Increasingly, non-Western militaries are identifying and internalizing the lessons of recent wars. Their most recent thoughts and writings concerning the operational and tactical problems confronting them in a fight against Western style military organizations suggests some clear warnings for the future. First, non-Western militaries understand that the West does possess vulnerabilities: an aversion to casualties and excessive collateral damage, a sensitivity to domestic and world opinion, and an apparent lack of commitment to prepare for and fight long wars. They perceive that Americans in particular still remain committed to a style of war focused primarily on the single dimension of precision strike. They are already thinking about how to target Western vulnerabilities while capitalizing on the three inherent advantages they possess: time, will, and the inherent power of the defensive. Taking a page from Mao and Giap, our potential future opponents have learned the value of time and patience. From their perspective, swift success is not essential to ultimate victory. In particular, the Chinese experience suggests that the maintenance of an army in the field at all costs, even in the face of the most damaging punishment, must be the first rule of war—a lesson not entirely surprising to students of the American Revolution.[13]

The second lesson apparent to our potential opponents is that it is imperative to interfere with an intruding power's intention to end the conflict quickly and at minimum cost. Thus, the logic of their strategy will lead to efforts that impede rather than prevent the intrusion of a Western opponent. In recent wars, non-Western armies have learned to limit the damage and duration of air campaigns by dispersing their forces in the field and by distributing telecommunications, logistics, and transportation infrastructures as widely as possible. Moreover, they understand that sophisticated air defense networks, whose effectiveness depends on airfields, surface-to-air missile sites, and complicated and vulnerable command and control nodes, have become more of a liability than an asset. Again, time, patience, and a willingness to sacrifice can substitute for technological sophistication. A few guns and missiles scattered about the countryside, capable perhaps only of shooting down the occasional intruder, may be enough to raise the level of frustration and impatience of the attacker sufficiently to limit an air campaign.

The experience of the Gulf War has also suggested to potential future opponents that they must not allow the United States unfettered use of air bases in surrounding territory. Their first option will be the use of intense diplomatic and political pressure to prevent U.S. forces from gaining access to airfields. Our recent experiences in the Gulf suggest how effective this approach may prove to be. But even if American air forces gain access to foreign bases, U.S. troubles will not be over. We can expect that through the means of ballistic missiles, cruise missiles, and special forces, any future opponent will attack the airfields from which the U.S. will conduct any future air campaign. Even the North Koreans, the sole remaining vestige of Stalinist militarism, are striving with their missile and weapons of mass destruction programs to ensure that they have the means to interfere with the movement of U.S. forces onto the Korean peninsula, should war break out.

Once conflict on the ground begins, potential opponents understand they must capitalize on their superior mass to offset the superior firepower and precision technology of Western armies. They will capitalize on the advantages of being on the defensive in or near their own territory. As they gain confidence, they will search for opportunities to mass sufficient force to achieve local successes. As in the air campaign, the enemy will seek to frustrate Western ground forces by employing just enough modern weaponry to extend the campaign indefinitely. A few precision cruise missiles against major logistic bases will add to the casualty bill that Western militaries must explain to their civilian populations back home. The object will not be decisive victory, but stalemate, stalemate that if continued for any prolonged period of time will inevitably result in the erosion of Western political support for the conflict.

Early Signals of Change

As non-Western militaries develop concepts for defeating the American firepower-centered method of war, the character and composition of their forces will slowly change. The impulse that existed during the Cold War to mimic Western force structures is rapidly disappearing. Foreign militaries that were once Cold War clones are taking on identities unique to their own culture and societies. The mountains of metal, consisting of expensive yet often second-rate air, sea, and ground machines of war that today serve as potentially lucrative targets in a conflict against modern Western militaries are rapidly disappearing. Non-Western armies, in particular, are getting lighter. The need to survive and remain effective against the threat of overwhelming Western killing power is forcing them to develop means to disperse, hide, or if possible eliminate the vulnerable logistics, transportation, and telecommunications facilities that now characterize the Western way of war.

Evidence of this trend lies in the shopping lists of many wealthier non-Western militaries. Instead of investing in sophisticated aircraft and blue water fleets, most are purchasing or developing cheap weapons of mass destruction and methods of delivering those weapons. Mines, both sea and land, as well as distributed air defense weapons add credence to the conclusion that the intent of these militaries is to use such weapons as a means to keep potential enemies at bay. Most money and attention is going toward land forces because armies provide political legitimacy in non-democratic states. They are the most useful instrument for regional wars of aggression, as well as the surest means for suppressing internal dissent and thwarting troublesome outsiders. For that reason the officer corps of non-Western states are becoming more mature, professional, and better educated. A visit to any of the more vigorous military educational institutions in the emerging world underlines a renewed sense of intellectual curiosity and a willingness to study the tenets and theory of war on their own terms. Younger officers, no longer fettered by the ideological constrictions of the Cold War, are seeking to discover ways of fighting that conform to their own unique cultures, local threats, and regional circumstances.

The Information Age—A Neutral Ally

At present there are too many in the U.S. and other Western military organizations who believe that they can best address the appearance of a major competitor in the next century by exploring the technologies of the information age to develop ever more effective means of finding the enemy and killing him from a distance. There are a number of troubling concerns with this premise. The most obvious is that the information revolution will be neutral in this looming competition; in fact it may favor the competition more than it favors Western militaries because potential enemies will be able to tailor new technologies to their particular style of war without becoming information-dependent. On one hand, the increasing flow of information is quite literally drowning commanders, staffs, and intelligence organizations. This is the crucial problem of the information age—one that we have yet to solve. The evidence is already clear that information technology will not simplify the decision-making process, but in fact makes it more complex. Our future opponents, however, given their expectations and aims, will require much less information to strike effectively—particularly since their aim is not to win a decisive victory. They will be, moreover, less dependent upon the microchip to conduct their method of warfare. A thinking opponent will quickly realize that our intensive reliance on information age technologies becomes a weakness that can become an asymmetric target.

A reading of current military writing from abroad, particularly Asia, reveals that many armies are already placing extraordinary emphasis on information operations and information warfare. At present American analysts are taking considerable comfort in the observation that few have made serious investments in information warfare and precision systems similar to those possessed by Western military organizations. What, however, they fail to see is that Asian armies already understand that advances in information technologies will favor their style of warfare just as much as it does the Western style. In particular, the internet and wireless, non-nodal communications will allow dispersed armies to mass rapidly. As information becomes more secure and information centers more dispersed and less vulnerable, potential opponents will wield more flexible and agile land forces. Moreover, they will be able to divide their forces into smaller and thus less detectable increments. In perhaps one of the strangest potential ironies of the future, Western information technology may well provide non-Western armies solutions to two vexing problems. First, cellular technology and the internet may allow them to maintain a concert of action for long periods among widely dispersed units. Second, these same technologies will allow them to orchestrate the rapid massing of dispersed units when opportunities arise to transition to the offensive.

The result may well be a technological foot race that either side could win. As we develop the technologies to find and kill an enemy, our potential opponents will develop the technologies to become even more difficult to find. The prospect becomes even more sobering when one considers the fact that the commercial sector is now in the process of providing future competitors with the tools they need, as our research centers continue to perfect non-nodal, distributed, and netcentric global information technologies for paying customers on a worldwide basis. Moreover, potential U.S. opponents do not have to spend a dime for the development of any of these systems. And again we must remember that such opponents have a very different strategy in mind for the next war. They have only to create a stalemate and inflict sufficient casualties on Western forces to raise political difficulties for the political leaders who decided to intervene (in the words of Nevile Chamberlain) in "a quarrel in a far away country between people of whom we know nothing."

The Warnings Are Real

Clausewitz provides us with a harsh and accurate warning about the fundamental nature of war:

> War, however, is not the action of a living force upon a lifeless mass (total nonresistance would be no war at all), but always the collision of two living forces. The ultimate aim of waging war . . . must be taken as applying to both sides. Once again, there is interaction. So long as I have not overthrown my opponent I am bound to fear he may overthrow me. Thus, I am not in control: he dictates to me as much as I dictate to him.[14]

It is this fundamental Clausewitzian point that Western, and American military organizations in particular, are in danger of forgetting. Our potential opponents in the next century will have thought long and hard about how to attack our weaknesses.

The less than sterling performance of the U.S. military in two recent wars against thinking, creative, reactive Asian militaries possessed with their own will, should make Americans cautious about an over-reliance on a style of war focused primarily on the advantages of superior firepower. There is no compelling evidence in the modern history of war to suggest that the killing effect of modern weapons is sufficient to break the will of a determined opponent. The survival of Waffen SS and Wehrmacht defenses, severely attrited though they might have been by the massive bombardment of Allied air forces, is one more indication of how tenacious the human will can be under the worst of circumstances.

To be sure, firepower can be paralytic in its effect. But paralytic effects by fire are always fleeting. Armies have shown time and again that they can become inured to the paralytic effects of fire and can even learn creative ways to lessen its destructive effects. Add to this factor the ability of non-Western armies to utilize the advantages of time, mass, will, and the power of the defensive, and the single American advantage of superior killing power becomes much less persuasive as an instrument of war than it appears on first consideration.

Our experience in wars recently passed should serve as both a guide and a caution as we prepare today for the prospect of facing some opponent on a future battlefield. The United States must choose its wars carefully and refuse to allow an inflated opinion on the utility and effectiveness of precision weapons to push for involvement in a conflict that precision strike and distant punishment cannot win by themselves. The experience of Vietnam should provide a sobering caution. To a considerable extent the American military embarked on that conflict believing that air power and technology could deliver far more than they actually could in the face of a clever and ruthless opponent who consistently adapted and changed to every new innovation the American military brought to the war.

Notes

1. Mao Zedong, "On the International Front Against Fascism," *Selected Works of Mao Tse-tung, Vol III* (Beijing: Foreign Language Press, 1967); William H. Whitson, *The Chinese High Command: A History of Communist Politics, 1927-1971*, (New York: Praeger Press, 1973).

2. Mao Zedong, *Selected Works of Mao Tse-tung, Vol I and Vol III* (Beijing: Foreign Language Press, 1975 and 1967).

3. Frederick Fu (F.F.) Liu, *A Military History of Modern China: 1924-1949* (Princeton: Princeton University Press, 1956).

4. Bin Yu, "What China Learned from Its Forgotten War in Korea," *Strategic Review,* Summer 1998.

5. Russell Spurr, *Enter the Dragon: China's Undeclared War Against the U.S. in Korea, 1950-51* (New York: Newmarket Press, 1987).

6. T.R. Fehrenbach, *This Kind of War* (New York: The Macmillan Company, 1963).

7. Bernard B. Fall, *Dien Bien Phu: Hell is a Very Small Place* (Philadelphia; Lippincott, 1967).

8. Earl H. Tilford, *Crosswinds: The Air Force Setup in Vietnam* (Texas: Texas A & M Press, 1993).

9. Cecil B. Currey, *Victory at Any Cost: The Genius of Viet Nam's Gen. Vo Nguyen Giap* (Washington, DC: Brassey's, Inc, 1997), pp. 274-280.

10. Don Oberdorfer, *Tet!* (New York: Doubleday, 1971); and James J. Wirtz, *The Tet Offensive: Intelligence Failure* in War (New York: Cornell University Press, 1991).

11. Robert H. Scales, *Certain Victory: The US. Army in the Gulf War* (Washington, DC: Office of the Chief of Staff United States Army, 1993).

12. *Ibid.*

13. Mao Zedong, On *Protracted War, Selected Works* of *Mao Tse-tung, Vol III* (Beijing: Foreign Language Press, 1967).

14. Carl Von Clauswitz, *On War*, ed. and trans. by Michael Howard and Peter Paret (Princeton: Princeton University Press, 1975).

Chapter Five

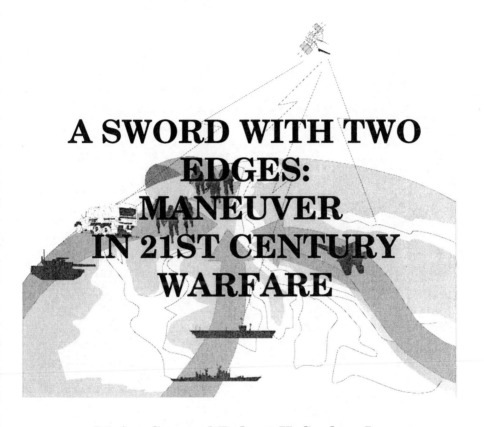

A SWORD WITH TWO EDGES: MANEUVER IN 21ST CENTURY WARFARE

Major General Robert H. Scales, Jr.

Reproduced with Permission Granted by:
Spring 1999 Issue
STRATEGIC REVIEW
Volume 27, Number 2

A SWORD WITH TWO EDGES:
MANEUVER IN 21ST CENTURY WARFARE

Battles are won by slaughter and maneuver. The greater the
general, the more he contributes in maneuver, the less he
demands in slaughter.[1]

Winston Churchill

An observer standing in the midst of the French
positions on the heights of La Marfee can clearly make out
the crossing points across the Meuse River seized by
German infantry on the afternoon of 13 May 1940. The day
was bright and cloudless. The French held the commanding
heights in strength. Their two hundred guns ranged the
ground over which German columns inched their way to
assembly areas on the east bank. Yet, the crossing
succeeded. Within four hours the 1st Rifle Regiment,
supported by Infantry Regiment *Grossdeutschland*, had
crossed the river in strength and ruptured French defenses
irreparably. Over the course of the evening, French troops,
who held most of the tactical cards, dissolved in panic. In
one of those rare moments of cataclysmic impact, a single
afternoon's combat sufficed to open the door to the collapse
of the most respected army in the world. The result sealed
the fate of the Third Republic.

How could it have happened? Any student of tactics
knows that a river crossing against a defended shore is the
most difficult of all tactical maneuvers. In such a maneuver,
the assaulting side requires overwhelming superiority in
firepower and mobility. Yet the Germans had neither.
Historians have tended to ascribe the German success to
superiority in mechanized warfare. In fact, the critical

---

1. Winston S. Churchill, *The World Crisis*, 1915 (New York, 1923), p. 5.

assault that broke the back of French resistance resulted from the efforts of infantry and combat engineers paddling across the Meuse in rubber boats. The battle culminated in the *Wehrmacht's* favor 12 hours before German engineers completed the bridges necessary to carry German armor across.

The Germans succeeded because of the excellence of their operational method—one that played out on the battlefield like a superbly orchestrated symphony. The instruments of blitzkrieg—tactical aircraft, tanks, infantry, sappers, and artillery—each added their own unique harmonic at the right time and in proper balance. They managed to balance the brute strength and psychological intimidation offered by firepower with the speed and physical paralysis provided by rapid movement. This fusion of fire and maneuver resulted in a seamless, unrelenting offensive that made the German assault on Sedan so overwhelmingly decisive. The German success was a triumph, not of overwhelming mass or firepower, but of both applied in harmony using intellect, foresight, imagination and will.

Victory in France had its roots in Germany's defeat in World War I. Decades of introspection and disciplined study during the inter war years taught the Germans a crucial lesson about the relationship between technology and the nature of war. Modern rifled weapons had upset the balance between the ability of armies to prepare the attack by fire and their ability to use maneuver against the enemy's vulnerable points. The battlefield had become so vast and lethal that soldiers attacking on foot could no longer cross no-man's-land with sufficient strength intact to achieve decisive results.

What the Germans understood in developing their doctrine was that, given the dispersion of troops, confusion, and chaos characterizing modern warfare, top-down control was no longer in the cards. It worked for Napoleon because he could see virtually the entire battlefield at Austerlitz.

But it was no longer a possibility on a battlefield where not only distance but the very violence and confusion of modern war separated soldiers and units. Troops now had to understand the objective and then, as the operation unfolded, adapt their responses to the tactical situation as it existed. Above all they must not wait for their commanders to tell them what to do. Rather, depending on circumstances, they had to act in accordance with their training, intuition, and understanding of the immediate situation.

The balance and harmony between maneuver and fire remained the essential imperative of maneuver warfare through the remainder of the machine age. They formed the nexus of American combat doctrine during the last decade of the Cold War. "AirLand Battle," developed jointly by the Army and the Air Force in the early 1980's, represented the final maturation of mechanized warfare, combining the aerial and ground dimensions into the instrument that proved so effective in the Gulf War. But, in retrospect, that doctrine and the Gulf War appear as the final refinements of a machine age fast disappearing. As the machine age fades with the appearance of a new millennium, the responsibility of U.S. military leaders is to anticipate and prepare for a new age.

The information age promises to change the context of war as decisively as the machine age altered war in the 19th and 20th Centuries. The challenge today is not unlike that faced by a previous generation of military thinkers who sought to anticipate how changes in technology and geopolitics would affect future wars. Unfortunately, the recent success of U.S. forces in the Gulf may well cause American military leaders to misjudge the course and duration of future war in the next century. The present fixation on firepower and bloodless wars may well cause the U.S. military to develop a 21st Century version of the methodical battle that brought catastrophe to the French Army and nation. History provides ample warning that a single-dimension approach to war is risky and dangerous.

Adaptive military organizations quickly learn how to counter technical and tactical advantages that often only provide their possessors fleeting advantage.[2]

War in the 21st Century: What Won't Change?

Thinking about war in the next century, military innovators need to grapple with a number of essential questions. The most obvious has to do with what will change and what will remain the same. On the answer to those two questions rides a host of others: What will be the role of technology? What kind of asymmetric possibilities are open to our opponents? What will be the underlying principles of command and control? What are the vulnerabilities of U.S. military forces, and perhaps most important, what is it that U.S. military power will need to achieve in terms of operational results? In the end American preparations and thinking about force structure and doctrine for the next century should aim at ensuring that at the tactical and operational levels of war, U.S. military forces will imitate the Germans and not the French along the Meuse.

As has been the case throughout the past 2,000 years, political concerns will undergird the conduct of war. Clausewitz' trinity of people, government, and military–and the ambiguities that relationships among them involve–will determine the parameters within which the United States will employ military force. And connected with the political dimension will be the will of the United States as well as of its opponents. In the Vietnam War the American military and government fought a limited war, while its opponents engaged in a war of "national liberation"–a total war.[3] Thus the political context within which America fights will prove as critical in the next

---

2. Major General Robert H. Scales, Jr., "Adaptive Enemies," *Strategic Review*, Winter 1999.

3. See in particular Harry Summers, *On Strategy* (Carlisle, PA, 1981).

century as it has in the past centuries. If the political will does not exist, then all the military power is of little use. Moreover, the United States will fight its wars in the next century for political purposes and that will demand the occupation of territory as opposed to simply smashing up the landscape.[4]

Equally important to thinking about war in the future is the fact that there are certain immutable facets to human conflict that technology cannot change. Contrary to the claims of some current theorists, technology alone will never eliminate the fear, confusion, ambiguity, fog and friction of battle. Such claims represent the rebirth of the technological mechanistic view of the world that the American military took with it to Vietnam.[5] Everything that modern science (not to mention history) indicates about the world is that mankind lives in a nonlinear universe of immense complexity. The American military can achieve superiority of battlefield information, and we must do so in order to exploit fully our technological superiority. But human beings will never gain anything approaching complete information dominance, because information alone does not, and will never equate to knowledge and wisdom about the enemy. As Clausewitz suggested in *On War:* "War ...is not the action of a living force upon a lifeless mass...but always the collision of two living [thinking] forces."[6] Our opponents will have limitless opportunity to

---

4. Paul Van Riper, USMC and Robert H. Scales, Jr., "Preparing for War in the 21st Century", *Strategic Review*, Summer 1997.

5. In his memoirs McNamara ascribes the American difficulties in Vietnam to the following cause: "Uncertain how to evaluate the results of the war without battle lines, the military tried to gauge its progress with quantitative measurements such as enemy casualties (which became infamous as body counts), weapons seized, prisoners taken, sorties flown, and so on". We later learned that many of these measures were misleading or erroneous. Robert Strange McNamara, *In Retrospect, The Tragedy and Lessons of Vietnam* (New York, 1995), p. 48.

6. Carl von Clausewitz, *On War* (Princeton, 1975), p. 77. For a clear discussion of why Clausewitz will remain as relevant in the next century as has been in this century see Alan Beyerchen, "Clausewitz, Non-Linearity, and the Unpredictability of War", *International Security* (Winter 1992/1993).

find a way to win regardless of whatever technological superiority we might possess. And as the Vietnam War suggests, they will react with intelligence, imagination and sophistication. The intellectual source of the German success at Sedan was derived from the 1933 edition of the German keystone manual, *Die Truppenführung* ("Troop Leadership"). It suggested all too accurately that:

> Situations in war are of unlimited variety. They change often and suddenly and are only rarely from the first discernible. Incalculable elements are often of great influence. The independent will of the enemy is pitted against ours. Friction and mistakes are everyday occurrences.[7]

Firepower and maneuver will continue to be the crucial determinates of how military operations play out on the 21st Century battlefields. The relationship between these two primal variables will also follow the patterns of past wars. Rarely has superior firepower determined the outcome of a war. Armies and nations have displayed remarkable resiliency in enduring sustained punishment wrought by bombs, artillery and missiles. In World War II four years of strategic bombardment were not sufficient to break the will of either the Nazi regime or the German people. Years of extensive bombing over Vietnam failed to reduce the flow of troops and supplies to support the war in the south. In the Gulf War, despite relentless pounding by coalition forces, Saddam Hussein refused to withdraw his forces from Kuwait.[8] While firepower kills, it cannot by

---

7. Chef der Heeresleitung, *Die Truppenführung* (Berlin, 1993), p. 1.

8. Robert H. Scales, Jr., *Certain Victory: The U.S. Army in the Gulf War* (Washington, DC, 1993), pp. 368-69. See also Williamson Murray, *Air War in the Persian Gulf* (Baltimore, MD, 1995), p. 307. Murray makes the point that if Saddam had been allowed to withdraw from Kuwait without a ground campaign, he would have been able to make the claim that his army had stood unbeaten and unbroken in the field. In effect the Iraqis would have been able to create another *Dolchstoß* legend, as the German Army had done after its defeat after World War I.

itself achieve the political objectives required for victory.[9] Even when delivered on a truly massive scale it has rarely succeeded in ejecting determined troops from the ground they occupy.[10]

But maneuver by itself also has inherent limitations. Depending on the experience of soldiers and their leaders, the unexpected presence of enemy forces in their rear or on their flanks, while disconcerting, rarely leads to total collapse. Stonewall Jackson's brilliant maneuver in hitting Hooker's exposed flank at Chancellorsville would probably have failed against a more resolute opponent.[11] While MacAuthur's success at Inchon began with a successful amphibious landing behind North Korean lines, the collapse of Communist forces occurred only after they had lost a bitter struggle to hold Seoul.

Decisive maneuver is extremely difficult to execute because the complexity of maneuvering many thousands of individuals across the landscape demands extraordinary skill and no small amount of luck. The risk is always high that the inherent friction so much a part of land warfare will quickly turn the most brilliant plan of maneuver into a costly slugging match where the victor will be the one willing to endure and suffer the most. Maneuver is made all the more difficult because it is inherently an offensive action and, as Clausewitz cautioned two centuries ago, the defensive is inherently the stronger form of war. The maneuvering side must by necessity risk exposure, detection and destruction to a much greater degree than the defender. Clausewitz' caution is made all the more sinister by a corollary which suggests that the power of the defensive

---

9. See William Hawkins, "Back to Vietnam? Iraq and the Limits of Air Power", *Strategic Review*, Spring 1998, pp. 43-50. See also Williamson Murray, "Air War in the Persian Gulf: The limits of air power", *Strategic Review*, Winter 1998.

10. See Paul Van Riper and Robert H. Scales, Jr., "Preparing for War in the 21st Century", *Strategic Review*, Summer 1997, pp.14-20.

11. It is worth noting that the majority of the Union Corps Commanders at Chancellorsville voted against a withdrawal.

becomes greater still when the state of weapons technology allows firepower systems to dominate the battlefield. The corollary has not been evident in our most recent conflicts because we were the only side to possess the most modern precision firepower weapons. But if the past is prologue this favorable condition cannot last for long. Eventually a future foe will copy or counter our precision advantage, and we may well discover the truth of the corollary painfully unless we find the technology to reverse the firepower advantage.

It is only when one side exploits the effects of firepower by maneuver that an enemy force begins to fall victim to the psychological dislocation of its fighting elements. The resulting psychological collapse spreads throughout the defeated force and eventually leads to paralysis.[12] Only when paralysis occurs can the attacking side gain the overwhelming decision it seeks at minimum cost to itself. Thus it is the combination, the subtle, symbiotic interrelationship between fire and maneuver that provide the decisive force necessary to end a contest quickly. Firepower temporarily paralyzes and impairs the enemy and thus creates opportunities to translate a temporary advantage into a lasting one through exploitation by maneuver.

War in the 21st Century: What Will Change?

Some aspects of future war will be decidedly different from today. For one thing, our enemies will be different. The American military is being carefully watched by those who some day might wish us harm. Potential opponents see opportunity and advantage in the way we have comported ourselves in recent conflicts. They are increasingly coming

---

12. As Clausewitz, who had experienced military catastrophe, suggests: "When one is losing, the first thing that strikes one's...intellect is the melting away of numbers. This is followed by a loss of ground...Next comes the break-up of the original line of battle, the confusion of units, and the dangers inherent in the retreat...The feeling of having been defeated, which on the field of battle had struck only the senior officers, now runs through the ranks down to the very privates." Clausewitz, *On War*, p. 254.

to believe that the American fixation on precision strike makes it possible to win simply by avoiding defeat. Tenacity, patience, and a willingness to sacrifice are effective counters to a high tech foe who has technology but little stomach for protracted conflict. The technological demands of hostile forces whose only objective is to avoid losing are most certainly modest.

A major war, anywhere in the world, may demand massive deployments of U.S. forces from North America into areas where no base structure exists or where, even if the bases exist, there will be direct threats from enemy cruise and ballistic missiles.[13] Moreover, the projection of U.S. military power may demand a forced entry into areas where the enemy has found the opportunity to hunker down and prepare defenses to meet an expected American thrust. Just enough precision or counterprecision weaponry will be sufficient to inflict unacceptable casualties on American forces. Sea mines, submarines, conventional brown water vessels and cheap weapons of mass destruction will keep intruders away from a hostile enemy's shore.

The Gulf War and the lethargic reactions of the Iraqi military to Coalition military operations should not suggest how future opponents will fight in the next century.[14] We must be prudent enough to give them credit for some substantial advantages. First we must assume that a prospective opponent will possess a high degree of political and military competence. If they are competent and well led, then we must also concede to them an advantage of will and tenacity to resist. Our future enemies understand clearly that in any conflict time will be our enemy and our enemy's friend. He may lose all of his battles and still win so

---

13. See among others on the changed strategic framework for war in the next century, Williamson Murray, "Preparing to Lose the Next War," *Strategic Review*, Spring 1998.

14. To understand the weaknesses of the Iraqi military before the Gulf War one must possess and understanding of the nature of the Iraqi regime and Saddam Hussein's tyranny. The best book on this subject remains Samir al-Khalil, *Republic of Fear, The Politics of Modern Iraq* (Berkley, 1989).

long as he preserves legitimacy by maintaining control of his army in the field.

In all likelihood he will field greater numbers. As we saw in the Gulf a mass of undisciplined, unmotivated, poorly trained soldiers can be as much an impediment as an advantage. But just enough training with equipment just modern enough to be marginally effective against a technologically superior opponent may well provide a less sophisticated but determined opponent with a force difficult to defeat quickly. Armed in all probability with advantages of massive numbers, determination and willingness to endure, a future enemy will not need to match us system for system to remain viable on the battlefield long enough for us to tire of the conflict and withdraw.

Regardless of advantages in mass and will, no thinking enemy will follow a doctrine that exposes his forces to destruction from American aerial delivered precision firepower. Over time he must transition from a Soviet style linear offensive doctrine centered around massive armored maneuvers to a more cautious doctrine that emphasizes the defense and control of broad areas of territory. Tactical units will disperse to the greatest extent possible while retaining the ability to mass on demand. The enemy will divide his combat forces into increasingly smaller increments with more and more empty spaces appearing between them.

The Size, Shape and Pattern of the 20th Century Battlefield

So what then might the battlefield of the next century look like, and how can the U.S. military leverage their capabilities to take advantage of a potential opponent's weaknesses? To begin with, we must understand what maneuver warfare aims to do and what its fundamental philosophy will remain. First, maneuver aims to disrupt and then to destroy the enemy's equilibrium. Consequently, it is not maneuver for its own sake that is the primary focus of maneuver war, but rather combining firepower and maneuver in such fashion that the enemy's entire command and control structure can no longer function. In other words he can no longer respond in a coordinated fashion to the moves of his opponent. This then will have important implications for how the American military should prepare forces to operate in the next century.

The first characteristic of future battle that will affect the nature of American war in the next century is that our battlefields will be very distant and, in all likelihood, located in regions of the world both remote and inhospitable. Getting to these places will in itself require an act of maneuver, in this case strategic maneuver, just as critical a task to success as maneuver on the battlefield. If we, as a nation, are to win quickly at minimum cost we must arrive early in a conflict, hopefully early enough to interfere with the deployment scheme of the enemy, perhaps early enough to place forces on the ground between the enemy and his operational objectives. Imagine how much more quickly and painlessly the Gulf War might have concluded if in August 1990 we had anticipated Saddam's intent and possessed a maneuver force with strategic velocity sufficient to have arrived in time to block the movement of the Republican Guard into Kuwait. To be sure, then as today, we can project both firepower in the form of tactical aircraft and presence in the form of light ground forces. But we did not have then nor do we yet have maneuver forces able to arrive quickly and fight enemy main force units decisively.

Well into the next century, once precision weaponry has reached the arsenals of the world's most prominent militaries, the shape and character of the battlefield will change fundamentally. Armies will adapt, as they always have, to revolutionary improvements in weaponry and develop effective ways to either copy or counter them. This process of adaptation is both natural and inevitable. The battlefield will continue to empty as armies seek to lessen the destructive effects of precision firepower. Again, this a continuing and spontaneous process that has been with us since the first precision revolution started thinning the battlefield with the introduction of rifled ordnance in the mid nineteenth century. Union and Confederate forces at Gettysburg were packed to a density of approximately 26,000 soldiers per square mile. On a World War II European battlefield a firefight on terrain similar to Gettysburg might involve several battalions of about 3,000 men. In Desert Storm the battlefield of Gettysburg could easily have been covered by a mechanized company in the attack.

On a future battlefield with precision weapons in the hands of both sides we can anticipate the battlefield spreading out even further. Gettysburg might well become a platoon position of perhaps three dozen soldiers and their weapon systems. With densities that thin, traditional forms of machine age maneuver will no longer be necessary. Armies spread over vast distances and divided into ever smaller tactical increments will no longer be assailable through the use of linear constructs of the direct attack, penetration or envelopment. Clausewitz' centers of gravity and Jomini's decisive points will no longer be easily identified, nor will they be geographically centered and concentrated. Highly rigid air defense grids, interconnected communications nodes and logistic networks of the past will give way to porous, distributed, and autonomous formations able to absorb repeated precision strikes with little loss of people or effectiveness. No amount of precision weaponry will be able to destroy robust formations divided into small increments spread over vast distances. The challenge of an enemy so arrayed will be to retain control and cohesion among so many dispersed and isolated elements on the battlefield. Curiously, information age technologies in the form of satellites and cellular telecommunications may well provide him with just the right tools to spread himself out and still retain the ability to mass on demand. As a testimony to the curious nature of our times, the technologies spawned by information based societies may well be turned against them on some future battlefield.

So how then must we operate in the future to achieve the moral and psychological collapse necessary for decisive maneuver warfare? Let's begin with a restatement of one of the immutable principle of warfare. War in practice requires the application in the proper balance between the ability to maneuver and the ability to destroy. As a side optimizes his operational method to accommodate one, he makes himself increasingly vulnerable to the other. Misjudgments concerning the true state of balance between fire and maneuver greatly increased the risk of catastrophic failure. The balance could get substantially out of kilter because of political or doctrinal misjudgments or by one side being too slow to adjust to opportunities offered by advances in technology. As the French demonstrated at Sedan, the natural response to the threat of an attack by fire was to hunker down, spread out and concentrate on dominating the battlefield by firepower. But this so called methodical style of war made them particularly vulnerable to assault by maneuver. The Germans saw opportunities for countering a method of war that had become unbalanced in favor of firepower and therefore vulnerable to maneuver. As our foes become more fixated on surviving precision strike, similar opportunities must inevitably arise.

To defeat a dispersed enemy we must disperse ourselves. Close combat will become a contest for control of territory. A vast battlefield thinly held will provide unoccupied spaces that can be assaulted and occupied at minimal cost. Thus the enemy can be collapsed by interposing forces between and among his widely scattered formations. We will possess the ability to see, sense, and track with great clarity, an ability secured by our control of the vertical dimension. Unblinking eyes in the exosphere and space will change how soldiers define key terrain. In past wars the decisive advantage went to the side occupying the high ground. Command of observation insured command of territory. Thus, from Little Round Top to Monte Casino to Pork Chop

Hill the infantryman's bloody obligation has been to take the hill. But our exploitation of the potential promised by satellites and high altitude remotely piloted vehicles will create a new high ground gained and dominated by information age technology rather than blood. Ground units will now be able to nest on almost any piece of ground and still command their surroundings. The enemy will no longer be able to predict when and where American forces will land in their midst. Frontal attack, ambushes and meeting engagements, long the most costly events in ground combat, will be less likely. Fewer soldiers in contact with the enemy and occupying uncontested ground events will surely reduce the cost of ground combat tremendously.

The ability to maneuver and occupy territory takes away from the enemy his first tenet of success: area control. A highly mobile and sophisticated ground maneuver force capable of operating in small units scattered across the countryside will deny the enemy refuge and source of sustenance. Our superior ability to see the battlefield with unparalleled clarity coupled with our ability to occupy or control key points will take away his ability to assemble his scattered forces without risking piecemeal destruction by fire. A soldier's eyes on every target will ensure that the right and most vital targets are hit. Our information advantage will help us to reduce the threat of surprise and ambush and will allow us to select and strike or capture an enemy's own centers of gravity and decisive points no matter how well hidden or scattered.

Regardless of how compelling the argument might be for maneuver as an essential component for achieving a decision on a future battlefield, the reluctance to put troops on the ground for fear of suffering excessive casualties continues to persist. Images of the first 20 minutes of the film "Saving Private Ryan" are compelling and chilling. But the information age promises to make ground combat considerably less destructive that the screen images of Utah beachhead in "Private Ryan." The film serves as a useful metaphor to explain the difference. Conjure the opening scene in your mind for a moment, but imagine that Captain John Miller knows exactly where the German defenses are located. Not only can he see them, but he has the ability to watch them move about and to anticipate where they might move next. He has at his command the ability to destroy some of the more critical static positions with precision munitions as his Higgins boat approaches the shore. He also can see well inland and knows with equal clarity where the enemy isn't located. Now imagine that Miller can lift his boat over the beach and land it precisely in a spot that is safe from enemy fire but positioned so that his platoon, once dismounted, can effectively block enemy egress from the beach. The enemy is now left with two unacceptable alternatives: either move out of his protected position into the open and face the certainty of destruction by fire, or stay in place and cede the initiative and the advantage permanently to the intruder.

Consider for a moment a more contemporary scenario. Recall our recent effort to intimidate and punish the Iraqis for not allowing full inspection of their nuclear, chemical and biological storage sites. Imagine how much more compelling the impact of military action might have been had we had the ability to follow tactical aircraft and cruise missile strikes with a sudden aerial assault by hundreds of individual ground units each capable of landing safely near a known or suspected site and commanding it by direct observation and covering it by fire.

Suppose further that each maneuver unit were robust enough to maneuver about for days if not weeks. Information age technologies will allow the tooth portion of a land power force to become extremely lean, self-contained and completely mobile. This capability will be achievable because most of the traditional impedimenta for a close combat force—-such as logistic and administrative facilities, higher command and communications centers and long range fire support units—-can be removed from the immediate battle area and held in a support base hundreds of miles distant from the battlefield. Only those few forces necessary to prosecute the close in fight would be placed in immediate proximity of the enemy's main force units.

The objective of blitzkrieg in the information age will be the same as its machine age predecessor, namely the rapid paralysis and eventual psychological collapse of an opponents will to resist through overwhelming application of a balance of firepower and maneuver. But technology and the nature of our future enemies will cause the new blitzkrieg to look considerably different. The aim will be different. As long as the enemy possesses precision weapons, no matter how primitive, the operational-tactical offensive that proved so successful for the Germans will prove to be too costly in future war. The dynamics of the future battlefield call for a return to the strategic offensive-tactical defensive approach where an offensive force uses its strategic mobility to place its combat units into positions so threatening to the enemy that he must either attack them or capitulate. Thus the most costly phase of the battle, the tactical offensive, becomes necessary for enemy, not friendly, forces to execute.

The requirement to overwhelm an enemy scattered across a vast area will require a maneuvering force to blanket or saturate a broad area with many small, autonomous and extremely mobile combat elements. Such an operation would play out more like a take down rather than a traditional linear movement through an enemy's defensive formations. Duration, timing and tempo would be different. Information age blitzkrieg would demand a continuous, relentless operation opened first with precision firepower followed immediately by a pattern of maneuver layered over the complete expanse of an the enemy's defenses in a single smothering act of aggression.

In order to overwhelm so much territory so quickly with so many discrete bits of combat power both fires and maneuver will increasingly have to be delivered from the air. An aerial maneuver force capable of operational maneuver of this sort will be costly to build. But remember, the armored formations that broke the back of the French Army made up less than eight percent of the total German army in 1940. Speed and agility count far more than sheer weight of metal if the objective is to collapse the enemy's will rather than slaughter him. Speed and agility also guarantee safety and lower casualties. A force mobile through the air will be practically immune from the threat of attack by missiles tipped with weapons of mass destruction. Aerial agility lessens the risk of defeat in detail. If surprised for any reason, the force possesses the mobility to shift quickly out of harm's way and approach the enemy from another direction. Aerial mobility permits a maneuver force to command more territory with fewer soldiers, thus limiting the number of soldiers exposed to enemy fires within the close combat area.

By the end of the next decade the maturation of the information age will provide the United States military with and even more remarkable ability to see the enemy and to strike him quickly with greater and greater precision. However, information age advances alone will not guarantee our ability to lift the Higgins boat over the beach or to coerce Saddam into doing our will through a credible threat of force. If we are to remain viable as a military power well into the next century, we must improve dramatically our ability to seize and control ground. We must build into our system of war the speed and agility to move unimpeded across large expanses of territory. We must be able to place combat formations at decisive points with the same precision and flexibility that we now have to place explosive killing power on distant targets.

The ability to complement precision fires with precision maneuver offers two essential advantages for warfare in the future. First, we would be able to beat an enemy at his own game of area control if we possessed the ability to array forces across a broad area yet retain the ability to mass them quickly at the point where the enemy is most vulnerable and weak. A balanced method of war that includes both of the timeless dimensions of fire and maneuver will greatly complicate the plan of an enemy who might seek to repeat the recent successes of others who have shown how to win against an approach to war centered principally around firepower.

An enemy who optimizes his operational method to remain viable and intact in the face of an opponent vastly superior in firepower, will by necessity make himself more vulnerable to assault by maneuver. If he disperses across a wide area to avoid the destructive effects of precision strike, he must suffer the loss of cohesion and control and thus be less able to mass against a threat from the ground. Dispersion will leave gaps in his ability to command his territory by observation and fire. These gaps will provide a maneuver force with the local sanctuaries he will need to occupy territory without having to fight for it. An expansion of forces over a wide area will increase the distances between each of his units in the field, thus making it easier for maneuvering forces to interpose themselves between the enemy's major units to paralyze them in place. If he disperses we disperse to check him at every decisive point, never allowing him to disappear into the shadows. If he masses we mass faster and bring to bear our overwhelming advantage in killing power. Facing two dimensions of threat rather than one, he will no longer be able afford the luxury of choosing the passive option of hunkering down to outlast and endure precision strikes. With troops in his midst he must act or lose. But if he attacks, our side then garners the inherent advantage of the defensive. To attack he must mass. But massing spells destruction by precision fires. Check by fires, checkmate by a balance of fire and maneuver.

A rapid orchestration of fire and maneuver on the battlefield is critical to winning quickly at minimum cost. Near simultaneous application of maneuver with fires allows an attacking force to sustain or make permanent the stunning yet transitory psychological effects of firepower. War is a test of will. The surest way to collapse an enemy's will is to control his territory. Without physical occupation warfare is nothing more than punishment from a distance, something that any nation with a will to resist can endure indefinitely.

Nevertheless, a word of caution is in order. The same technologies that will allow us to accelerate strategic and operational maneuver may also, if we are not careful, slow us down and impede our ability to maneuver with the precision we will require to achieve decisive results and win quickly. Too much information received through too fine a telecommunications instrument will create the temptation to micromanage the battle. This at a time when maneuver intended to paralyze an enemy spread over vast distances demands decentralized command and control at the lowest possible levels. Without the ability to out think the enemy by exercising superior agility and initiative, greater speed of maneuver will only shorten the path to defeat. A commander who lets some higher authority do his thinking for him and who waits for orders before acting will never be able to use the instruments at his command effectively.

This is not to say that higher commanders must take a hands-off approach. To the contrary, future war will demand that commanders manipulate a huge mechanism composed of enormously more parts spread over vastly greater distances and moving at vastly greater velocities than today. The challenge to a commander of applying precision firepower and maneuver will be all the greater because, if he is to gain the most from each, he must deliver one immediately behind and in close proximity to the other. Therefore, a commander, in order not to become his own worst source of friction, must learn to think ahead of his opponent and to orchestrate his symphony rather than play each bar one instrument at a time. Otherwise he will never be able to react to the inevitable uncertainties and surprises in war. The 1933 edition of *Truppenführung* still carries with it the essence of maneuver warfare, and its cautions continue to resonate from one age of warfare to the other: "situations will be of unlimited variety...the independent will of the enemy will always be pitted against ours...friction and mistakes will continue to be everyday occurrences."

A final word of caution. Regardless of how successful we are at restoring the balance between fire and maneuver in the future, we must accept the truth that all future victories will not be cheaply won. A thinking enemy willing to sacrifice and fortified with enough technology to deny us unlimited domination of the battlefield will most certainly cause us damage. If we hope to restore a range of balanced, offensive options to American commanders beyond the Year 2010, the power of the information age must be harnessed to develop a new generation of maneuver platforms that will be able to place close combat soldiers into commanding positions on the battlefields at the least possible cost. Tomorrow's battlefield success will be achieved by Joint Task Force Commanders who have the ability to orchestrate precision strike with precision maneuver. The leap ahead in situational awareness guaranteed by improvements in information age technologies promises to provide us with the instruments necessary to add physical agility to our future force as well as superior killing power. The dawn of a new age of warfare and the anticipated emergence of clever, adaptive enemies will require an order of magnitude increase in strategic and operational speed of maneuver if we hope to strike the enemy quickly and preemptively and collapse his will to resist.

The corollary to Newton's fundamental law of physics echoes with a sense of urgency: every successful technical or tactical innovation that provides a dominant military advantage eventually yields to a countervailing response that shifts the advantage to the opposing force. America's military dominance in firepower and attrition warfare has been on display for almost five decades. We must anticipate a future military challenge that will attempt to defeat our preoccupation with precision strike. We must use the time we have in the decade ahead to restore balance in our future method of war. Our future arsenal of military capabilities must include a 21st Century sword with two equally compelling edges: precision maneuver as well as precision firepower. Without these two applied in balance and harmony, future conflicts might well devolve into massive wars of attrition. Churchill's understanding of the relationship between slaughter and maneuver is both propitious and sublime. Great generals win with maneuver. Let's begin now to take on the challenge of a future competitor and begin now to build a balanced force to defeat him.

Chapter Six

FROM KOREA TO KOSOVO: HOW AMERICA'S ARMY HAS LEARNED TO FIGHT LIMITED WARS IN THE PRECISION AGE

Major General Robert H. Scales, Jr.

Reproduced with Permission Granted by:
December 1999 Issue
ARMED FORCES JOURNAL
INTERNATIONAL
Volume 137, Number 5

FROM KOREA TO KOSOVO: HOW AMERICA'S ARMY HAS LEARNED TO FIGHT LIMITED WARS IN THE PRECISION AGE

Author's Introductory Note

This article was written after a visit to Albania in May 1999. During that trip, I developed the central thesis for this essay: In wars of limited liability, success must be gained with a limited expenditure of means. A brief review of recent history clearly tells us that we have been practically learning this lesson in real wars for half a century, beginning with Korea. The imperative to prepare for a full-scale war against the Soviets, however, has effectively impeded our ability to embed this lesson into our warfighting doctrine. Kosovo is a wake-up call.

The Cold War is over. Thankfully, we expect it will be some time before we have to face the prospect of fighting another major military competitor who can threaten our vital national interests. But recent events such as Kosovo seem to be telling us that lesser conflicts fought for less than vital interests will continue to challenge us. We must improve our understanding of these conflicts. We must also develop a realistic doctrine for winning them based upon our own practical experience. This article addresses these issues and concludes with a proposed maneuver warfare concept for this new era of limited liability wars in the Precision Age.

FROM KOREA TO KOSOVO: HOW AMERICA'S ARMY HAS LEARNED TO FIGHT LIMITED WARS IN THE PRECISION AGE

> Every age has its own kind of war, its own limiting conditions, and its own preconceptions. Each period, therefore, would have held to its own theory of war.[1]
>
> Carl Von Clausewitz

Many in the professional ranks of the American military see the reluctance to put soldiers on the ground in Kosovo as a disturbing precedent that calls for future wars to be fought and won by air power alone. A close examination of American battlefield performance, however, suggests that the Kosovo experience marks nothing more than another data point, albeit a dramatic one, along a clearly defined continuum of transformation by the United States. Since the end of the Second World War, America's military forces have adjusted their unique capabilities to produce a new style of warfare. This is the result of a fundamental shift in the relationship between the dynamics of firepower and maneuver. When the dynamics of combat undergo substantial transformations, radical shifts in doctrine must be made to accompany and capitalize upon them. During this last half-century, the principal factors affecting the conduct of war—geostrategic, political and technological conditions—have been altered by the events of our time.

Geostrategy:

The end of the Cold War stand off between the two major global powers removed the protective blanket that had

---

1. Carl Von Clausewitz, *On War*, edited and translated by Michael Howard and Peter Paret, Princeton: Princeton University Press, 1976, p. 593.

dampened all of the old ethnic, tribal and religious embers left smoldering since the end of the Second World War. Lifting great power control gave the green light for aggressive regimes to set about righting perceived regional wrongs. Frustrated autocrats felt free to satisfy their hegemonic ambitions usually at the expense of some less powerful neighbor. At home, national paranoia over the threat of a great cataclysmic war gave way to social outrage directed at powers who tramp on the territory, rights, or well-being of lesser states.

No longer are our wars desperate struggles to preserve our right to exist as a nation. Instead, our most recent conflicts have been fought as wars of conscience to further peripheral interests in many diverse corners of the globe. Our potential enemies are increasingly being perceived as local tyrants who are intent upon gaining hegemony over some part of the world only tangentially important to our domestic welfare.

Technology:

The course of war would be difficult enough to anticipate if the shifting relationships between international actors were the only significant factor to influence change in the future. But we must also account in our calculation for the fact that we live in a transitional era set within a crease between the machine age and the information age. The microchip is altering the way armies fight just as thoroughly as did the gasoline engine and radio by lifting armies off their feet and mounting them inside land and aerial vehicles.

We know enough now from field experiments and practical experience with information age warfare to anticipate with some clarity how the microchip will continue to alter the course of war. The battlefield will continue to expand, perhaps geometrically, now that communications no longer effectively limit the amount of territory a military force can occupy and control. The ability to see with great clarity and strike with even greater precision will force ground units to take full advantage of the opportunity to spread out and disperse in order to survive. Fear of destruction in detail by precision strikes, principally from above, has already made linear, echeloned, massed armored formations an anachronism of a machine age that is now just passing.

Domestic Politics:

Both the geopolitical and technological trends of the recent past have raised expectations by the American people that our wars will be fought in a manner such that the political ends are worth the costs and the costs are increasingly measured in terms of expenditures of human life. Casualties soon may represent a dominant, perhaps the dominant measurement of success or failure in wars of limited ends and means such as Kosovo. Dead Americans are becoming our most vulnerable center of gravity—and our enemies know it. As we have seen from recent events, serious doubts on the part of our national leaders about casualties may not only delay, but may well prevent commitment of ground forces.

The tolerance bar that we use to measure our casualties has been driven ever downward by America's changing attitudes toward conflict. Since our most recent wars have been fought increasingly to further peripheral interests abroad rather than for national survival, we are less willing as a nation to send our sons and daughters into harm's way. Likewise, modern weapons technology has also raised the expectation that precision weapons can now substitute explosive killing power for manpower on the ground.

Limited War Precedents: Korea to Vietnam:

To its credit the American military began, intuitively at least, to sense these shifts in battlefield dynamics as early as the Korean War, the first of our modern wars in which limited strategic interests did not justify unlimited commitment. Combat commanders in the field, quick to recognize the importance of preserving the lives of their soldiers, routinely modified their way of fighting to achieve success at minimum cost. The most pervasive doctrinal adjustment made during our first two experiences with limited war was to increase the firepower available to support maneuver forces in close combat and to lessen the exposure of close combat soldiers to direct attack by the enemy.

Early battles in Korea began with the application of doctrinally correct proportions of firepower to maneuver inherited from the Second World War.Very quickly, however, field commanders increased their demand for artillery and air power to support ever more compact and self-contained assault forces. What began as traditional dismounted infantry assaults in 1950 soon became elaborate tank, infantry, and firepower intensive demonstrations intended to gain the objective with minimum cost in lives.

During the Battle of Soryang in the spring of 1951, twenty-one battalions of artillery fired over three hundred thousand rounds in five days in support of a single push by X Corps. Two years later, at Pork Chop Hill, nine battalions fired over thirty-seven thousand rounds in less than twenty-four hours in support of a single regimental assault. As the weight of firepower increased, the densities of infantry formations decreased in proportion. By the winter of 1950-51, General Ridgway conducted most of the Eighth Army counter attacks at regimental level. That spring, Ridgway consistently used nothing larger than company teams to spearhead his advance to the Han River.[2]

2. Billy C. Mossman, *Ebb and Flow: November 1950-July 1951*, Washington, DC: U.S. Army Center of Military History, 1990, pp. 238-239, 350-354, 442; S.L.A. Marshall, *Pork Chop Hill: The American Fighting Man in Action, Korea*, New York: Morrow, 1956, p. 196.

Similarly in Vietnam commanders learned quickly and adapted a European style, maneuver- centric method of war to match the realities of limited war in constricted Asian terrain. Close combat units gradually increased the proportion of supporting fires and lessened the exposure of lead elements moving into contested areas.

General William DePuy, commanding the First Infantry Division in 1966-67, realized quickly that artillery and tactical aircraft were responsible for most enemy casualties. His casualties, on the other hand, came principally from three sources: enemy mortars, concentrations of enemy small arms fire delivered against infantry units in set-piece ambushes, and mines. His common sense solution was simply to use much smaller infantry units to locate and fix the enemy, usually squads or platoons, and then orchestrate a varied medley of supporting firepower systems to do most of the killing.[3]

Once the enemy was located, the infantry's task was to stay out of the killing zone, avoid decisive engagement and pull back just far enough to allow effective delivery of ordnance, but not so far as to allow the enemy breathing space to disengage and escape the firepower trap. The old infantry adage "close with and destroy the enemy" became simply get close enough with as few forces as possible to "find, fix, flush and set up the enemy for destruction by fire."

DePuy was among the first to grasp the fact that modern firepower technology and the imperative to win at lower cost together were sufficient to cause a shift in the relationship between firepower and maneuver. In later years he was fond of saying "On a battlefield increasingly dominated by lethality, if you can be seen you can be hit, if you can be hit, you will be killed." Whether traditionalists liked it or not,

---

3. Paul H. Herbert, *Deciding What Has To Be Done: General William E. Depuy and the 1976 Edition of FM 100-5, Operations,* Leavenworth Papers, No.16, Fort Leavenworth, KS: Combat Studies Institute, 1988, p. 19-23.

DePuy believed that the balance had in fact shifted to the point that firepower systems, not infantrymen, had now become the central instrument for achieving decisive effect on the battlefield. To DePuy, the doctrinal maxim that firepower supported maneuver may well have been reversed.[4]

While seeming to offer the promise of less costly victories, DePuy's concept of maneuver supporting fires failed to last as a viable doctrine much beyond Vietnam. There were cultural objections. Commanders rightfully feared that training combat soldiers not to close with the enemy might diminish fighting spirit and create hesitation and a loss of decisiveness and *élan*.

Experience in real combat also demonstrated shortcomings of a firepower-centered doctrine. The most persistent complication was offered by the enemy who learned over time how to lessen the killing effects of our fires. After suffering horribly from American firepower during the Tet offensive in 1968, the North Vietnamese quickly changed their fighting doctrine. They learned to "hug" close to units in contact and to keep larger formations dispersed and positioned just out of artillery range. The enemy soon became very adept at hiding in built-up areas and the jungle. They also learned imaginative ways to deceive reconnaissance and spoof even the most sophisticated detection technologies.

Second, pressure late in the war to reduce casualties served to pervert DePuy's intent. As the war dragged on, firepower became too much of a good thing. Maneuver commanders began to complain that a firepower intensive doctrine had become a millstone around their necks. A single example serves to make the point. The "force-feed-fire support system" used by the 25th Infantry Division

---

4. John L. Romjue, *From Active Defense to Airland Battle: The Development of Army Doctrine, 1973-1982*, Fort Monroe, VA: U.S. Army Training and Doctrine Command, 1984, pp. 8-9.

toward the end of the war relegated the control of every contact, however minor, to the duty officer at division headquarters. He was instructed automatically to dispatch a stream of firepower systems into the fight to include Air Force gunships, tactical airpower, attack helicopters, and even "flame bath" helicopters equipped with napalm. The firepower would come even if the battalion commander felt that such a rich dose was either wasteful or counter to his scheme of maneuver.[5]

Another extreme example of the debilitating influence of firepower late in the war comes from a corps artillery commander in the Central Highlands region of Vietnam who reported that his command fired almost two million rounds in seven months of relatively inactive combat equating, by his best estimate, to a ratio of 1,000 rounds or roughly $100,000 per kill. Lives were saved to be sure, but the resulting loss of flexibility and control was rightfully lamented by infantrymen on the ground.[6]

Yet in spite of these shortcomings, maneuver commanders returning from Vietnam supported DePuy's hypothesis. The new limited war imperative to win at minimum cost demanded that the traditional balance between fire and maneuver be altered significantly just as DePuy suggested. A remarkable study done by a group of returning infantry commanders at the Army War College in 1969 concluded that firepower was now the dominant factor on the American battlefield. They wrote that *maneuver is performed primarily to pinpoint the location of the enemy, and to increase the effectiveness of the massive application of fire on the enemy. Ideally the enemy should be killed at the maximum effective range of organic weapons. The need to advance infantry to "zero" range will proportionately*

---

5. Robert H. Scales, *Firepower in Limited War,* Washington DC: National Defense University, U.S. Government P:rinting Office, 1990, pp. 287-296.

6. Scales, p. 143.

increase friendly casualties and decrease the ability of foot
infantry to maneuver or use fire support.[7]

Post Cold War Precedents:

Practical experience in subsequent wars continued to
reinforce the lesson that the cost of a conflict must remain in
proportion to the perceived value of the endeavor. The Gulf
War in particular taught the value of a protracted
preliminary aerial bombardment to wear down and
demoralize the Iraqis sufficiently to make the land
campaign as casualty free as possible. The battlefield
continued to thin in the Gulf as the firepower quotient rose.
The range and lethality of modern tanks and the ability of
maneuver forces to see vast distances in the desert allowed
armored formations to open up to an unprecedented degree
thereby exposing forward maneuver elements as little as
possible. What might have constituted a battalion front in
World War II was now occupied by a force as small as a
platoon. Instinctively when faced with the realities of real
war against a thinking enemy the Army returned to
DePuy's maxim of minimum exposure for maximum killing
effect.

The loss of eighteen rangers in close, back alley fighting
in Somalia dramatically underscored a corollary to DePuy's
maxim: a tactical engagement fought for too high a price for
too little return might very well by itself determine the
strategic outcome of a national endeavor.

Recent experience in Kosovo now seems to suggest that
the bar continues to lower as the country begins to accept
the burden of limited liability wars fought to prevent harm
to one ethnic or cultural group by another. Some even
suggest that the bar has been lowered so much for wars like

---

7. Richard E. Cavazos, *et al.*, "Analysis of Fire and Maneuver in Vietnam:
   June 1966 - June 1968," unpublished Student Research Paper, U.S. Army
   War College, Carlisle Barracks, PA, 1 March 1969, pp. II-v and II-210,
   II-212.

Kosovo that a ground campaign with its attending risk of casualties is a thing of the past at least for American troops. Perhaps, the argument goes, the precision revolution has given us the ultimate tool, the silver bullet, to win future wars by firepower alone.

However, a closer look at Kosovo suggests that, while improvements in precision munitions may continue to tilt the firepower-maneuver equation in favor of the former, the nature of the enemy and the immutable character of war continue to argue for the preservation of balance between the two classic components of war. The Serb reaction to firepower dominant assault was remarkably similar to the North Vietnamese over a quarter century before. The Vietnamese realized that overwhelming firepower alone could never compensate for the presence of an aggressive force on the ground to find, fix and fight them in close combat. Without a ground threat, they merely had to array their forces in order to endure punishment by fire alone.

Serb tactics followed the Vietnamese example with remarkable fidelity. Units went to ground and dispersed over wide areas. Soldiers hid their equipment with great skill and constructed dummies that proved effective at spoofing aerial observers and image interpreters. Trouble for the Serbs arrived with the ground threat from the Kosovo Liberation Army. However amateur and ineffective, the presence of the KLA in their midst forced the Serb army to come out of hiding and begin to mass. Once in the open, the Serbs were obliged to trade the security of their hiding places for battle in the open.

If Kosovo suggests that maneuver still remains essential to a balanced approach to war, how then do we resolve the problem of maneuvering without suffering excessive casualties? Back to DePuy and his maxim. DePuy's maxim correctly grasped the trend of the expanding battle area as the range and lethality of weapons continues to increase. Soon the battlefield will become so expansive and porous that the conventional schemes for ground maneuver may well play more to the advantage of the enemy rather than to ourselves. On an expanded battlefield an adaptive enemy, armed first and foremost with patience and guile, might well be able to offset our advantage of superior firepower with a countervailing strategy centered around the occupation and control of large thinly occupied areas of territory. His tactic will be defensive and centered on controlling ground. He cedes the other dimensions of war because he knows he cannot compete against a technologically superior enemy on the sea and in the air. On the defensive, he may appear to lose the initiative and with it, in the conventional wisdom, the ability to win, but like George Washington during our Revolutionary War, not losing either forces or ground becomes the effective equivalent of a new kind of winning. So his object is not to win but to avoid losing by holding on and preserving his forces in the field just long enough for the enemy to tire of the conflict and go home.

DePuy's maxim, reinforced by experience in Kosovo, suggests that as an enemy disperses across a broad area and goes to ground in order to avoid destruction by fire he makes his force increasingly vulnerable to defeat by maneuver. A dispersed enemy force cannot mass quickly, nor can it cover all of its territory by fire from static positions. An enemy gone to ground cannot see beyond the end of its nose and cannot react in time to turn back forces which might suddenly rush to occupy the uncovered, unprotected terrain in its midst.

But DePuy also demonstrated that a ground force must change its style of maneuver to gain full advantage of the potential provided by modern firepower systems. A force optimized to fully exploit precision fires must be able to maneuver quickly against a dispersed, static enemy. This can only be done if that force has adopted new methods of warfighting at the strategic, operational and tactical levels of war.

Strategic:

The surest way to win at minimum cost is to win quickly. A decisive, quick victory can best be assured by an early arriving force of overwhelming power capable of conducting a strategic takedown. A "strategic preemption" force would first seek to use airpower to frustrate enemy deployment long enough for early arriving ground forces to position themselves between the enemy and his initial operational objectives. Enemy ground forces caught in the act of deploying or moving forward in the attack can be easily targeted and destroyed by precision weaponry.

Time is a particularly critical factor on a battlefield dominated by firepower. As we have seen in Korea and Vietnam too long a delay in collapsing an enemy greatly heightens the risk that an act of strategic preemption will be stretched into a wasteful war of attrition—a war the enemy knows we cannot win. As we have seen from our own recent experience with limited wars of attrition, given enough time an enemy will learn to avoid destruction by dispersing and burrowing into the countryside or by massing inside his urban terrain.

Our difficulties with projecting forces to Korea, Iraq, Kosovo and elsewhere, tell us that quick victories are hard to achieve when an intervening power like the United States is an ocean away from an enemy who perhaps has only to violate a neighbor's territory to fulfill his aggressive intentions. An enemy acting unilaterally can mobilize quickly and achieve almost total surprise. A major power like the United States, on the other hand, can respond only with great deliberation. Time must be taken to build political consensus for action both at home and within the international community. Thus the chance exists that an enemy will be able to initiate aggressive actions, or even possibly gain his initial objectives before we can intervene.

The example of the Serbian dash into Kosovo demonstrates the particular futility of attempting to preempt an enemy force using airpower alone. Similar experiences with strategic intervention by air in previous limited wars suggests that such an effort can be made orders of magnitude more effective if aerial platforms are guided to their targets by eyes on the ground. Special operations forces planted deep inside North Korean, North Vietnamese, and Iraqi territory have proven their ability repeatedly both to survive and to take away the enemy's ability to hide from or spoof attacking aircraft.

Given the right strategic conditions and resources, however, strategic preemption can succeed and succeed decisively. Our strategic takedown in Panama took only a day to cause the collapse of Noriega's army of thugs. The secret of success lay in the ability of the American command to synchronize the delivery of overwhelming power simultaneously against a multitude of objectives spread throughout the entire Republic. That power was an effective mix of air operations to paralyze and disorient through selective destruction and ground operations to seize, hold and ultimately to confirm the effects.

Before the Panamanian forces could even begin to comprehend what was happening, they found themselves surrounded, overwhelmed and blocked at every turn. Victory, as evidenced by the disintegration of the PDF, came, not with physical destruction so much as with the utter inability of the enemy to react effectively in any direction, leading to the ultimate collapse of his will to resist.

Operational:

The apparent shift in the firepower-maneuver balance in favor of firepower works to the disadvantage of a force which seeks to intervene in a distant theater and operate offensively against a static foe. It has been a long-standing tenet of warfare in the modern age that a firepower dominant battlefield environment favors the defensive. Experience has shown that the surest way for an offensive force to overcome this disadvantage and succeed on a firepower dominant battlefield is to employ an operational offensive-tactical defensive method of war. The concept is both simple and timeless. An attacking force maneuvers to place himself between the defender and his line of communications. The defender then can either remain static and wither or leave the security of his defenses to attack the force to his rear now set firmly in place and ready to receive him. Defenders like the Serbs who must disperse and go to ground in order to survive a precision attack are particularly vulnerable to such a stratagem because the attacker can take advantage of the enemy's thinly occupied battlespace to locate and then occupy voids left uncovered by fire and observation.

The secret of success against an enemy gone to ground would be to paralyze him with precision fires just long enough to allow an early arriving ground force to simultaneously occupy multiple points throughout the enemy's area of operations and saturate the enemy's most vital areas with small, discrete, autonomous and highly lethal, mobile combat elements.

In order to gain and maintain maneuver dominance ground combat units would not need to physically occupy key terrain or confront enemy strong points directly. Instead, an intervening force would occupy uncontested terrain close enough to control and thus dominate these vital centers through direct observation and the use of short-range precision weapons. Such a violent, unanticipated and overwhelming act would take the form of a strategic takedown or coup de main rather than a conventional form of linear maneuver.

A once cohesive body of enemy forces would now be divided into isolated pockets, each a sub-critical mass severed from its parent body unable to communicate or maintain itself for very long without resupply and unable to be reinforced. Once the intervening force gains the advantage of position over the enemy the factor of time also shifts to his favor. The enemy cannot linger very long in a fractured state. His choices are either to fight or wither. But fighting will be a problem. Once set within the enemy's critical area the intervening force is in a position to call the tactical shots now that he can leverage the power of the defensive to his advantage.

Modern precision technology strengthens the inherent power of the defensive phase of an offensive-defensive stratagem. The range and lethality of our superior firepower weaponry expands the killing zone making it far more expensive for a less sophisticated enemy to move unprotected against us in the open. The static side has the advantage of watching and engaging with firepower from positions well out of the enemy's much shorter lethal reach while remaining relatively secure in fixed, covered positions. The enemy is trapped and can only escape by massing to attack. If he masses he becomes a perfect target for destruction by precision strike. Check and checkmate.

Our dominance in situational awareness given to us by our overwhelming advantage in information technology will help us solve the problems that DePuy and other American field commanders found most vexing in this new style of war. DePuy realized that a change in tactics alone could reduce casualties only to a limited degree. In Vietnam, no matter how small and protected he made his lead elements, the cost of the initial contact was still too high. Also, DePuy was frustrated by the ability of the enemy to escape before his supporting firepower became most effective. The enemy could slip away because ground forces could be not be assembled quickly enough or spread thin enough to cover all avenues of escape particularly in the rugged wooded terrain in Vietnam.

The Army learned from its experiments with digitization at the National Training Center in 1997 that a properly internetted maneuver brigade provided with an immediately available suite of aerial sensors could expand its area of control by a factor of four or more. Superior situational awareness allowed units to locate all friendly units and most of the enemy immediately around them. The ability to see the battlefield with great clarity and immediacy allowed them to anticipate each enemy movement and avoid being surprised. Also, units participating in these force-on-force experiments discovered that the ability to spread out, yet still remain cohesive and able to maneuver, freely allowed them to outflank and surround much larger units in open combat.

Tactical:

If we have been successful at gaining positional advantage and paralyzing the enemy at the operational level then we must seek to finish the fight in close combat with the smallest possible loss of life. Once secure in operational sanctuaries, tactical units will expand outward to find the specific location of previously unlocated enemy ground units. These tactical scouts will be preceded by aerial eyes in the form of Unmanned Aerial Vehicles (UAVs) or other downlinked aerial sensors. These sensors must be capable enough to find small discrete pockets before the scouts stumble within the range of enemy direct fire weapons. The scouts' mission will be to define the outline of the enemy formation clearly and then locate and destroy all significant points of resistance without the finding force becoming decisively engaged or suffering casualties.

Seen from a point high above, the battlespace in a culminating campaign against a dispersed enemy might appear in the mind's eye like a distant prairie ablaze with a thousand fires. All of the individual fires would be surrounded simultaneously by groups of firefighters building fire lanes and pouring on flame retardant selectively in order to keep the smaller fires from combining to form larger conflagrations.

Most enemy points of resistance would be left to burn themselves out, particularly those in difficult areas such as close terrain, forests and cities. Those which threaten people or property would be fought aggressively, but from a distance. Firefighters would move in close enough to be effective but not so close as to be trapped by the flames.

Close combat of this sort will be decisive to be sure, but decisive from a distance. Close combat units will maintain just enough contact to surround, contain and feel out the shape and size of each enemy formation. As precision strikes begin to wear away the will of the enemy, close combat forces converge methodically with deliberation. By this stage of the fight time becomes our ally. The initiative belongs entirely to us. We can only lose now if impatience causes us to be careless and allows a desperate enemy to inflict more casualties than we can afford. Eventually, surrounded, unable to mass, out of touch with adjacent units and higher authority, each discrete enemy force slowly collapses.

Finding the Balance:

Our Cold War fixation on fighting the big battle has impeded the development of weapons appropriate for fighting limited liability wars just as surely as it has impeded our ability to internalize and accept limited war fighting doctrine. This has lead to some curious ironies.

Recent experiences have taught us that the surest way to win limited wars is to win them quickly. Time is our greatest enemy and our enemy's greatest friend. Yet as our experience in Kosovo has shown, we still lack the means to transport decisive landpower to even a local theater of war in time to preempt or preclude the offensive actions of a minor tyrant.

We seek to win at minimum cost. During wars in this century the overwhelming majority of battlefield deaths have been suffered by infantrymen in close combat. The greatest killer of American infantry has been the homely and unglamorous mortar, followed closely by the rifle and machine gun. Yet while today we possess the technology to remotely locate strategic targets in Belgrade or Baghdad, a platoon leader must still rely on DePuy's tactic of direct observation and contact in order to locate a machine gun position. We can strike strategic targets with precision from thousands of miles distance but our platoon leader has no way to destroy a mortar over the next hill with any degree of precision.

Recent post-Cold War experience in Kosovo and Iraq have shown that even an army of inept petty tyrants can, if given time, adapt and learn to counter our unique method of fighting limited wars. Add to this uncomfortable truth the realization that the American people will continue to demand cheap victories and it seems absolutely apparent to those who have studied recent history that the United States will no longer have the luxury to improvise on the battlefield. Fortunately, the recent history of limited wars offers more than just a warning. It offers us a historical trail of practical and empirical evidence which provides a path to guide us into an uncertain era. In sum the recent past seems to be telling us that:

• A battlefield dominated by precision fire favors the defensive. Therefore, the surest way to win at acceptable cost is to employ an operational offensive-tactical defensive strategy whereby the attacker uses superior mobility to place his forces amongst and between the enemy such that the enemy is forced to wither and concede or to attack in the most disadvantageous circumstances.

• Firepower intensive wars must be won quickly. Over time, the effects of firepower diminish. Therefore, decision on the battlefield must be achieved before the weight of munitions needed to achieve effects exceeds the practical limit of the force to deliver them. However, the promise of a geometric increase in killing power for a given weight of munitions offered by cheap distributed precision weaponry will relieve us at last of the millstone of the ammunition train. Infantrymen will now be able to kill the enemy effectively in the close fight without suffering substantial loss in mobility.

• The enemy must be located precisely and fixed with the smallest possible exposure of the maneuver force. In the long term this finding function might well be performed remotely from air or ground vehicles.

• An adaptive enemy will most likely counter our superior precision strike capability by dispersing, hiding and going to ground. While such a posture limits his vulnerability to precision, it also makes his force extremely vulnerable for exploitation by maneuver forces capable of controlling his most vulnerable points from the ground.

• The object of close combat in the future will be to find and fix the enemy without closing to within decisive distance of the enemy's weapons. Decisive range is defined as the practical limit of the enemy maneuver unit's organic weapons.

• Maneuver forces must be provided the tools to adequately support an offensive strategy that is dominated by precision firepower. We can kill very deep targets with great precision, principally from the air. Likewise, combat units can kill with precision very close using direct fire from guided anti-tank missiles. But the firer is exposed and vulnerable during this direct exchange. We lack the ability to kill with precision in the zone between these two extremes—just where this new style of warfare needs precision most—close enough to find, fix and track directly without being so close as to become vulnerable to the enemy's direct fire systems.

A Cautionary Conclusion:

DePuy's doctrinal method is best suited for wars of limited liability which clearly occupy only a narrow segment of our potential future conflict spectrum. Surely, for the near term at least, America's soldiers will find themselves most involved in non-shooting peacetime contingencies.

True, but we already have shown that we can do presence, peacekeeping and peace enforcement missions well as demonstrated by the performance of American soldiers in Bosnia, Kosovo, Haiti and elsewhere. We can do better to be sure. But our past performance tells us that our doctrine for stability operations today is fundamentally sound. Improvement is always needed but the imperative for changing the way we conduct these kinds of operations is not pressing. Our most serious doctrinal challenge starts when bullets begin to fly. Recent history tells us that limited wars are what we do most often with least success. These kinds of wars need the most attention to insure that we will be able to win them at the least possible cost in the future.

A second caution deals with the perception that Americans are no longer willing to expend blood in foreign adventures. The day may well come soon when a serious competitor threatens an interest vital enough to allow a serious sacrifice in blood. However, while the American people may someday allow military professionals to spend lives more freely, they will never again allow soldiers' lives to be wasted. So even in a major war we will continue to shoulder the obligation to fight and win at minimum cost.

Our experience in recent war tells us that regardless of how intense the combat, cheap victories will come only if we change our warfighting doctrine to accommodate the new realities of the precision age. Modern weapons technologies have changed the dynamics of battle. The relationship between the dynamics of firepower and maneuver has shifted fundamentally. We must begin now to alter the way we fight in order to stay ahead of potential enemies who, as we have seen in Kosovo, already have begun to understand and exploit our tendency to rely on firepower alone to win on the battlefield.

Chapter Seven

CLASHES OF VISIONS: SIZING AND SHAPING OUR FORCES IN A FISCALLY CONSTRAINED ENVIRONMENT

Major General Robert H. Scales, Jr.

Reproduced with Permission Granted by:
CENTER FOR STRATEGIC
AND INTERNATIONAL STUDIES
Washington, DC

CLASHES OF VISIONS: SIZING AND SHAPING OUR FORCES IN A FISCALLY CONSTRAINED ENVIRONMENT

Author's Introductory Note

In the Fall of 1997 the Center of Strategic and International Studies put together a panel to debate the conflicting views that the three services had about the nature of future war. I was joined by Major General Charles Link, U.S. Air Force, Retired, and Lieutenant General Paul Van Riper, U.S. Marine Corps, Retired. We were scheduled for about an hour but the exchange became so passionate that it lasted nearly three times as long and could have gone much longer had the schedule permitted.

General Link gave a presentation that argued that the recently completed Deep Attack Weapons Mix Study (DAWMS) conducted by the Joint Staff was seriously flawed in that it failed to give air power sufficient credit for its destructive power against a postulated ground force invading South Korea. He contended that, in fact, air power would have been sufficient to "halt" the enemy force short of its strategic objectives and thus would have provided the American leadership a viable alternative to the immediate introduction of ground forces into the theater.

Needless to say, General Van Riper and I took a conflicting position. The excerpt that follows was the last presentation of the day and it is a fairly concise encapsulation of my retort to General Link's depiction of what has since become commonly referred to as the Air Force Halt Strategy.

***

A Soldier's View

Let me begin by addressing a couple of points. The first is the issue of gaming: the problem we have with DAWMS and all the other games over the years is that we are using what, in essence, is an analytical training tool that has evolved over 20-25 years, based on old, Lanchestrian models—force-on-force engagement; in short, the old force application models that go back to World War II. We then take attrition-based models and apply them to the art of war. Of course, the further we get into warfare, the more it is an intellectual rather than a physical exercise; and the more that information will determine your ability to win on the battlefield, the less viable force-on-force attrition-based models become. This is a given.

The second issue is that of the sequence of operations. Again, particularly as we look toward warfare in the future, I agree with General Link 100 percent: the days of the sequential linear joint operations are over the moment the enemy gets the opportunity to buy even a nickel's worth of precision or counter-precision. We have to get beyond the old Desert Storm models of how to fight wars. Making yesterday perfect is a portent for disaster, and I am going to tell you not necessarily how to rearrange deck chairs, which is what General Link has talked about for the past hour, but how to design a new ship to carry the deck chairs to victory.

General Link said something, perhaps inadvertently, that I haven't heard him say before. He talked about the need for operational art, the services' need to maintain the hands-on experience, the *fingerspitzgengefuhl,* that's so necessary for an understanding of the operational art within the services. I do not know whether he intended to say this, but our view of operational art is subjective rather than objective. We are not looking for the golden ball bearing factory here. We approach warfare as a holistic act in which the object is not butchery, but the collapse of an enemy's will to resist. It is an art rather than a science. And if Johnny can't dive bomb, that's too bad; but if Johnny does

114

not understand the fundamental character and nature of war in the future, then all the precision and all the dive bombing in the world will lead you up a blind alley.

The object of war is not to kill everyone: is not butchery; is not genocide. We in the Army maintain that the object of war is the destruction of the enemy's will, not his physical destruction. The purpose of combat is to convince the enemy that he has lost. And the enemy, in terms of the American art of war in the 21st century, is time. General Link has that dead right: the longer a campaign is drawn out—the more a campaign becomes a sequential battle of attrition that is determined by the pace of buildup and counteroffensive—the more likely we are to suffer unnecessary casualties. Why? Look at the Firepower Curve chart.

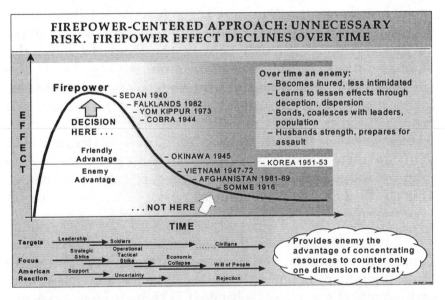

Unless your object is to kill everyone, then the principal impact of killing power, or precision firepower—call it what you want—is psychological and not physical: over time, in every war in which firepower ever has been applied alone, to include the Gulf war, the psychological effect of firepower decreases over time.

What we seek is a Sedan, not a Khe-Sanh. We seek to have the ability to compress that cycle of war and apply maneuver and firepower—the components of combat power—not sequentially, but simultaneously. Because remember, over time the enemy bonds himself to his leaders. Anthropologists call that *terror bonding*. The enemy becomes inured to war. A good example of this is the image of the British soldier brewing tea on the firestep in the middle of a German bombardment. More important than his apparent comfort, he learned how to deal with it.

After the terrible disaster of Saipan in 1943, the Japanese 32nd Army under General Cho—when he was ordered to defend Okinawa—figured this out. He learned how to handle it. In the Battle of Shuri Castle, U.S. forces suffered 9,000 dead and 90,000 casualties in 89 days of combat because the Japanese had figured it out. They got it right. Fast-forward to the time after the terrible slaughter of the spring offensive of 1951 in the Huan Ju Bowl; the Chinese got it right. They figured out how to deflect the killing power of U.S. aerial firepower. Once they did that, what did we have? A stalemate for the next year and a half that caused far more casualties from that point forward. After the terrible slaughter of North Vietnam's Tet Offensive in spring 1968, General Giap got it right. He figured it out and changed his strategy to be able to achieve his political and military aims by ceding U.S. dominance on the firepower battlefield.

We need to be careful. If you take a single-dimensional approach to combat, you give the enemy the opportunity to take a single-dimensional counter. If you do that, an enemy with a nickel's worth of technology is going to beat you every time. History tells us this is true.

I am going to talk to you about the Army After Next. I am not simply going to rearrange the deck chairs. What is important is what happens next. What sort of enemy do we face in the years ahead?

Here is where I disagree with General Van Riper a bit. The information revolution will give us mental agility and "information dominance," but sometime in the future, probably after 2010, our potential foe—someone I will call a major competitor, not a peer competitor—will have the ability to apply combat power effectively on the battlefield. So, by 2010, to have information no longer will be enough; this will result simply in building an Army that only will die smarter. You have to have the ability to act on what you know, to balance your ability, to put speed into the equation so that you can exploit "information dominance."

I think we agree on everything we have heard so far. But the enemy we will face in the future after 2010 will not be a peer competitor. No one else will buy carrier battle groups, infantry divisions, and stealth fighters to compete with us in the next 20 to 25 years, but the threat is even more sinister because it is a threat based around an asymmetric approach. I have seen from my tours around the world over the past two and a half years that many of our future competitors have it right; they have figured us out. A little bit of technology applied in the right direction—for example, cheap cruise missiles; distributed air defenses that have no nodes; the ability to place both sea and land mines; the use of cellular telephone technology; and so on—will make an enemy very difficult to take down with a single-dimensional approach, and the enemy then can apply his own advantages. The number-one advantage that we will have in the future is defeating the enemy's will—the ability to collapse the psyche of his people. To try to destroy that will with firepower alone, as the British learned in London, the Germans in Berlin, and the North Vietnamese in Hanoi, will serve only to steel that will rather than break it.

The enemy also has the power of the defensive. So, in order to win, he doesn't have to beat the Americans any more than George Washington had to beat the British after Long Island. If he can achieve a halt phase in a future war, he wins! Because halt means he's been able to extend the campaign out, and time is on his side.

If all this is true, then how do you take on that strategy after 2010?

The answer is speed: speed to balance knowledge; the ability to seek protection and to achieve a decision in times and order of magnitude quicker than our ability to conduct campaigns today; the ability to move about the battlefield and to exploit what you already know.

Why is speed important? The challenge we face is very similar to the challenge that armies have faced for hundreds of years. In order to collapse the enemy's will to resist, we have to cross a deadly zone. We have to be able to get through the enemy's area of effectiveness to strike at his operational center of gravity and collapse it in order to achieve victory.

The muzzle-loading rifle extended the killing zone of the infantryman from 150 meters to 1,000 meters or more. Back then, armies moved at two and a half miles an hour. Americans learned at Gettysburg and at Antietam exactly what the price for that was. It is no different today.

Today, we have an Army, or a land power, that moves at 20 kilometers an hour, and the killing zone is thousands of miles wide. We can achieve a decisive effect on a future battlefield with a 20-kilometer-per-hour Army no more than we could at Le Mans and Le Chateau with a two-and-a-half-mile-per-hour Army in 1914. We must accelerate the pace of movement in order to be able to achieve decisive effect. How do you do that? By strategic, operational, and tactical speed.

What is the long pole? Logistics. Not technology, logistics. We took 640,000 tons of ammunition with us to Desert Storm. It took 40 tons of fuel to drop a single ton of bombs. We took 28,000 containers with us to Saudi Arabia. That is why the campaign buildup took six months, because we had an Army—I would say a military—that was much too heavy. An Army division weighs 94,000 tons. It takes another 90,000 tons to sustain it for six weeks. No matter how much you know, you can't inject speed into that equation with a military that is heavy and immobile.

Finally, as Lenin said, quantity has a quality all its own. The bottom line is this—and here I agree with General Van Riper—ultimately, close combat is a blue-collar business. If the density of the battlefield becomes too thin, factors other than technology and physical effect begin to determine how effective you are on the battlefield (such things as bonding, cohesion, leadership, the ability to control and deal with the fear of violent death). So even an army that thins out on the battlefield, so to speak, still will have to be able, when the close fight occurs—and it always does—to be able to coalesce and bond units together.

Let's talk about strategic speed—getting there "firstest with the mostest," to quote General Nathan Bedford Forrest. The first element of winning wars after 2010 against a major competitor will be to get to the theater of war very quickly to begin the process of the collapse of will from the moment you leave the continental United States.

How will you do it? You can put air power, sea power, and land power into this equation, but this is how we do it today: you have a line in the sand with forward-deployed forces. Early-arriving forces give you a political statement, and maybe they will be able to survive, but they certainly are not able to achieve decisive effect. As General Link said, an enemy force has the opportunity to set itself operationally. Whether it is in Kuwait, in Budapest, or along the Pusan perimeter, the enemy has the ability to set himself operationally. Therefore, subsequent operations—what he calls the counteroffensive—is reactive. You are trying to reestablish yourself in a theater of war.

What we need is the ability to preempt the enemy on the battlefield. Here is where General Link and I agree. It is the ability to arrive on the battlefield and, through an act of strategic preemption—a strategic takedown operation— keep the enemy from his operational objectives and destroy him in detail, to disintegrate his force—not to butcher it, but

119

to disintegrate his force in the field. When you do that, campaigns go from months to weeks, in some cases from weeks to days. The operational level of war takes hours and, in some cases, perhaps days, depending on the nature of the terrain.

How will you do it? You have to break that logistical umbilical cord. You have to accelerate the pace of movement by an order of magnitude. The only way to do that is to go up. Here again, General Link and I agree. If you can go up—if you can exploit the "surface-to-space continuum," as we call it—you can gravitate many of your combat support functions outside the immediate confines of the battle area and you can gravitate many of the combat support functions upward—including logistics, intelligence, communications, and fire support (to some degree).

So it is conceivable, then, that you could build a force that is split, much as it appears in the following chart. In fact, we saw hints of this in Desert Storm: the ability to split a force. Keep in the battle area only those forces that kill, sense, move, and fuse information. That's it. Move everything else outside the battle area. How far? That depends on technology. Probably outside the immediate reach of weapons of mass destruction.

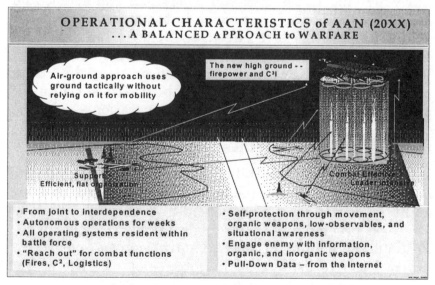

120

The left part of the above chart is an industrially efficient organization that provides just what's needed, just in time. The right side of the chart is a military force that is extremely small, extremely lean, very agile, and able to move operational distances at hundreds of kilometers an hour.

We conducted an operational war game in early 1997. As a matter of fact, we conducted seven iterations—one Marine and six Army. I will not go into the details, but allow me to give you some insights.

The first thing we learned is that the art of war does not change. The second is that, if you do not control space, you lose. You must be able to know more than the enemy does, and that difference needs to be on the magnitude of six, seven, or eight to one. When we fought RMA forces that were roughly equal, we had something like the *blitzkrieg*. When we bumped up the information advantage by about a factor of two, we saw a very fluid, dynamic battlefield. When we pushed it up to six to seven to one, the whole character of warfare changed.

If you can apply killing power and maneuver nearly simultaneously and lay that over an enemy force across the entire spread of his operational array, it is like putting a wet blanket over a fire. You snuff it out and you collapse it. It is the double shock of destructive power and a maneuver force that surrounds you and occupies all positions of advantage. This is what collapses the enemy's will to resist—not constant butchery. That is what does it. I think the war game showed that.

General Van Riper and I were raised in an era in which we saw enemy units aggregated in rectangles displayed on a piece of acetate on a map. The information was always wrong, it was always old, and we never trusted it. The aggregations we saw of the enemy—and even of ourselves—were always in blocks.

121

But what happens if you can see the enemy in exquisite detail, in near-real time? What if, instead of seeing, squares on a map, you can see individual units and individuals, just as General Link mentioned? If you can do that, then you can take the Blue force and break it down into aggregations that correspond to the Red force. Then you have command and control again, thanks to the information revolution, to coordinate all that and apply it as a single blanket of maneuver. If you can do that in a very short period of time, a campaign goes from a month-long, exercise, a bloody exercise, to something that lasts hours.

In the six iterations that we ran, we fought in Central Europe, Southwest Asia, and Northeast Asia. The operational phases lasted from two hours to two weeks. The enemy did what you would expect it to do: he went straight for the cities and more complex terrain. When he did that, he stretched out the length of the campaign considerably. By the way, another point to General Link's idea, if you are going to model future conflicts, it has to be free play, force on force; fixing the enemy does not give you insights if the coin of the realm is information.

Go to the strategic game. If you can pick up a strategic force and move it—in this case, to Europe in about 36 hours—and have it in combat immediately, it makes you more efficient militarily, but it also makes your diplomacy and political problem infinitely more complex. We learned that during our strategic war game at Carlisle Barracks in January 1997. So if you are not careful and you don't build coalitions carefully over time, you run the risk of either going to war alone or going to war without the preconditions properly set. The enemy knows this; therefore, he knows that our strategic center of gravity is our ability to build a coalition and to do it quickly.

Jointness becomes interdependence. Listen to me now, because this is important. We cannot fight a campaign— whether the center of mass is air, land, or sea—in the traditional building-block, phased, time-sequenced manner that joint doctrine calls for today. If you do this, as we learned in our war game, the biggest source of combat friction is ourselves, *not* the enemy. It is ourselves, because of this obsession we have with putting everything in a matrix. We have to learn to get beyond joint doctrine and come to something that my war gamers call *interdependence,* or the ability to orchestrate killing power and a positional advantage concurrently.

Our Achilles' heel was space, and the enemy knew that. The Red commander in this game was James Blackwell, formerly of the Center for Strategic and International Studies—and you trained that diabolical bastard well because he attempted immediately to collapse this surface-to-space continuum. As soon as he started to do that, that became our center of gravity, and we had another Pearl Harbor in slow motion. The lessons are that we must protect our space assets, and there is no such thing as space war, air war, or ground war—it is a single continuum in 2020.

Operational impressions: speed and mobility. If you can't combine the two together, all the firepower in the world does not help. There is great synergy when you mix maneuver and firepower. The more killing power you can bring from outside the battlefield into the battlefield, the smaller and more agile your operational force becomes.

Special operations forces are our global scouts. I could go into a great deal of discussion about this, but the people who made the coalition possible and allowed us to fight with coalition partners effectively with a high-tech/low-tech mix were the special operations forces that we employed in the game.

How about technology? How do you build a force like this? Just as General Heinz Guderian learned in the 1920s that the diesel engine and metal roads in Central Europe were going to give him the *blitzkrieg* irrespective of whether he wanted it, the information revolution is going to allow us to build flexibility and "information dominance" irrespective of whether we choose to do so. Much of the technology I am talking about is derivative as outlined in the following chart. How do you project a force overseas in a day and a half rather than six months? You do it by exploiting the work that is being done as we speak today by General Michael Loh and others to exploit the so-called middle market. Aircraft and high-speed sealift will allow us to pick up strategic forces and move them very quickly directly into an operational area and free up what formerly were strategic assets to move forces within the theater of war.

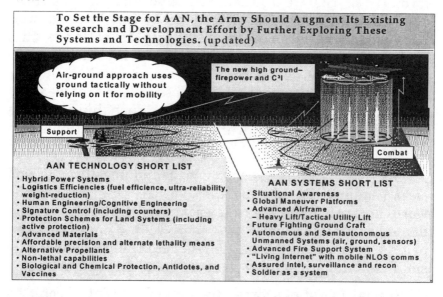

To Set the Stage for AAN, the Army Should Augment Its Existing Research and Development Effort by Further Exploring These Systems and Technologies. (updated)

Air-ground approach uses ground tactically without relying on it for mobility

The new high ground— firepower and C³I

Support

Combat

AAN TECHNOLOGY SHORT LIST
- Hybrid Power Systems
- Logistics Efficiencies (fuel efficiency, ultra-reliability, weight-reduction)
- Human Engineering/Cognitive Engineering
- Signature Control (including counters)
- Protection Schemes for Land Systems (including active protection)
- Advanced Materials
- Affordable precision and alternate lethality means
- Alternative Propellants
- Non-lethal capabilities
- Biological and Chemical Protection, Antidotes, and Vaccines

AAN SYSTEMS SHORT LIST
- Situational Awareness
- Global Maneuver Platforms
- Advanced Airframe
  – Heavy Lift/Tactical Utility Lift
- Future Fighting Ground Craft
- Autonomous and Semiautonomous Unmanned Systems (air, ground, sensors)
- Advanced Fire Support System
- "Living Internet" with mobile NLOS comms
- Assured intel, surveillance and recon
- Soldier as a system

That is a fast and dirty Army After Next. Suffice it to say that what you have just heard is not the idle ramblings of some gray-headed, two-star general, but the culmination of a great deal of work done by a team of people who, for the past two years, have worked very hard and approached this from a holistic, eclectic perspective in which we started with the art of war and geostrategy and worked back toward technology, instead of going into some technological toy store and pulling the things off the shelves that we thought were the neatest. The result, we, at least, believe, is an image of war as it begins to unfold through the murky future that will look increasingly like the cycles of war to come.

Chapter Eight

AMERICA'S ARMY: PREPARING FOR TOMORROW'S SECURITY CHALLENGES

Major General Robert H. Scales, Jr.

Strategic Studies Institute
U.S. Army War College
Army Issue Paper Number 2
November 1998

AMERICA'S ARMY: PREPARING FOR TOMORROW'S SECURITY CHALLENGES

Every age [has] had its own kind of war, its own limiting conditions, and its own peculiar preconceptions.[1]

Carl Von Clausewitz

Introduction:

The chronicles of military history teach us the importance of preparing for future security challenges. It would be unrealistic to anticipate the next 25 years as the beginning of a peaceful century void of conflict. As Clausewitz observed, every age has indeed been marked with its own kind of war. While the means change over time, warfare will remain "An act of force to compel our enemy to do our will."[2]

America's elected leaders should expect numerous international security challenges as the new millennium witnesses continued racial, economic and religious tensions. Some of these conflicts will be so severe that our very national viability and existence could be in jeopardy. The United States, moreover, must anticipate the rise of regional hegemons[3] who will undoubtedly challenge our vital national interests. In some instances, these security threats will require resolution by using the element of military power.

The Army is preparing to meet tomorrow's security challenges by implementing a strategy that will transform

---

1. Carl Von Clausewitz, *On War*, edited and translated by Michael Howard and Peter Paret, Princeton, NJ: Princeton University Press, 1976, p. 593.

2. *Ibid.*, p. 75.

3. For purposes of this discussion, regional hegemons are defined as nation-state actors who attempt to dominate their respective region of the world by either threat or use of military force.

it from a heavy, forward-deployed force to a lighter, more versatile, power projection force. The knowledge-rich attributes of Force XXI will be enhanced with the physical agility of Army After Next Era Battleforces. These new capabilities, in combination with a fully trained force consisting of high quality people from both active and reserve components, will enable America's Army to remain the world's dominant strategic land power during the 21st Century.

The World Beyond 2010:

While the first decades of the 21st Century will reflect dramatic social and economic change, some things will remain predictable. There is little evidence that suggests the Information Age will alter the perpetual characteristics of geopolitics.

Geopolitical interactions based upon the pursuit of international order, stability and the balance of power will continue to influence the national interests of the United States. The nation-state will remain fundamentally the same. These states will be identifiable political entities bounded by geographical parameters. They may exercise sovereignty in new ways as the old Industrial Age bureaucracy designed to regulate commerce and industry is pushed aside by Information Age innovations.

Global restraint, maintained through the balance of power during the Cold War, will be more difficult to achieve as the world is likely to disintegrate into areas of multipolar tensions with competing regional hegemons. Reduced influence of a bi-polar strategic balance has already allowed the world to return to its pre-Cold War natural condition. Competing states will seek to gain dominance over their neighbors. Conflicts will abound as some nations redress historic grievances and others open old wounds that have been festering for hundreds of years. The proliferation of information, while increasing knowledge and understanding among nations, also galvanizes ethnic groups and contributes to cultural friction within troubled regions. Some states may disintegrate into smaller, ethnically based units. This fragmentation will cause both interstate and intrastate conflict.

What is different today is the fact that, thanks to the growing interdependence of world markets and the expansion of information, even the most local source of friction may spark sympathetic heat in distant places. The thousand year conflict in the Balkans has become more than a localized squabble between conflicting ethnic and religious groups. What goes on there affects relations among the West, Russia and the Muslim countries of the Middle East. The lingering territorial dispute and nuclear arms race on the Indian subcontinent, the conflicting interests over the Spratly Islands among China and other Southeast Asian nations, and the continuing issue of the relationship between Taiwan and China point to other likely areas of regional strife and disharmony.

Future conflicts will most likely occur along the same geopolitical and cultural fault lines that have separated civilizations for millennia. These historic lines extend across northern and southern Europe, converge in the Balkans, and traverse through the Middle East; continuing beyond Eurasia, turning south toward the Pacific Rim, down the Malay Peninsula and into the Indonesian Archipelago. As in the past, these geopolitical fault lines will continue to witness ethnic, religious, economic, and political confrontation. [4]

As the competition for resources and regional dominance intensifies, hegemons will likely develop where the intersection of sociopolitical zones collide. Since these regional fault lines contain abundant natural resources, particularly petroleum, these economic attributes will continue to capture the interest of the United States and other advanced countries. Between now and 2025, it is

---

4. For greater detail see Samuel P. Huntington, "The Clash of Civilizations," *Foreign Affairs*, Summer 1993, p. 25.

- Fracturing and Regionalization.
- Diffusion of Threats.
- Rise of Regional Hegemons.
- Resurrection of Lingering Hostilities dormant during the Cold War --- return to normal global chaos
- Anti-Access Strategies.

Conflict continues to center around States or State-Like Actors.

reasonable to assume that if an aspiring regional hegemon emerges to threaten either our interests or the interests of our friends and allies, conflict will likely occur.

Future militaries throughout the world will continue to reflect the societies they defend. Just as the Agricultural Age and Industrial Age affected how armies fought, information technologies will have a dramatic impact upon the character of military organizations and force structure. The power of the microchip already makes it possible to know much more about the location of both enemy and friendly forces. This enhanced situational awareness requires us to begin thinking in terms of a surface- to-space continuum that will transform the traditional battlefield of the past into a future "battle-space" that will be more vertical than linear.

This enhanced knowledge will mean American forces will strategically deploy with greater speed to the theater of operations and then act with greater speed throughout the operational and tactical battle-space. Digitization not only improves the ability to communicate, it fundamentally alters the relationship between fire and maneuver. With the capacity to attack an enemy's center of gravity with great precision, our forces will maneuver with greater dispersion and protection to overwhelm the opponent's ability to resist.

130

Just as societies and states will reflect various stages of economic development and modernization, global militaries will likely retain elements of older, industrial armed forces while selectively buying state-of-the-art technology. In all likelihood, the proliferation of weapons and technologies will continue, thus contributing to the potential destabilization within regions of interest to the United States. For example, warriors from failed states might equip themselves with outdated weapons yet have access to weapons of mass destruction and employ the latest technology to exploit our information systems.

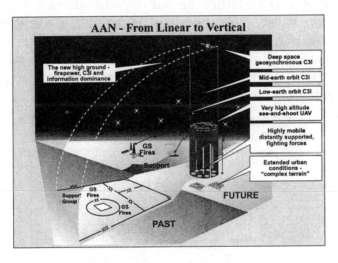

America's Vital National Interests in the 21st Century:

The United States has little choice but to remain globally engaged beyond 2010. America is expected to maintain one of the world's largest economies, and we can assume with some certainty that the United States will continue to actively promote democratic principles, free market economies and human rights.

For the American military, the Third Millennium began in August 1990 when GEN(R) Colin L. Powell, Chairman of the Joint Chiefs of Staff, shifted the United States from threat-based planning to capabilities-based planning. This approach reflected the changing strategic landscape resulting from the fall of the Berlin Wall and the end of the Cold War. For the last several years this methodology has been the basis for determining the required forces needed to secure America's national interests.

The President's National Security Strategy defines vital national interests as those of such importance that we, as a nation, will do whatever is necessary to defend them whenever our national survival is at risk. Vital interests include the physical security of our territory and the security of the territory of our formal allies. They also include the safety of American citizens at home and abroad. Part of insuring our security is maintaining access to trade and resources that are vital to our economic well-being. To defend these vital interests we are, and will remain, ready to use military force "unilaterally and decisively."[5]

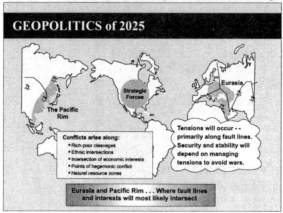

Important but not vital national interests are those that affect our national well-being and the character of the world, but do not threaten our national survival. We may or may not use military force to address these interests, depending on the costs and risks and how these measure against the interests at stake.[6] Many of the threats to our

5. See *A National Security Strategy for a New Century*, Washington, DC: U.S. Government Printing Office, October 1998, p. 5.

6. *Ibid.*

interests through 2010 and beyond will fall into this gray area of "important" but not "vital."

The third level of interests addresses humanitarian concerns. These interests stem from our historical idealism and our democratic values and heritage. As a nation we will continue to stand for what is good and right. If people need our help, we may act because our values demand that we do so. Often, we will try to avert humanitarian disasters through diplomacy or by cooperating with a wide range of international and non-governmental organizations. In many cases, it will make more sense to take action early to alter a situation which, if left unattended, might grow into a disaster requiring a massive intervention, which might be costly in terms of both treasure and lives.[7]

Our national interests will remain focused on Europe, East and Southwest Asia.[8] These regions are strategically important to the United States because most of our vital interests extend from the continental United States to Europe, Asia and the Pacific Rim. The United States must be prepared to act wherever vital national interests intersect with regions of potential conflict. Latin America is certainly important to the United States, as stated in the Monroe Doctrine, and we are mindful of events in Africa. But, not every conflict will require U.S. military action. Military intervention, however, may be required if an outbreak of conflict within these regions jeopardizes our national interests.

Future Threats: Who Might Oppose the United States?

We can postulate with some degree of certainty that a major military competitor is not likely to arise from modern democratic states. Although warfare among or between democracies is not impossible, because of mutual economic

---

7. *Ibid.*, p. 6.
8. *Ibid.*, p. 12.

interests and the similarity between political and social culture, such a prospect is highly improbable.

It seems almost a certainty that current threats will continue from hostile subnational groups, criminal cartels, and transnational terrorists. While each group may possess the capacity to cause great mischief, they are not expected to pose a threat to our continued existence and viability as a nation. Various rogue states may possess the will, but their lack of means to do us harm will not allow them to be more than a temporary threat to any vital national interest.

Probable Long-Term U.S. Strategy (to 2025)

- **Security Policy will center on:**
  - Security of the United States.
  - Stability overseas in areas of vital national interest.
- **Military Strategy will center on:**
  - Defense of United States; land, sea, air and space.
  - Forward engagement (stationing) in vital regions.
  - Projectable Military Power.
- **Engagement & Enlargement will continue worldwide across the full spectrum of operations.**

Likewise, failed states are not likely to pose a significant threat. Although there may be plenty of people in these states who have very little regard for our nation or its values, the only way they can threaten us will be through criminal activity involving various forms of terrorism. Although this is an area of concern, the states themselves will simply lack the means to threaten our vital interests.

The proliferation of weapons of mass destruction is a particular concern but this activity is not expected to threaten our national survival. It would be threatening to our homeland and overseas interests if any of these entities gain access to either chemical or biological weapons of mass destruction. However, delivery systems with limited range, along with the increasing sophistication of detection capabilities, constrain their viability as a weapons system. Moreover, there is no basis to assume that the current policy of deterrence will not continue to be effective as the United States has declared that the use of such weapons against our forces and homeland will incur a rapid and deadly retaliation.

The Rise of a Major Competitor:

A major competitor, however, with both the will and the means to oppose us, could become a significant threat to our vital national interests and possibly to our continued viability as a global power. While we do not predict the emergence of a peer competitor, one that could match the United States in all military categories, certain regional states have both the national will and the convincing military means to challenge and threaten the regional interests of the United States and our commitment to favorable world order. These countries would not try to match American air, land, and sea capabilities. Instead, as regional powers, their conventional center of gravity would be protected by a large army and reinforced by selective investments in key systems such as missile defense, or cheap but effective air and naval counter measures. These resources would feature just enough precision and lethality to deter outside incursions and achieve regional dominance.

The famous study of strategy and warfare, written by Sun Tzu, warned: "In battle one engages with the orthodox and gains victory through the unorthodox."[9] The most dangerous future opponent will heed the lessons from the Gulf War and will subsequently design a strategy that avoids our strength and uses indirect means to erode our national will. This opponent will exploit perceived American weaknesses such as an over-reliance on

---

9. Sun Tzu, *The Art of War*, translated by Ralph D. Sawyer, Boulder, Colorado: Westview Press, 1994, p. 187.

More than 8 YEARS into the 21st CENTURY we see a RISING PATTERN of ASYMMETRY

- Shedding Cold War Impedimenta
- Streamlining forces: Less weight, more mobility
- Less corrupt, more ideologically tuned
- From internal security to regional projection
- More mature, professional, educated
- Doctrinal focus on Operational Art. - Deflect air/seapower to preserve "Armies in being"
- Off-the-shelf information age technologies
- Just enough conventional weapons technology to keep low tech forces viable
- Offensive strategy: Satisfy long simmering hegemonic ambitions
- Defensive strategy: Primitive strategic forces to prevent interference from abroad.

	Army	Asymmetric Investments
India	980,000	
North Korea	1,000,000	
Pakistan	520,000	
Iran	345,000	
Iraq	350,000	
Russia	670,000	
China	2,200,000	

technology, an aversion to casualties and collateral damage, a lack of commitment for sustained campaigns and sensitivity to world opinion. Willing to invest a disproportionate amount of resources into advanced weaponry, this potential adversary will not seek to defeat our military forces in the field. Rather, he would adopt a defensive-offensive strategy that seeks to counter critical American advantages and deter, or, at the worst, attain an operational stalemate.

Without question, beyond 2010, America should expect the new century to bring a new kind of war that will threaten a number of vital national interests. The most serious threat will likely arise from a transitional state bent on becoming a regional hegemon. This potential enemy may feature a partially modernized military, specially tailored to counter American technology and enriched with just enough Information Age advancements to seize the initiative. Such an adversary will not try to defeat us, but will seek to deter our incursion into a regional crisis, or make our involvement so costly that we withdraw. These opponents will realize that a stalemate can be defined as a victory. These nations and actors with revolutionary impulses are going to be difficult to deter and defeat in the coming century.

National Security Policy Beyond 2010:

As the world leader of democratic principles, our security policy serves three objectives. First, it must provide for the physical security of the United States by making sure our military capability is strong enough to deter aggression and protect our national interests. Second, we seek stability in those areas of the world where American vital interests are at stake. Third, we will promote democracy abroad and bolster economic vitality along the cultural fault lines where American interests and potential instability converge. Only a long-term commitment of American power to those regions will foster the kind of stability that will ensure that U.S. vital interests are not threatened.

Our national military strategy must further reflect our commitment to deter aggression and preserve our way of life. As a global power, the United States must be unmatched in its ability to defend U.S. interests by air, land, sea and space. It is no longer useful to think of this nation as a "maritime" or "continental" power. Air and sea lines of communications are the interior lines of a world where our far-flung interests may be threatened.

The Army of the 21st Century will use those air and sea lines of communications to move where it must to secure our interests. In the Roman Empire, the Mediterranean Sea both facilitated commerce and allowed for the movement of troops. The Empire was sustained for nearly four centuries largely because Rome was master of both the sea and the land. The Army will never participate in operations that are completely independent of the other services. During the next century, the United States must continue to be a global maritime and aerospace power. Joint, Unified and

America's Strategic Challenge Might Play Out Like This...

Threat

Constrained Competitors	Regional Competitors	Major Competitors
• Industrial-Age Forces	• Industrial-Age Forces	• Information-Age Forces
• Very Limited Precision	• Selective Precision	• Precision and Mass
• Asymmetric Strategies	• Asymmetric Strategies	• Hegemonic Ambitions,
• Quasi-Professional	and Investments	"Anti-Access Strategies"
• Sparse WMD	• Quasi-Professional	• Professionalized
	• Limited WMD	• Proliferated WMD

2000 ——————— 2010 ——— MILITARY PREEMPTION CAPABILITY BECOMES ESSENTIAL ——— 2020 ————————→

Response

• Tension Management	• 2-MRC Strategy	• Major War-Winning
• Engagement and	• Improved Forces	Capabilities
Enlargement	• Improved Strategic and	• Precision, Mass, Speed
• Peacekeeping/Peace	Operational Mobility	• Strategic Maneuver
Enforcement	• Improved Situational	• Information Dominance
• OOTW	Awareness	• Jointness to
	• Forward Presence	Interdependence

Coalition action will be necessary to secure our worldwide interests and respond to future threats.

Developing the Army's Long-Range Vision:

America's Army will continue to be the only element of military power prepared to exercise direct, continuing, and comprehensive control over land, its resources and its people. During the next 25 years, the Army will exist to deter aggression and to fight and win the nation's wars. Other requirements will include providing options during small-scale contingencies and peace operations such as humanitarian and domestic assistance. Despite the infusion of technological systems, the Army of the future will be a total quality force seamlessly integrated with active and reserve components. More importantly, it will continue to rely on a strong value system that demonstrates an organizational commitment to take care of people.

As the long-range transition from Force XXI to Army After Next continues, great change will occur in the Army's physical, technological and cultural makeup. Beyond 2010, the Army must complete the metamorphosis from the rudimentary efforts initiated with Force XXI to the fully integrated force envisioned within the Army After Next. These changes will physically alter the institution's war-making sinews and will ensure the Army's viability well into the next century. While a future enemy may gain competencies that would counter American technical advantages, we must retain a dominent ability to win quickly and decisively at low cost. Moreover, the Army must have the means to conduct battle rapidly and to end it while the paralytic effect of firepower is greatest.

To fulfill its role as the land component member of the joint team, the 21st Century Army must acquire a number of mental and physical capabilities that will ensure full-spectrum dominance. The Army must be sufficiently versatile to operate effectively across a wide range of missions as part of a joint force or multinational coalition that can win quickly and decisively. Combat elements will incorporate the effects of knowledge and speed to gain positional advantage while protecting the force within an environment of near total strategic, operational and tactical battle-space awareness. This force will be capable of moving rapidly to any point where conflict threatens our vital interests. The 21st Century Army will combine the effects of battle-space awareness and precision fires to derive the full potential of strategic speed and dominant maneuver. As these changes become fully integrated, the synergistic effects derived from these various capabilities will enable

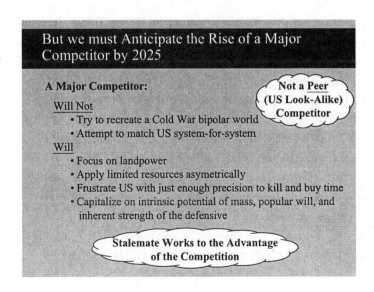

the Army to be the nation's force of decision on the 21st Century battlefield.

The objective must be to use all the capabilities of a balanced military force so that the final outcome of any war will be decided before the first engagement. The way to do that is to collapse the enemy's will to resist. Strategic preclusion is a process that involves marshalling forces rapidly and moving them to points of conflict quickly.

In Operation Desert Storm we saw a glimpse of this. As soon as the decision was made to deploy American forces into the Persian Gulf in great numbers, the television news programs showed troops getting on airplanes, tanks on flatcars moving toward ports, aircraft taking off for bases in Saudi Arabia, and ships leaving port. Iraqi leadership saw a formidable force building and moving inexorably toward them. The psychological destabilization of the enemy begins with mobilization and deployment, and culminates with the total collapse of the enemy brought about through an integrated attack that combines the destructive effects of maneuver and precision engagement.

The Army's Contribution To Our National Military Strategy:

In the 21st Century, the twin pillars of our national military strategy will continue to be forward presence and power projection. Both active and passive deterrence will be essential throughout the regions where we maintain vital national interests. After more than three years of active investigation, we are convinced that four major categories of military forces will be required in order to effectively execute a comprehensive National Security Strategy.

Global scouts are a key resource and part of the Army's effort to bridge active and passive deterrence measures. Consisting of attaches, foreign area officers, conventional and special operating forces, global scouts build and nurture a reservoir of trust and goodwill with potential coalition partners. These soldiers seek to favorably shape the strategic environment. While these teams teach the fundamentals of combat, they also seek to educate other cultures on democratic values and governmental procedures.

Forward presence forces demonstrate our national resolve and commitment to maintain peace and stability within a region. These resources serve to deter aggression and they help prevent major crises through aggressive engagement programs and coalition building. Either through the foresight of our predecessors or fate, we currently have forces throughout the world stationed in

Beyond 2010 Knowledge Dominance will no longer be enough. We must have:....

Speed -- to Exploit Knowledge:

- Forces must move to survive and succeed
  - Linear Speed -- Strategic preemption
  - Angular Speed -- Anticipate, out think, gain positional advantage
- Pulsed, continuous operations
- Agile, high operational transition capability
- Adaptive, full-spectrum force

regions where our vital national interests endure. These forces are deployed on foreign soil and their presence is usually enough to deter hostile actions. If necessary, they can provide an immediate response to acts of aggression and stabilize the situation until reinforcements arrive. American forces stationed in South Korea are an excellent example of strategically positioned forward-deployed forces.

Because of its current forward positioning along historic lines of conflict that are of great interest to the United

141

States, the 21st Century Army will play the largest role of all the services in favorably shaping the geo-strategic environment through peacetime engagement activities. Most countries throughout the world depend on large land forces to define and defend their way of life. Very few nations, in contrast, have significant navies or air forces as part of their military structure. In the eyes of our friends and allies, and even our potential enemies, troops stationed overseas represent the ultimate American commitment to peace and stability.

Global scouts and forward deployed forces will only be effective if they are backed with a credible reservoir of over-the-horizon forces that can mobilize and deploy from the United States to wherever acts of aggression occur. The essence of our military credibility will be continental-based forces that can rapidly deploy to either preclude aggressive actions or defeat an opponent before his forces have time to achieve complete victory.

Charting the Road Ahead–
The Army as an Integral Member of the Joint Team:

During the next 25 years, the world's security environment will be shaped by the interaction of nations undergoing various stages of national economic and social

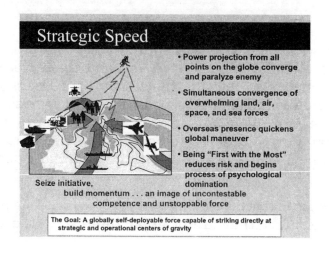

Strategic Speed

- Power projection from all points on the globe converge and paralyze enemy

- Simultaneous convergence of overwhelming land, air, space, and sea forces

- Overseas presence quickens global maneuver

- Being "First with the Most" reduces risk and begins process of psychological domination

Seize initiative, build momentum . . . an image of uncontestable competence and unstoppable force

The Goal: A globally self-deployable force capable of striking directly at strategic and operational centers of gravity development. While the information revolution will undoubtedly affect most societies, only a few nations will have transitioned into the Information Age by 2010. For those nations that make this leap, information technologies will also permeate their older industrial production facilities as well as their agricultural sectors. In some nations, these effects will be positive, fostering greater socio-economic progress. In other societies, people may suffer while their government pours resources into building a military machine that could transform these nations into regional hegemons.

With few exceptions, major conflict between states will occur in the vicinity of long-standing geopolitical and cultural fault lines that separate civilizations. Nations and groups will continue to seek ways to impose their wills upon each other and when they do, war will result. American involvement will occur whenever its vital national interests intersect with conflict along these tectonic fault lines.

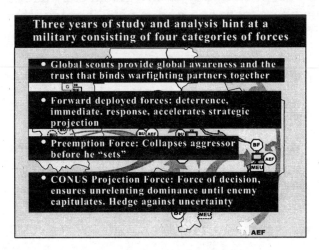

Three years of study and analysis hint at a military consisting of four categories of forces

- Global scouts provide global awareness and the trust that binds warfighting partners together
- Forward deployed forces: deterrence, immediate. response, accelerates strategic projection
- Preemption Force: Collapses aggressor before he "sets"
- CONUS Projection Force: Force of decision, ensures unrelenting dominance until enemy capitulates. Hedge against uncertainty

Certain nations will choose to invest in conventional military forces, information technologies and selected weapons of mass destruction. Their purpose will be to dominate selected regions while deterring American incursions. If confronted, they will employ an asymmetric strategy that seeks to avoid America's military strengths

143

and exploits perceived weaknesses. Nations that follow this pattern represent our most significant future threat.

While the world beyond 2010 will present a number of strategic security challenges, America will remain as the single global military power. Although the fundamental nature of war in the 21st Century will not change, new weapons will alter the traditional relationship between fire and maneuver.

During the early decades of the 21st Century, the Army of 2025 will differ from today's Army in two distinct ways. First, it will achieve unprecedented strategic and operational speed by exploiting information technologies to create a knowledge- based organization. Second, it will exhibit tremendous flexibility and physical agility through streamlined, seamlessly integrated organizations that use new tactics and procedures. The collective result will be a versatile, full spectrum, capabilities-based force that can decisively respond to any future global contingency. As the world begins a new age and a new century, the Army is preparing for the next kind of war that will emerge.

Chapter Nine

THE DAWN OF A NEW AGE OF WARFARE: AND THE CLARION CALL FOR ENHANCED MANEUVER CAPABILITIES

Major General Robert H. Scales, Jr.

Reproduced with Permission Granted by:
Spring 1999 Issue
DEFENCE SYSTEMS INTERNATIONAL
Sterling Publications Ltd.
London, England

THE DAWN OF A NEW AGE OF WARFARE:
AND THE
CLARION CALL FOR ENHANCED
MANEUVER CAPABILITIES

The Information Age will alter modern warfare in the 21st Century just as the Industrial Age altered 20th Century battlefields with new forms of integrated mechanization. Armies reflect the cultural fabric of their sponsoring societies. There is a historical and symbiotic relationship between advancing technology and the evolving means of warfare. As Clausewitz observed, every age has indeed been marked with its own kind of war. The information revolution promises to deliver a watershed of change that will again significantly alter the context of future war.

During the past 50 years, much of the talent, energy and national resources of the free world were invested within the Defense Community to ensure that the battlefield advantage resided with the armed forces who were compelled to fight from defensive positions. The military threats of the Cold War Era required this type of operational capability. For more than two generations, democratic nations invested their military research and development funds to improve precision strike capabilities. The dividends from this investment strategy yielded a suite of weapons with unprecedented lethal range and accuracy. The Cold War, consequently, ended with defensive forces enjoying the battlefield advantage.

The Battle Trumpet Sounds Anew

If we hope to restore a range of balanced, offensive options on the battlefield of tomorrow, the power of the microchip must be harnessed to develop a new generation of maneuver platforms that will be able to counter precision fires while making contact with the enemy. Precision strike only brings a single dimension of offensive heft to the battle. To be sure, firepower can be paralytic in its effect, but these effects are always fleeting. Firepower alone will not collapse an opponent's will to resist nor will it bring the coalition commander certain victory. The clarion call for a new generation of maneuver platforms sounds anew. Tomorrow's battlefield success will be achieved by commanders who have the ability to orchestrate precision strike with precision maneuver. As computer technology enhances both situational awareness and precision munitions, soldiers of tomorrow will simply die smarter if we fail to develop this leap-ahead physical agility. The dawn of a new age of warfare and the anticipated emergence of clever, adaptive opponents will require an order-of-magnitude increase in strategic and operational maneuver speed.

Almost 10 Years into a Strategic Pause

We are now experiencing a period of strategic calm very similar to the interwar years of 1918 to 1939. The end of the Cold War and the defeat of Iraq's Republican Guard marked a major geopolitical transition that has introduced an era of global harmony. The world beyond 2010, however, promises to become a complex web of international security concerns. Global restraint, maintained through the balance of power that existed during the Cold War, will be more difficult to achieve as long-standing multipolar tensions fester and competing regional hegemons attempt to dominate their respective corners of the world. Conflicts will abound as some nations redress historic grievances and others open old wounds that have been simmering for hundreds of years.

Future conflicts will most likely occur along the same geopolitical and cultural fault lines that have separated civilizations for millennia. These historic lines extend across northern and southern Europe, converge in the

Balkans, traverse through the Middle East, continue beyond Eurasia, turning south toward the Pacific Rim, down the Malay Peninsula and into the Indonesian Archipelago. As in the past, these geopolitical fault lines will continue to witness ethnic, religious, economic and political confrontation.

The Rise of Major Military Competition

If the past is an indication of the future, this global vacation from military violence will end eventually. It is too soon to postulate whom the significant challengers might be, however, we have started to develop some emerging insights regarding the origin and context of future regional conflict.

During the next two decades, states will continue to cluster in one of three major groups based upon their political, economic and social differences. It seems reasonable to anticipate with some degree of certainty that major military threats will not likely arise from the approximately two dozen developed, industrialized democracies. Although warfare among or between mature democratic states is not impossible, such an outcome is most improbable. Likewise, at the opposite end of the have-and-have-not continuum, there is a large number of states who struggle for survival and they will not have either the economic or military means to challenge our vital national interests. Without question, these "have-not" nations will certainly continue to need humanitarian and peacekeeping assistance.

In between these two extremes there is a group of "transitional" states most likely to become candidates for serious military competition in the next century. These evolving states, located primarily in Europe, the Middle East and Asia, are already beginning to develop the economic means that will generate the expandable income to support more sophisticated militaries. We should anticipate, by the end of the next decade, a few of these transitional states to become adaptive enemies with both the national will and military means to challenge us. These competitors will enjoy both the positional advantage of the defense and the technical advantage of newly emerging precision munitions to challenge our interests within their respective regions of influence.

Without question, the United States Army expects the new century to bring a new kind of war that will threaten a number of vital national interests. The potential enemy of the early 21st Century may feature a partially modernized military, specially tailored to counter American technology and enriched with just enough Information Age advancements to seize the initiative. Such an adversary will not try to defeat us, but will seek to deter our incursion into a regional crisis, or make our involvement so costly that we withdraw. These opponents will realize that a stalemate can be defined in their terms as a victory.

The Microchip is a Neutral Ally

Presently, many military organizations believe that they can best address future competition with technologies that improve our ability to find and kill the enemy from a distance. This superior knowledge, unfortunately, will not be sufficient to ensure future success. Even the great chess-masters, who have 100 percent clarity and real-time vision over their battlefield, must cope with the unexpected moves from a thinking opponent.

The information revolution, at best, will be neutral as military competitors challenge each other. It will alter the nature of warfare and potentially do more for our opponents than it will do for us. A thinking opponent will quickly realize that our intensive reliance on information age technologies becomes a weakness that can become an asymmetric target.

One of the potential ironies of the future may occur because western information technologies could provide non-western armies with solutions for two of their most vexing problems. First, cellular technology and the Internet may allow them to maintain a concert of action for long periods of time with widely dispersed units. Second, these same technologies will allow them to orchestrate the rapid massing of dispersed units when opportunities arise to transition into offensive operations.

The prospect of this scenario becomes even more sobering when one considers the fact that many commercial ventures already provide future competitors with the tools they need while commercial research centers continue to perfect non-nodal, distributed and net-centric global information technologies. All of these resources will be available to paying customers without one developmental dollar spent by our potential opponents. The technological foot race is underway and either side could win. As we develop the technologies to find and kill the enemy, our potential opponents will develop the technologies to become even more dispersed and difficult to find.

Charting Tomorrow's Capabilities Today

The Information Age beckons the Defense Community with a clarion call for innovative thought and experimentation. Increasingly, the dominant means of warfare will become less anchored within existing industrial age impedimenta and more reflective of new systems, innovations and adaptations launched by the unfolding march of the information revolution. As the size and lethality of the deadly zone increases, our industrial age experience becomes less relevant as a means of determining the future course of modern war. During the peaceful interlude that we currently enjoy, it is important to examine new ideas and evaluate the merit of new concepts. Fortunately, we have a rich historical roadmap of experiences that give us a sense of direction. The chronicles of military history teach us the importance of developing a vision for the future of landpower that will guide technological developments and assist with the development of new fighting doctrine. The blueprint for successful Armies beyond 2010 will be discovered through both analyses of military history and an organized experimentation effort that must be sustained over a period of many years.

The imperatives for charting tomorrow's capabilities today are imposing. The secret of future victories will be discovered if we are willing to foster innovation and support experimentation during the next decade. A revised blueprint for tomorrow's Army is possible to imagine if new concepts, doctrine and structure are investigated. Certain victory in 2025 can only be assured if we accept the premise that the era for industrial age warfare is passing quickly while we are just witnessing the dawn of information age warfare.

Chapter Ten

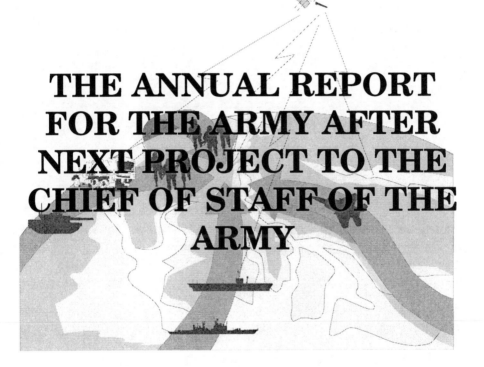

THE ANNUAL REPORT FOR THE ARMY AFTER NEXT PROJECT TO THE CHIEF OF STAFF OF THE ARMY

Major General Robert H. Scales, Jr.

The Army After Next Project
Deputy Chief of Staff for Doctrine
Headquarters, Training and Doctrine Command
Fort Monroe, Virginia

The Annual Report for
The Army After Next Project
to the Chief of Staff of the Army

July 1997

Contents

INTRODUCTION

The Chief of Staff of the Army and the Commander, Training and Doctrine Command established the Army After Next project in February 1996 to help the Army leadership craft a vision of future Army requirements. The project connects the process of change represented by Army XXI and guides future Army research and development programs. This is the TRADOC commander's second annual overview of the AAN program.

Visualizing the future requires a process that anticipates the nature of warfare in the next century and the evolution of U.S. national security requirements. For that purpose, AAN conducts broad studies of future warfare to frame issues vital to the development of the U.S. Army and to provide those issues to the senior Army leadership in a format suitable for integration into TRADOC combat developments programs. These studies focus on, but are not constrained to, the period 2010 and beyond. The choice of a 30-year point of focus is intended to place a distant intellectual beacon far enough in front of the pace of change so that ideas and a vision of the future will not be constricted by near-term budgetary and institutional influences. Such an approach is needed to break free of the action-reaction cycle of incremental change, which can only hold the future hostage to the past. To ensure a comprehensive and holistic perspective focused on 2025, the program is organized around four broad research areas: the geostrategic setting, the evolution of military art, human and organizational issues, and technology trends.

By 2010, the Army will exploit the Force XXI effort to achieve nothing less than a technological and cultural metamorphosis. By then, over a decade of experimentation and field exercises will create a knowledge-based force, Army XXI, balanced across our traditional imperatives and possessed with a clarity of observation, degree of decentralization, and pace of decision making unparalleled in the history of warfare. AAN simply seeks to provide the Army of 2020 with the physical speed and agility to complement the mental agility inherited from Force XXI.

Following the conceptual direction set by Force XXI's advanced warfighting experiments, AAN's primary research mechanism is a series of free-play tactical, operational, and strategic war games and war-game excursions designed to explore the character of future warfare and to provide an in-depth joint and multi-disciplinary examination of political, social, demographic, and technological trends likely to affect the future of war. Insights derived from games conducted to date comprise the heart of this report. Because they reflect only the first cycle of AAN studies, these insights should be considered suggestive rather than conclusive. Future AAN war games can be expected to refine them significantly.

THE PROCESS OF CHANGE

The history of warfare reveals a cyclical pattern of military change in which evolving technology alternately favors attack or defense. Before the Industrial Age, such cycles alternated slowly because innovation developed and spread slowly. After the Industrial Revolution, the cycles began to accelerate, though they were still somewhat retarded by political and institutional conservatism and the uneven development of military technologies. By the American Civil War, rifled muskets—the precision weapons of the day—had greatly extended the deadly zone troops had to cross to close with an enemy, a condition favoring the defense. Subsequent advances in artillery led European armies to believe that superior firepower would restore the power of the offensive and with it the possibility of quick, decisive victory. Events proved them wrong. While lethality skyrocketed, the pace of movement across the widening deadly zone remained that of a marching soldier. Technology thus served only to increase the slaughter and

157

to mire armies on both sides in a conflict of attrition to which there seemed no alternative.

By 1918, the Germans had found a partial solution—a method of opportunistic infiltration allowing infantry to transit the deadly zone intact—but they lacked the technology to accelerate the advance enough to reach decisive objectives before the defender could recover. By the onset of World War II, the internal combustion engine, armor plating, and the wireless provided the means to accelerate maneuver. Mechanization allowed troops to cross the deadly zone protected and at high speed. Large units could dash great distances into the enemy's rear. Victory thus came from disintegrating the coherence of the defense and collapsing the psychological will of the defender. Through rapid maneuver supported by mobile firepower, the offensive once again came to dominate warfare.

In the postwar years, the United States and its NATO allies applied microchip technology to develop precise, long-range killing power in an effort to successfully defend against a Soviet-style *blitzkrieg*. The cycle of warfare had turned yet again in favor of the defense. By the mid-1980s, technology had extended the tactical deadly zone to what were once operational and possibly strategic distances. As this trend continues, long-range, precision firepower systems will maintain the defensive as the dominant form of warfare.

To restore the advantage to the offensive, we believe that the Army must devise the means to accelerate the speed of movement across the deadly zone by an order of magnitude or greater. The union of knowledge and speed will do more than increase linear velocity; it will also quicken a commander's ability to divine and exploit an enemy's weaknesses and to offset the influence of chance and uncertainty. The American method of war-making in the future must rely on the offensive if this nation intends, as a matter of policy, to retain the ability to strike rapidly, decide quickly, and finish wars cleanly with minimal loss of life to all sides. Current AAN research is directed at this most vital and pressing challenge.

THE RATIONALE FOR CHANGE

The historical record of military change is mixed. Some changes, like the Navy's development of carrier aviation in the mid-1930s, Germany's *blitzkrieg,* and the Army's development of airmobile operations in the 1960s, have succeeded. Others, like France's Maginot Line and the U.S. Army's Pentomic reorganization of the 1950s, have not. Generally speaking, those that have failed reflected either too narrow a view of warfare or else a faddish preoccupation with untested theories. The AAN Project consequently embraces a broad view of warfare, particularly since the Army must win wars as well as battles. Accordingly, AAN studies consider warfare in all its dimensions, beginning with its most likely strategic conditions. Fundamental to this perspective is the belief that even the smallest element of the Army must reflect a common unifying thread, beginning with the vital interests of the United States and proceeding through national security policy, military strategy, long-term operational objectives, and, ultimately, the design and employment of every tactical unit.

Based on its broad study of future warfare, AAN research to date indicates that the Army should expect dramatic changes in the dynamics of battle in the period beyond 2010. The remainder of this report discusses those changes as we currently understand them. While many aspects of the future remain indistinct, others have already become discernible. The Army can and should begin now to prepare for the future, even if our desired end state remains only dimly perceived. We can adjust our glide path as our vision of the future gains clarity. Inaction is a decision we cannot afford. The Army must change soon for three reasons:

First, every revolution, whether political, economic, or military unfolds in evolutionary steps. Generally, at least half a generation, about 15 years, is required for vision and ideas to mature into secure and irreversible change. It takes about that long to grow a battalion commander or platoon sergeant or to develop, test, and field major systems. It may take even longer to truly alter the institutional culture sufficiently to internalize revolutionary change. In addition, the Army today finds itself very much a fellow traveler in a grander societal revolution. Global institutions and cultures are busily shifting from the Industrial to the Information Age. The Army today has a foot firmly planted in both ages. Materiel and structures developed in the era of the recent past must now either be modified or replaced to prepare for conflict in the Information Age. Central to this decision is whether current and programmed systems will satisfy the requirements of a 2025 battlefield. Since current AAN research suggests that tomorrow's battlefield will differ from today's in revolutionary ways, the Army's leadership must soon determine how to apportion research and development resources among a host of competing technological alternatives. Also, it must determine how much of the Army to modernize along current lines before *leapfrogging* Army XXI systems with entirely new technologies and significantly different operational and organizational concepts.

Second, the United States currently enjoys unrivaled military supremacy, but this condition may well erode after the turn of the century, Many analysts see both China and a recovered Russia as having the economic potential to become major military competitors. Yet, any number of military challengers might arise. Such challengers need not seek to match the U.S. in every military category. Instead, they merely need to acquire capabilities intended to counter critical American advantages—in sensor technology, for example—depriving U.S. forces of the assurance of rapid battlefield dominance and raising the political costs of military intervention. That approach would especially appeal to armies building or rebuilding from a relatively small technology base, as the Germans did after World War I. Such armies would have few sunk costs. Indeed, current AAN research strongly suggests that any serious military threat between now and the 2025 period will very likely involve asymmetric forces designed specifically to threaten U.S. superiority in areas requiring long development and deployment lead times.

Third, if not corrected soon, the current emphasis on a method of warfighting that emphasizes firepower at the expense of maneuver may well result in a protracted war characterized by stalemate, attrition, and unacceptable loss of life to both sides. Recent experience in war and insights from the AAN series of war games demonstrate that, even in the age of precision warfare, the principal benefit to be derived from firepower is the psychological paralysis of the enemy, not his physical destruction. Unfortunately, this benefit decreases over time as an enemy inures himself to the shock of firepower and learns to "maneuver under

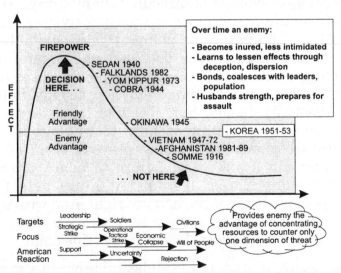

In war, the psychological dominates the physical. Since the psychological effects of firepower erode over time, decision should be sought quickly. To do otherwise invites unnecessary risk.

precision" through the use of deception, dispersion, and maneuver by infiltration. Quite likely by 2025, a competent enemy may also be able to counter American advantages in precision firepower with a variety of precision and counterprecision technologies of his own. If American military forces are to win quickly and decisively at low cost, they must have the means to conduct battle rapidly and to end it clearly at the moment when the paralytic effect of firepower is greatest. As the figure above demonstrates, to delay beyond the high point of effect only prolongs the killing and stiffens the enemy's will to resist. Decisive victory ultimately must be achieved by forces on the ground. Psychological collapse—the breaking of an enemy's will to resist—results when an opponent finds himself challenged and blocked wherever he turns. Restoration of the balance between fire and maneuver will take time, at least a decade or more, and the process must begin soon.

THE PACE OF CHANGE

Adapting to change is difficult for any army. At best, changing a military organization too quickly may result in acquisition of immature or inappropriate capabilities. At worst, it can threaten the doctrinal and organizational cohesion on which any fighting force depends. But as armies throughout history have learned to their dismay, failure to adapt is equally deadly. Sunk costs or budgetary penury may preclude adoption of new technologies, while institutional conservatism may prevent their effective exploitation. In either case, failure to adapt ultimately results in squandered lives and military defeat. Our challenge today is to get the balance right. And with system wear-out only about 12 years away, we have just enough time to do it. The diagram below makes this point.

The steep axis of change is undesirable because too great an angle encourages too rapid a lock on systems that might be quickly outdated. Another risk on this axis—perhaps even greater than premature materiel lock-in—is that of

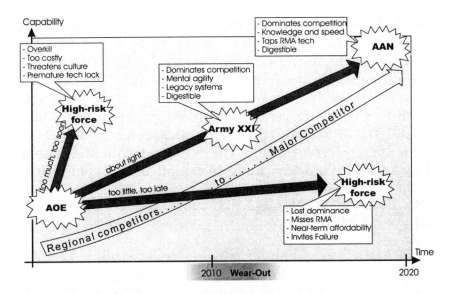

Capability

- Overkill
- Too costly
- Threatens culture
- Premature tech lock

- Dominates competition
- Knowledge and speed
- Taps RMA tech
- Digestible

AAN

High-risk force

- Dominates competition
- Mental agility
- Legacy systems
- Digestible

Army XXI

too much, too soon

about right

Major Competitor

too little, too late

to . . . .

High-risk force

AOE

Regional competitors . . . .

- Lost dominance
- Misses RMA
- Near-term affordability
- Invites Failure

Time

2010 Wear-Out   2020

The challenge is to change the force without putting it at risk.

disrupting the organization without achieving a real increase in fighting capability; simply to be seen to outside audiences as "doing something." The Pentomic reorganization of the 1950s was perhaps the clearest recent example of such a misplaced impulse.

The shallow axis is equally undesirable because too slow a rate of change may miss the revolution altogether. For years after World War I the tank was widely seen as an infantry support weapon, though hindsight proved its value as a primary instrument of maneuver. When the dynamics of the battlefield change rapidly—and we believe such change is occurring now—so also must the rate of adaptation. Rapid military change is not unprecedented. But too often in the past, its driving impulse has been prior defeat. We believe effective adaptation is possible without that unpleasant incentive.

As a general observation, near-term change tends to focus on force structure and equipment. Planning for more distant futures tends to concern capabilities and

163

possibilities—the *how* rather than the *who* or *what*. While pragmatic near-term planners try to improve existing systems, longer-term visionaries can deal in theory and emerging capabilities in a more abstract fashion. The challenge is linking the two without allowing the present to consume the future, or the vision to become intellectually sterile. While focusing on capabilities, AAN seeks at the same time to think through the organizational and human changes that will be required to exploit those capabilities.

THE PROCESS OF CHANGE: MID- AND LONG-RANGE

TRADOC's commander once commented that the AAN was about "ideas, not concepts." That is a succinct description of AAN's orientation. The AAN Project has become a laboratory—part technology-oriented, part military science—in which the Army works with other services and agencies of government, academic institutions, and civilian industry to build ideas about the future. AAN differs perhaps from the efforts of other futures groups in that its participants take extra care to subject ideas to both the considered experience of military history and the analytical rigor of state-of-the-art gaming.

AAN is the flagship program among several studies whose purpose is to assist the Army's leaders to establish priorities and earmark resources to maintain force readiness today and in the future. The findings and analyses developed by the AAN Project and provided to the planners of the DCSOPS Office of Strategy, Plans, and Policy help set the more distant parameters that will guide Army long-range planning.

As a result of this year's study, a more complete understanding of the Army's long-range process of change is beginning to emerge. In general, the process divides into three *armies:* the current force, the programmed force, and the potential force.

164

The *current force is* today's Army in the field, ready to fight. TRADOC's obligation to this army is training and doctrine. Pursuant to that obligation, TRADOC soon will publish the newest edition of FM 100-5, *Operations,* the Army's keystone doctrinal manual, last revised in 1993.

The second force falls under TRADOC's combat developments responsibility. Roughly equivalent to the *programmed force,* it is the army in near-term development, which is undergoing upgrades to existing systems in order to take advantage of new technologies and opportunities immediately available for organizational improvement. This force falls within the influence of the Program Objective Memorandum, which tends to lock large programs within a 5-to-7-year period to compete within the budget process. The programmed force is aimed at the midterm future. In 1940, this would have been the Louisiana Maneuver force. Today, it is Army XXI. TRADOC's *battle labs* were established specifically to extend as far as possible the period of experimentation within the POM's influence. Programmed force development is guided by TRADOC Pamphlet 525-5 and addresses the familiar TRADOC requirements: doctrine, training, leaders, organizations, materiel, and soldiers.

The third or *potential force* is the one with which AAN is primarily concerned. Here the focus shifts from improvement of fielded capabilities to long-term research and development programs; and from current and programmed force structures to as-yet-unspecified capabilities associated with our emerging vision of future warfare. Implied is a similar shift from the sorts of Cold War challenges that shaped the creation of today's Army, to the more ambiguous and variegated global military challenges likely to confront America and her allies in the next century. Hence, while some of the associated technologies may be revolutionary, the potential force itself should be viewed essentially as the next logical step in a continuing adaptation of military capabilities to the changing dynamics of war and requirements of national security.

Next summer TRADOC will publish a new pamphlet, 525-6, that will capture the emerging ideas of AAN in order to help the senior leadership craft its vision of future warfighting. The pamphlet will serve as the Army's *distant beacon* to guide the combat developments process for the mid- to long-term future.

Because of this anticipatory function, AAN furnishes the primary link to other DOD agencies engaged in long-term development—for example, Defense Advanced Research Projects Agency projects and various Defense Science Board studies. As with AAN, such efforts typically aim well beyond DTLOMS and frequently push the outer bounds of practicality. Moreover, because the potential force is not hostage to the POM, it represents the most promising opportunity for true integration with sister service concepts, such as the Air Force's ultra-high-altitude UAV and the Marine Corps' small-unit operations study.

The wellspring of AAN is the Army leadership's vision of the role and function of land power in the 30-year future and beyond. AAN's four broad areas of study all seek to clarify developments in geopolitics, military art, human and organizational issues, and technology that are today only dimly perceived, and then integrate those insights with those of other services into a cohesive joint view of future warfare. At the same time, AAN is closely connected with *futures* programs in DOD and other government agencies, including partnerships with AAN *franchise* programs in the U.S. Army Space and Strategic Defense Command (SSDC), U.S. Army Special Operations Command, and TRADOC's Combined Arms Support Command.

In sum, AAN's objective is to provide the Army's leadership the raw materiel for a vision of war, and thus of land-power's role, in the 30-year future. To accomplish that objective, the AAN process must be continuous, year after year, so that the Army's vision is always extended and linked to developments in other services. Provided it remains solidly connected to technological and organizational development, such a process is the Army's best assurance of a smooth and effective glide path to the future.

A GEOSTRATEGIC VIEW OF 2025

The most difficult yet essential aspect of defining land-power capabilities 30 years in the future is forecasting the security requirements those capabilities must satisfy. Clearly, we cannot predict with precision the future geostrategic condition of a world that even today is changing at an unprecedented pace. We can however recognize those enduring national interests that any future land power force must be able to support.

AMERICAN NATIONAL INTERESTS THROUGH 2025

For the purpose of AAN studies, interests subdivide into *vital* and *important*. The boundary between these categories is neither rigid nor immutable, particularly since statesmen have a habit of transmuting important into vital interests when the former are challenged. But the categories at least help distinguish objectives for which the nation is willing to risk unlimited liability from others whose importance tends to be more circumstantial. Among vital interests, AAN recognizes—

- Deterrence and prevention of nuclear, biological, or chemical attack on the United States and its allies, and continuing reduction of the threat of such attack. Implied is the maintenance of effective control over formerly Soviet nuclear weapons and weapons-usable materiel.

- Prevention of the rise of a powerful, hostile hegemony in Asia or Europe. Implied are the continued safety, freedom, and prosperity of friendly nations in both regions, maintenance and improvement of effective alliances like NATO, and deterrence of hostile ambitions on the part of any potential aggressor.

- Continued unhindered access by the United States and our allies to global resources—especially energy resources—essential to our economic health.

In addition to these overriding interests, the United States will continue to pursue objectives that are less vital, but still important enough to justify the selective use of force. Examples might include preventing the emergence of a hostile regional hegemony in the Persian Gulf and maintaining the peace and security of the Korean peninsula, the Taiwan Straits, and the South China Sea. The U.S. will also continue current efforts to suppress and combat international terrorism, drug trafficking, and transnational crime.

Given these interests, the United States can be expected to remain heavily involved in the world of 2025—a leader in both multinational and bilateral defense arrangements and an active promoter, as we are today, of democratic principles, free market economies, and human rights. Were the United States to renounce global leadership and turn inward as we did in the 1930s, the effect would be felt profoundly throughout the world, creating a power vacuum almost certain to produce uncertainty and unrest— historical precursors of global conflict.

There is, however, no reason today to suppose that the United States will turn inward even if we could. On the contrary, every indication is that we will continue to maintain sufficient power to play a decisive international role. Thus AAN assumes a world in which the United States remains engaged, retaining the military power to support regional alliances and to deter or defeat major military competitors. In this year's studies and war games, our analytical focus was on hypothetical challenges to vital interests in 2021. This summer, the study effort will expand to include examination of potential conflicts involving

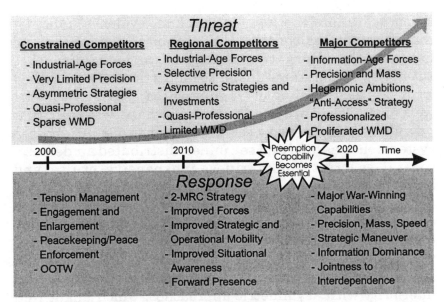

Threat		
Constrained Competitors	**Regional Competitors**	**Major Competitors**
- Industrial-Age Forces - Very Limited Precision - Asymmetric Strategies - Quasi-Professional - Sparse WMD	- Industrial-Age Forces - Selective Precision - Asymmetric Strategies and Investments - Quasi-Professional - Limited WMD	- Information-Age Forces - Precision and Mass - Hegemonic Ambitions, "Anti-Access" Strategy - Professionalized - Proliferated WMD
2000	2010	Preemption Capability Becomes Essential 2020 Time
Response		
- Tension Management - Engagement and Enlargement - Peacekeeping/Peace Enforcement - OOTW	- 2-MRC Strategy - Improved Forces - Improved Strategic and Operational Mobility - Improved Situational Awareness - Forward Presence	- Major War-Winning Capabilities - Precision, Mass, Speed - Strategic Maneuver - Information Dominance - Jointness to Interdependence

America's strategic challenge is to prepare for the rise of a major military competitor.

less-than-vital interests. The following chart summarizes the expected features of the threat spectrum associated with pursuit of both vital and important national interests during the next 30 years.

RISE OF A MAJOR MILITARY COMPETITOR

From the beginning, the AAN Project has found problems with the term *peer competitor*. While a mirror-image peer may serve DOD and service programmatic objectives, AAN believes that the term *major military competitor* better characterizes the military challenge to the United States for the next 30 years.

Peer competitor implies the mirror-image, action-reaction stasis inherited from the Cold War. In fact, due to disparities in disposable wealth and the competence of the American technological base, current U.S. military superiority will continue to discourage would-be aggressors from engaging in head-to-head competition. Today, already seven years into the new millennium, evidence indicates that many states concede U.S. technical dominance and have sought alternative strategies to neutralize U.S. strengths. These states do not seem particularly concerned with the acquisition of sophisticated, state-of-the art weaponry. They are inclined to purchase weapons that provide relatively cheap counters against our air and sea systems such as land and sea mines, distributed air defense, coastal seacraft, submarines, inexpensive cruise and ballistic missiles, and unsophisticated weapons of mass destruction. Such strategies offer a less sophisticated enemy the ability to dampen, delay, and disrupt the high-tech offensive power of an advanced military force without the inherent expense of purchasing battlefield symmetry. These states will likely offset technological inferiority with asymmetric approaches, which might well include the ability to field mass armies, to incite popular will, and to exploit the inherent strength of the strategic defensive.

Control or deterrence of military hostilities will undoubtedly remain an objective of future American national defense policy. Furthermore, AAN believes that there is a high probability that one or more major military competitors will arise by 2025. For purposes of this study, AAN defines major military competition as "first-tier state with a modernized military establishment and cultural and strategic predilections counter to the vital interests of the United States or its allies."

NATIONAL SECURITY STRATEGY IN 2025

Ideally, the pursuit of national interests is translated into action through a coherent national security strategy that balances requirements against capabilities. AAN assumes that U.S. national security strategy through 2025 will continue to exhibit a fundamental continuity. While incorporating new capabilities and operational techniques, U.S. military forces will continue to support allies, deter potential adversaries, and respond as required to unforeseen military and humanitarian contingencies. Forward-based forces will continue to play a vital role in supporting these objectives, not only in terms of their operational effectiveness, but even more importantly as the clearest demonstration possible of U.S. national will and commitment to the defense of its allies and interests. Yet, as events in the recent past have shown, even the best positioned and most potent military force can fail to deter, particularly if an opponent misjudges American resolve because of his own ignorance or cultural bias. Therefore, actual or threatened military aggression will usually require the deployment of major fighting forces from the United States directly into threatened regions to resolve the issue.

MILITARY ART AND SCIENCE IN 2025

The proliferation of precision weaponry by 2025 will expand the battlespace enormously in terms of size and lethality—conditions that will favor the defense. Additionally, the ability to see the battlefield more clearly through information technology will heighten the defender's advantage by making attacking forces easier to detect and by allowing the defender to mass battlefield fires and other effects more accurately. This year's AAN war games indicate that, unless the speed of movement increases substantially, those improvements in detection and the precision-fire delivery will make offensive action infinitely more difficult.

Fortunately, knowledge—battlefield information—is a two-edged sword. Mating superior knowledge with speed of movement can provide the means to frustrate the defender's ability to acquire and mass fires and thus allow an attacker to cross the deadly zone intact to accomplish an operationally decisive maneuver. Since operational art, by definition, entails employing tactical successes to achieve strategic ends, increasing the speed of movement across all three levels of warfare must become the driving imperative of future military development.

THE FY 1997 WAR GAME SERIES

During FY 97, AAN conducted a series of futuristic war games to frame strategic and operational issues likely to influence war against a major competitor in 2020. The three TRADOC-organized war games consisted of operational-level, force-on-force games at the TRADOC Analysis Center at Fort Leavenworth (the Leavenworth Games), the Winter War Game at Carlisle Barracks (WWG 97), and a series of excursions derived from the WWG to provide a sensitivity check of the WWG major events. All games were open-ended, free-play exercises with an active and unfettered Red force. All services participated. The WWG included world-class representatives from the executive branch, industry, academia, the military, and other government agencies.

The games played a 2020 Blue force capable of order-of-magnitude increases in speed, which we propose can only be achieved by rotating the traditional two-dimensional orientation of land forces upward into the atmosphere and space. A more refined understanding of the character of this force emerged during the course of the war-game series. An independent contractor associated with the DOD Revolution in Military Affairs (RMA) study effort constructed a hypothetical Red force designed to present an asymmetric threat to U.S. 2020 force structure.

THE LEAVENWORTH GAMES

The Leavenworth games explored force-on-force combat between notional forces at the tactical and operational levels. The principal objective was to develop a basis for determining conflict resolution in the WWG. Four subgames took place. The first pitted an Army XXI division against a Red 2020 force. The second and third placed a Blue 2020 force in opposition to the Red force in two different

172

combinations of terrain. The last evaluated enhanced Marine Corps capabilities against the Red force. The games involved four variables: terrain, including urbanized areas; size and posture of the enemy force; support available but located outside the engagement area; and the level and quality of information dominance on both sides.

The principal finding of the Leavenworth games was that mobility, characterized predominantly by speed of maneuver, proved to be the most important factor contributing to battlefield success. Further, battlefield knowledge actually enabled speed, though the precise relationship to date remains difficult to determine. To help isolate the contribution of knowledge to combat outcomes, the AAN staff defined three tiers of relative battlefield knowledge. A tier-one force possessed limited knowledge of the enemy plan and intent, but could achieve information dominance for specific periods of time; this force could exploit certain limited windows of opportunity. With tier-two capabilities, a force could understand significant aspects of the enemy's plan, could recognize his intentions at key decision points, and could react to take advantage of those decisions. With tier-three capabilities, the force could see the enemy as an organizational whole, including his pattern of operations, task organization, phasing and tempo; in short, Blue could understand Red's intent and could develop and execute a plan to counter that intent. The introduction of a force capable of tier-three knowledge superiority changed the time cycles and patterns of maneuver between opposing forces fundamentally and dramatically; Blue could enter the engagement more quickly, achieve decisions more rapidly, finish the fight faster, and reengage the enemy elsewhere. The Leavenworth games offered the following insights.

Maneuver

A significant finding of the AAN war games was that superior knowledge permits a commander to apply each discrete part of his force in a single simultaneous act of overwhelming fire and maneuver. Knowledge dominance on the battlefield will allow a dramatic increase in the speed of maneuver. A relationship exists between knowledge and precision that permits maneuver forces to employ an ambush dynamic against opponents on an almost routine basis. Precision in maneuver might take any number of forms. One example is highly refined targeting and maneuver directed against individual enemy elements by small units moving at great speed under leaders following mission orders. After several game turns, the Red commander knew that a Blue force with knowledge advantage and speed was unstoppable, and that his only options were to hold in place and concede or execute a series of disjointed, uncoordinated attacks and suffer defeat in detail. In either case, the practical result on the battlefield was always the same: immediate and dramatic disintegration.

Blue forces employed an air-ground tactical method of maneuver that combined lighter surface fighting vehicles with advanced airframes capable of transporting them at speeds as great as 200 kilometers per hour over distances in excess of 1500 kilometers. This method allowed, among other things, a more extensive use of the vertical dimension of the battlespace which, coupled with superior levels of information dominance, permitted greater speed and precision in maneuver. Terrain came to serve a protective and concealing function without restricting mobility; and the resultant ability to accelerate movement through the battle zone enhanced force survivability by frustrating the enemy's capability to detect, track, and engage Blue forces.

Asymmetric Responses

Red's learning curve rose sharply as the games progressed. Confronted by overwhelming combat power, he resorted to asymmetric responses in an effort to offset Blue's advantages. He recognized early on that Blue's superiority, particularly in firepower and information dominance, eroded over time. Any action that heightened ambiguity or complexity, and thus increased the time Blue needed to gain control of the situation, benefited Red. Therefore, Red moved rapidly to complex terrain—urban, suburban, and, in some cases, forests and mountains. He used his limited information warfare capabilities to slow Blue maneuver through electronic warfare and deception. Although Red lost, his asymmetric responses partially succeeded: he managed to degrade Blue's precision, to slow his operational tempo, and to significantly increase the damage to the Blue force. The lesson is obvious. For the 2020 Blue forces, time is the worst of enemies.

THE WINTER WAR GAME

The strategic, or winter, war game forms the capstone event in the annual AAN cycle. This year's WWG focused on the whole realm of political, strategic, and operational levels of a *most vital* war in 2020 to identify issues related to the changing character of warfare in about 2025.

The Blue force employed in the WWG represented a multifunctional *total* army concept. It consisted of Special Operations Forces providing an essential *global scout* function, forward-deployed Army XXI forces performing deterrence and condition-setting roles, a global strike force composed of AAN battle forces, and a force of decision consisting of CONUS-based Army XXI units operating as a consolidating force that insured the ability to fight sustained combat should the campaign last longer than expected or take an unexpected turn. In effect, the WWG Blue force represented an army in transition, from the Army XXI legacy force to the notional 2020 AAN battle force of the Leavenworth games.

A portion of the legacy force was deployed in Europe, but scattered in partnership-for-peace packets—so dispersed as to offer the capacity for only limited resistance when Red began threatening aggression. Modernized 2020 forces were concentrated in CONUS, with the exception of a 2020 force deployed in Korea as part of the Army's 2020 modernization plan. Special Operations Forces were present in Europe prior to hostilities. They established close and trusting relationships with nontreaty states in the region and this provided the *glue* that held together a quickly assembled coalition of warfighting partners. They also provided the first reliable theater-level eyes-on-target and helped prepare for the arrival of Blue forces. In deployment into battle, the Blue 2020 forces reached conflict termination before the legacy systems could close on the theater. The WWG offered significant insights on the influence that speed and knowledge will have on a future battlefield.

Speed

Speed emerged once again as a dominant factor at the strategic-political, strategic-military, and operational levels of war. Technology's impact on the speed of political decision making during crisis complicates the National Command Authorities' problems of deterrence and response and the always-difficult problems of forming coalitions of willing allies and reluctant friends. Paradoxically, the very capabilities that allow future forces to increase speed and tempo may contribute to hesitation on the part of political leaders.

Strategic speed—very rapid deployment directly into a theater of operations—as played in the WWG allowed political leaders and military commanders to accelerate movement to a theater of war before the enemy can set or make a preemptive move. In a subsequent war game excursion, an earlier Blue deployment effectively deterred Red's aggression. Concerns emerged during the game over an obvious disparity between the strategic speed of an AAN force—arriving from CONUS ready to fight within 48 hours—and the follow-on CONUS-based Army XXI force. To allow the ability both to preempt an enemy from setting his force in a theater and to continue unrelenting sustained pressure over time, the projection schemes of both forces should be seamless and firmly joined. It became clear during the game that by 2020 a mature Army XXI force must be much more projectable than heavy forces are today, inferring perhaps the requirement to move globally from a staging point to a distant battlefield in no less than two weeks. Also the war game reinforced the observation that most of the information technologies inherent in AAN should be present in an Army XXI force to ensure that both can act in harmony on the battlefield and collectively exploit the advantages of a knowledge-based force.

The challenge of connecting the deployment of forces with dramatically different strategic speeds was exacerbated by the requirement that arose during the game to approach the theater by infiltration rather than by staging. During the Leavenworth games, it became apparent that even when opposed by an enemy possessing primitive weapons of mass destruction, the risk of mass casualties prohibited the use of major ports and airfields. The enemy quickly realized that his greatest opportunity for success when facing a force of such enormous capability was to defeat him before arrival in theater. Therefore, early-arriving AAN forces were obliged to set down at scattered locations deep inside the theater of war just beyond the reach of the enemy's operational forces.

Operationally, the WWG suggests that sequenced operations, as understood today, should occur in a more seamless and simultaneous manner at theater level, melding the application of firepower and maneuver into a single culminating act and thereby reducing the duration of campaigns from months to days or hours.

The geostrategic position of the United States has committed the Army in this century to rely on strategic maneuver to win wars on the ground. The major difference between General Marshall's concepts of power projection in 1942 and the Army's of 2025 is the speed with which forces can be deployed and employed in a single, unrelenting, sustained act of global maneuver. Early discussions of global force projection indicate that the worldwide structure that will enable Army forces of 2025 to conduct high-tempo strategic maneuver must be in place prior to deployment. The early placement of logistics, communications, and intelligence may play a more significant role in the pace and effectiveness of strategic maneuver than the deployment of the fighting force itself.

Logistics in the WWG, the Leavenworth games, and the war-game excursions were played primarily as a function of deployment. AAN's hypotheses, which require further testing in FY 98, posit that to achieve the speed necessary to cross the deadly zone intact, operational-level forces require a radically streamlined logistical tail. Second, strategic-level deployment requires new technologies and methods of projection that get a fighting force from its CONUS base into combat in a few days. Current deployment systems, based on an outmoded Cold War view of strategic maneuver, will only present the enemy with targets in a precision-rich theater of war.

Knowledge Sensitivity

In the WWG, Red reacted to Blue's deployment by immediately attacking the systems that Blue relied on for knowledge dominance, especially space-based systems. Reds all-out attack in space caused policy and warfighting dilemmas for Blue. The erosion of Blue's ability to use space-based assets would have, over time, significantly reduced Blue's knowledge advantage. As it happened, Blue's war with Red ended before attrition of space assets could influence events on the battlefield. Forces already in contact mitigated the loss of satellites to some extent by using organic means, such as high-altitude UAVs, to maintain tactical knowledge dominance. Strategically and at the theater level, however, the loss of specific systems would have had a cumulatively harmful, though not disastrous, effect. Blue's Pacific campaign against Pink, just getting underway when the game ended, was partially blinded by Red's actions. The effect on global logistics would have been felt immediately. A subsequent war-game excursion that varied the nature of Red's attack on space-based assets did not materially affect the outcome of the game. Nonetheless, in both war games Red commanders understood how vital information dominance was to Blue force effectiveness. Both aggressively sought to collapse Blue's protective shield of knowledge. The insights from the games suggest a serious need to protect information flow through robust, resilient, and redundant infrastructures that can be reinforced with a *bodyguard* of deception and disinformation and easily regenerated if damaged.

EMERGING CHARACTERISTICS OF THE FORCE

Thus far, AAN study results indicate that success on the 2025 battlefield will require force characteristics that emphasize a robust surface-to-space continuum, split-based operations, interdependence, hybrid forces, and mature leaders leading cohesive units.

Surface-to-Space Continuum: The New High Ground

In order to achieve the degree of knowledge dominance and operational speed postulated in this paper, by 2025 the Army must have shifted upward from its traditional two-dimensional spatial orientation of land forces into the vertical or third dimension. In particular, the deep-strike operational maneuver function must be able to occupy the third dimension from just above the surface through the exosphere into space. Future land combat units will exploit terrain by maneuvering for tactical advantage within the folds and undulations of the earth's surface without suffering the restrictions imposed on mobility by contact with the ground.

The vertical component should also include tactical UAVs, exospheric long endurance UAVs, and space vehicles

179

in various orbital configurations extending to geosynchronous orbits. This constellation of aerial vehicles should allow traditionally land-bound functions—intelligence, all forms of communications, and fire support delivered from unmanned platforms orbiting continuously above close combat forces—to move upward. Many of the elements in the continuum will come from other services and from the civilian telecommunications industry.

Split-Based Operations

A robust surface-to-space continuum—consisting of a constellation of UAVs and space-based telecommunications satellites—will also permit an order-of-magnitude reduction in the size of the tactical force arrayed in close contact with the enemy. *Reach-out* communications, intelligence, and fire support, combined with *just-in-time* and *just-what's needed* logistics, will eliminate all baggage not directly related to closing with or gaining positional advantage over the enemy. To achieve a relative degree of protection and security, support units will operate from separate locations, possibly hundreds of kilometers from the theater, beyond the effective range of weapons of mass destruction.

Interdependence

Time is the enemy of a force that depends on knowledge and speed for effectiveness. The effect of time on the conduct of battle is corrosive and gradual rather than dramatic. As we learned in the Leavenworth games and subsequent analyses, the shock effect upon which much of the effectiveness of U.S. combat power depends dissipates as the enemy becomes inured to the psychological impact of precision fire and learns to lessen its destructive effects through counteraction. Also, as the Red commander demonstrated, even a tier-three knowledge advantage inevitably erodes as the enemy learns our patterns of operations and begins to predict our actions.

Finally, the strategic game suggested that in a future era of informal and ad hoc military relationships, coalitions may become more difficult to create and harder to maintain once combat begins. Lingering too long on the battlefield opens the opportunity for an enemy to split an opposing coalition. Saddam Hussein taught this lesson very well.

Therefore, in 2025 even more than today, U.S. forces will not be able to afford linear, sequential campaigns that require discrete staging and phasing. To defeat this corrosive enemy of time, the operational level of war must be pushed toward the execution of near-simultaneous campaigns that, at the theater-operational level, will take on the characteristic of a *coup de main*. Operational acceleration of this magnitude can only be achieved by moving beyond joint toward interdependent operations. Interdependence suggests the need for a level of interoperability between land, sea, and aerospace mediums that will allow a near-simultaneous application of precision fires and maneuver applied in a broad pattern of effects that strike and check the enemy everywhere he can be seen and engaged. Sequenced campaigns, depicted today by delivery schedules and broad arrows on a map, will be replaced by an expansive takedown operation where the enemy's will to resist collapses when he finds himself smothered by fire and surrounded everywhere by maneuver forces occupying positions of advantage.

Interdependence also has programmatic implications. AAN believes force structures of the 2025 time period will also need to be interdependent, that is, whole functions may migrate from one service structure to another in favor of speed, agility, and economy. For example, space-based systems may well provide communications and other functions now associated with land systems. If this model holds up, quite possibly future land forces may require less expense to field and operate than previous Army forces.

Hybrid Forces

The U.S. Army has always gone to war as a hybrid force. Traditionally, dissimilar forces—heavy and light, regular and reserve, legacy and modern—have fought side by side. The problem in the past has been to get the most out of such a disparate force. In the Winter War Game, the total land force that Blue employed consisted of a mix of Army XXI units and AAN battle forces. In the environment postulated for 2025, the capabilities of these forces complemented each other very well. AAN battle forces executed rapid, strategic maneuver, while Army XXI units functioned as a force of decision, providing the total force with heft, flexibility, and a hedge against uncertainty. The challenge in this scheme will be to ensure a proper fit between the early-deploying AAN force and the slower-deploying Army XXI forces. While the former must arrive quickly to collapse the enemy, the latter must possess enough strategic agility to follow immediately behind to guarantee unrelenting long-term pressure on the enemy and to limit risk to the early arriving force.

The Human Dimension

Although discussed in greater detail further in this report, the human dimension bears mentioning here as well. AAN research indicates that battle leaders will have to function in very compressed planning and operating cycles and at very high tempos. Indications are that battlefields of 2020 will require cohesive units and leaders with higher levels of maturity. This research does not necessarily mean that the Army will require a higher leader-to-led ratio, only that it needs a more mature, better-experienced leader and soldier than is the norm today.

MODELING, SIMULATION, AND FUTURE GAMES

After a year of intense study, wargaming, and work with the other services and agencies of government, it is becoming apparent that present-day tools and perceptions only lead to more questions about the effects of technological change, the human and organizational dimension of future warfare, and the character of warfare itself.

Two-sided, open-ended war games continue to prove their worth as research tools for framing issues in the 25-year future. Free play is essential to understanding future warfare—even if Blue loses—because future success at the strategic and theater levels will increasingly depend on knowledge and other nonquantifiable advantages rather than on the more familiar attrition models that tend to favor bigger, more powerful forces. The key to gaming at strategic and theater levels is to make interaction between models and human experts as realistic as possible. WWG 1997 utilized an interactive global model with more advantages than drawbacks, but as games increase in complexity and focus, they will require more realistic models that effectively stretch a combat environment from surface to space. AAN will take this issue on as a major portion of its 1997 effort.

The Winter War Game this year postulated a war for vital interests. Consequently, game play centered at the most violent and intense end of the conventional scale of warfare. The AAN study group recognizes that to meet the needs of American defense policy in 2020, the Army must be extraordinarily *capable,* to be sure, but it must also be *adaptable* enough to be useful at the lower end of the conflict spectrum. Intuitively, an AAN force built around knowledge and speed would seem to possess characteristics essential to prevail in a conflict for "less-than-vital interests." Exceptional mobility across inhospitable terrain, speed of deployment, and the ability to observe with exceptional clarity and to maneuver and strike with great precision all give promise that the AAN battle force postulated here would be decisive in stability and security operations against a less sophisticated enemy. The Summer War Game (SWG 1997) has been designed to test this hypothesis under conditions differing markedly from AAN games to date. The

Army Special Operations Command will play as equal partners in this important exercise, and AAN will provide an analysis of the game separately and in the June 1998 report.

SOLDIERS AND UNITS IN 2025

The war games demonstrated that Blue's tactical success depended to a great extent on his ability to execute decentralized operations. His strategic and tactical speed would have required an exceptional degree of mental agility and psychological resilience. We believe that the development of these qualities by 2025 will require nothing less than a cultural change within the Army that embraces a philosophy of decentralized action based upon a high degree of professional trust and confidence between leaders and led.

Situations changed quickly and sometimes dramatically in the war games, which suggests that commanders will have to make decisions at consistently faster rates. Real-time battlefield knowledge may require AAN leaders to rapidly digest and act upon an indeterminate and ever-changing amount of information. In addition, the heightened speed of AAN operations may generate higher levels of physical and emotional stress, thereby creating a greater risk of cognitive and psychological impairment. AAN battle units employed a larger number of *moving parts* functioning at higher rates of speed, which in the future may force leaders at all levels to cope with increasing levels of complexity. Even armed with the advantages of sophisticated information aids, AAN leaders may find their decision-making capacities quickly overwhelmed. To execute the precise and dispersed maneuver that characterized Blue operations in the tactical war games, crews and teams will very likely be obliged to fight in a degree of isolation far more psychologically demanding than in past wars. The war games suggested that Blue forces would also need a high level of mental agility and psychological resilience to operate effectively in discrete, self-reliant, well-informed, autonomous small units.

EXPERIENCED LEADERS

One way the Army can achieve and maintain the mental agility necessary for success on tomorrow's battlefield is by cultivating mature, highly experienced leaders. Such leaders provide at least four benefits: 1) mastery of increased skill sets; 2) greater experience in both command positions and staffs; 3) a firm foundation from which to exercise battlefield intuition; and 4) the ability to successfully withstand higher levels of stress due to psycholoical maturity and experience.

COHESIVE UNITS

Stable, cohesive units can provide the requisite foundation for developing mental agility and psychological resilience. Soldiers who train together for long periods tend to adopt a shared view of the battlefield, to include their environment and their unit's ability to respond to specific combat challenges. This shared view allows leaders, peers, and subordinates to act effectively, with little or no communication, even in rapidly changing situations. Likewise, cohesive units offer the Army a greater reservoir of psychological resilience—a safety net—that offsets, to a great degree, battlefield fear, fatigue, stress, and isolation. Such units remain mentally agile even under severe circumstances. They require less supervision, handle complex tasks effectively, and exhibit mutual trust, confidence, and loyalty.

SOLDIER TRAINING AND EDUCATION

Synthetic training environments, in the form of virtual, constructive, and live simulators, may allow highly effective training under conditions both safe and, in some cases, nearly indistinguishable from actual combat. In the future, newly formed units or staffs may build trust, confidence, and a state of constant readiness by working through a series of increasingly demanding exercises in a synthetic environment. Live training will remain necessary in the future to be sure. But, realistic simulators will allow live training to be reserved for *finishing exercises*. The Army should develop synthetic training to assist it in meeting the demands of the 2025 battlefield.

AAN soldiers and their units will require higher levels of mental agility and psychological resilience to successfully meet tomorrow's battlefield challenges. Experienced leaders and cohesive units should serve as the foundation for the Army's effort to develop and maintain these qualities. The goal of the AAN human and organizational effort should be to build units capable of operating within their optimal range while forcing the enemy to operate beyond his own.

TECHNOLOGY: THE PATH TO KNOWLEDGE AND SPEED

The Army of 2025 will probably differ from today's Army in two fundamental ways. It will achieve unprecedented strategic and operational agility by exploiting information technologies to create a knowledge-based Army. But to know and see with greater clarity is not enough. The Army must possess a complementary capacity to act on its superior knowledge by building into its structure the physical agility to move rapidly and adroitly across a larger and more lethal battlefield. An essential body of technologies is emerging that offers the potential to create a knowledge-based army capable of strategic and operational maneuver by 2025.

THE TECHNOLOGICAL CHALLENGE

The AAN study expresses tomorrow's technological challenges in terms of the need to achieve greater knowledge and speed.

Knowledge

Knowledge will proceed from a robust, redundant, and flexible network of communications and intelligence systems interwoven into a seamless surface-to-space continuum. This continuum will feature *nets* of surface sensors connected electronically to a series of interlinked UAV fields, ranging from low to very high altitudes, covered by an umbrella of space-based systems. This constellation of systems will provide an *unblinking eye* capable of constant surveillance over the battlespace and will connect the combat force with its distant support and sustainment base. It should serve as a living internet of connectivity immediately responsive to soldiers on the ground.

However, as the WWG demonstrated, an adversary may attack space systems immediately, and perhaps repeatedly, to deny knowledge dominance. Work should therefore continue in TRADOC and SSDC to identify specific land-power requirements in terms of space systems and to develop relationships that carry those needs into space technology initiatives in other services and agencies. WWG experience and follow-up research also indicate that low-, mid-, and high-altitude UAVs will become essential to maintaining knowledge dominance. Internetted UAVs serve to thicken the communications infrastructure in the event of a loss of space systems.

Mechanisms also must be established for both rapid replacement of degraded systems and seamless substitution of one information source for another. Finally, doctrine and training must accommodate the possibility of a degraded information environment; and soldiers, units, and leaders must be deliberately conditioned to sustain operational tempo notwithstanding system interruptions.

Speed

The AAN views speed in strategic, operational, and tactical dimensions. The Army must pursue ways to accelerate pace of movement so that, in the tactical dimensions, close combat forces can frustrate enemy acquisition, targeting, and precision weaponry and, in the operational and strategic dimensions, can rapidly counter, check, and ultimately collapse enemy maneuver forces.

Technologies related to self-deploying tactical forces, fast sealift, and airborne large-capacity lifting bodies currently support the acceleration of strategic projection. Although the Army does not develop new concepts or vehicles for air and sealift, these capabilities will become essential to the effective use of land power in 2025.

At the tactical and operational levels, three technologies offer possibilities for shrinking the logistical tail of fighting organizations. First, alternative power sources and fuel-efficient ultrareliable fighting vehicles will allow combat forces to operate longer and over greater distances than today. Second, cheap precision warheads, long-range fire support located outside the combat area, and alternative propellants will allow reductions in the weight and bulk of ammunition trains. Third, energy storage systems and hybrid power systems can reduce fuel and electrical power requirements and eliminate most of the weight and bulk of today's power generation and storage systems.

In addition, future ground craft, composed of advanced, lightweight materials, will enjoy greater firepower, mobility, and speed. Advanced airframes will possess increased capacities for heavy lift and tactical utility lift. These greater lift capacities will allow a marriage of ground and air systems that permits commanders to use the ground tactically for cover and concealment without suffering a degradation in mobility. Protection schemes for land power will include a host of new active protection and signature control systems. While the 2025 battle force will protect itself primarily through knowledge and speed, several emerging technologies promise to further enhance force protection. Advances in antidotes and vaccines will reduce vulnerability to chemical and biological weapons. Speed also includes rapid strategic deployment. All of the lightening technologies already mentioned have the potential to enhance deployability as well as battlefield mobility. In addition, future technology must concentrate on enhanced means of self-deployment, ultrafast sealift, and improved high-capacity airlift. Although the Army is not directly responsible for the last two, no service has a greater interest in them.

THE AAN SCIENCE AND TECHNOLOGY LINKAGES

Throughout the past year, AAN has established close relationships with the science and technology community, academia, and several DOD and non-DOD government scientific agencies, most importantly, the Assistant Secretary of the Army (RD&A), Army Materiel Command, DARPA, HQDA DCSOPS, and members of the TRADOC combat developments community. AAN operational requirements influence the research efforts of the science and technology community through these relationships. Just as importantly, this collegial cooperation ensures that AAN remains apprised of further emerging technologies that might enhance its operational concepts and requirements.

As the process matures, the AAN will become part of a growing number of science and technology decision-making teams. Through AAN, TRADOC has participated in the 6.1 basic research triennial review and has influenced the direction of defense strategic resource objectives and the creation of Army SROs. AAN has also provided a perspective on 6.2 science and technology objectives and advanced concepts technology demonstrations.

The Army must continue to develop partnerships within the science and technology community to create a focused set of technologies for future warfighting. Key among these is DARPA, which is already working with the Army to explore innovative concepts and technologies that apply to small-unit operations. As the pace of technological advance continues to accelerate, perspicacity in acquisition will become a strategic imperative for the Army.

THE ROAD AHEAD

Although the Army in the field is operating at a very high tempo, the next few years will find the Army in a position of unchallenged military superiority and with breathing space to consider the next challenge. This window of opportunity will not last long; perhaps by the end of the century the next major military competitor will begin to show itself. In the meantime, the Army can begin to reorder its house for the challenges ahead.

Since the opportunity is fleeting, changes of the magnitude tentatively envisioned in this report must begin soon. Issues of force structuring and budget management must be addressed within the tenure of this CSA if a new force is to begin fielding around 2010. The AAN process and its estimation of the future will continue to develop, but the AAN staff is satisfied that the major issues outlined above will remain valid. The challenge now is to begin to move from ideas and vision into action.

Chapter Eleven

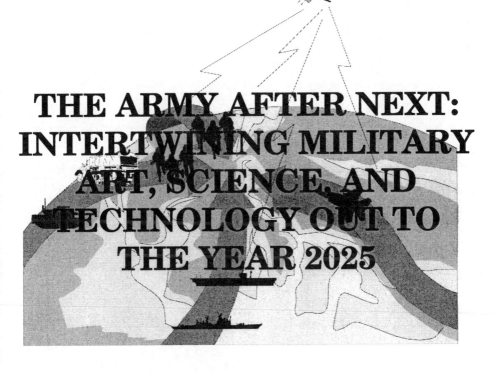

THE ARMY AFTER NEXT: INTERTWINING MILITARY ART, SCIENCE, AND TECHNOLOGY OUT TO THE YEAR 2025

Major General Robert H. Scales, Jr.

Dr. John A. Parmentola

Reproduced with Permission Granted by:
May-June 1998 Issue
ARMY RD&A JOURNAL

THE ARMY AFTER NEXT: INTERTWINING MILITARY ART, SCIENCE, AND TECHNOLOGY OUT TO THE YEAR 2025

Introduction

The Army After Next (AAN) Project Office at Headquarters, U.S. Army Training and Doctrine Command (TRADOC) is conducting broad studies of future warfare for the year 2025 timeframe. The purpose is to isolate the issues vital to the development of the Army. The vision generated from these studies will be integrated into future TRADOC combat developments programs.

Several important dimensions motivate the focus on the 2025 timeframe for AAN. First, given our available lead time and the rapid pace of economic development in a number of evolving countries, it is likely that the United States will encounter a major military competitor or, at the very least, confront significant asymmetric threats in this period.

Second, the year 2025 enables military art and technology experts to divert their thinking from concepts and capabilities associated with the programmed force of Army 2010 to more novel approaches to achieve the AAN vision. It also provides ample lead time to incorporate innovative technologies and unanticipated revolutionary discoveries into this vision.

Finally, it provides an opportunity to refocus Army basic and applied research on efforts that have significant potential for advancing critical AAN enabling technologies. Thus, TRADOC's AAN efforts will enable the Army to refine its choices as a function of time and optimize its investment decisions to achieve critical AAN warfighter capabilities.

This article describes the assumptions, arguments, and challenges that form the basis for conceptualizing the Army's warfighting capabilities out to the year 2025 and the science and technology support and activities that will enable the Army to eventually realize these capabilities.

Speed, Knowledge And The Lessons Of History

Cycles of change in warfare are particularly difficult to comprehend and even more difficult to anticipate because, unlike endeavors in finance, medicine, or law, active experience in war is, thankfully, infrequent. Because warfare is not frequently practiced, soldiers must rely on the laboratory of past experiences to gain vicarious experience in war. To be sure, the frenetic pace of technological change in the modern world has compressed the interval and stretched the amplitude of the cycles of change. Nonetheless, undeniable cycles remain, and we should be able to search the recent past to identify these new cycles.

With the rise of industrial production and the appearance of precision warmaking machinery such as rifled weapons in the mid-19th century, technology began to dominate patterns of change. Such weapons extended the deadly zone, or the distance that soldiers had to cross to engage a defender, from 150 meters in Napoleon's day to 1,000 meters or more by the end of the American Civil War. As the deadly zone increased by nearly a factor of 10, the risks of crossing it were further multiplied by the lethality induced through the precision and volume from the massive proliferation of repeating arms. Thus, technology favored the defender. Images of the terrible slaughter of World War I remain as testimony to the cost in blood exacted by an operational method that relied on a killing effect to achieve decisive results.

The Germans first conceptualized the solution in 1918, and it was deceptively simple: short, highly intense doses of firepower to prepare the assault, small units to exploit the

194

shock effect of firepower to infiltrate and bypass centers of resistance, and operational formations to move through exposed points of weakness and push deep into enemy lines. After the war, the further development of the internal combustion engine provided the means to translate the theory into effective action and restore the dominance of the offensive. Motorized armored vehicles allowed soldiers to cross the deadly zone protected by enormously greater speed while employing blitzkrieg to gain victory. This was achieved through psychological paralysis induced by movement, rather than through butchery induced by massive application of firepower.

After World War II, the challenge was to halt a Soviet-style blitzkrieg across the Northern German Plain. Tactical forces needed defensive killing power to absorb the initial Soviet-armored shock and hold their defensive positions. This led to the defensive forces' return to dominance. The operational problem, however, was to strike deep offensively below the rate of arrival of follow-on armored forces at the front line. The resulting AirLand Battle Doctrine of the 1980s suggested a swing of the pendulum back toward offensive forces. Operation Desert Storm added momentum to the pendulum swing with ground and air forces overwhelming static defenses with unprecedented speed and intensity. Nonetheless, even Desert Storm produced troubling hints that evolving defensive systems threaten to reimpose strategic and operational paralysis. Iraq's SCUD missile attacks on Saudi Arabia and Israel, had they been more accurate or included chemical or biological warheads, might have strengthened Iraq's defense considerably. The proliferation of such systems will substantially raise the stakes of future interventions.

Two key attributes of future U.S. Armed Forces, if harmoniously developed, would firmly re-establish the dominance of the offensive forces. The information revolution will likely allow us to define and track the elements of a force with exquisite clarity and detail, but

195

knowledge of the enemy, alone, is not enough. We must possess the means to act on what we know, and action depends on speed. The combination of knowledge and speed of movement will allow a future battle force to anticipate enemy movement and turn costly force-on-force engagements of past wars into surer and less costly engagements by choice.

Much like the evolution of military and private sector capabilities in the 20th century, an important physical parameter influencing the Army After Next is the compression of time. For the Army, this means taking advantage of future advancements in information technologies while concurrently increasing speed or equivalently reducing the time required to strategically deploy, tactically maneuver, traverse the killing zone, deliver metal on target, and provide timely logistic support to the battleforce. To that end, information technologies will allow us to position outside the combat zone all but those forces necessary to move, observe, and kill.

The imperative for speed in this new form of warfare begins at home ports, airfields, and installations. A highly lethal force, shorn of its Cold War impedimenta, will be able to project itself from the homeland or from strategic points overseas in days rather than weeks or months and arrive in the operational theater ready to fight. Strategic speed will allow theater war to take the form of a *coup de main.*

Our goal in applying firepower must be to exploit its substantial paralytic effects to gain advantage. To win quickly and decisively at low cost in the future, we must have the means to conduct the battle quickly and end it cleanly, preferably at the moment when the paralytic effect of firepower is greatest. Victory is best guaranteed through maneuver of forces on the ground. Psychological collapse, the breaking of an enemy's will to resist, comes when an opponent is challenged and blocked at all points. A commander with the dual advantage of speed of maneuver and killing power will dominate the battlefield. If these two essential elements of combat power are orchestrated skillfully, an unfettered battle force will be able to strike multiple vital points simultaneously or in a sequence of their choosing. In a very short time, perhaps only hours, such a force would be able to quickly disintegrate an enemy's warfighting structures, producing an unequivocal military decision with minimum cost.

The fourth cycle of war, therefore, should seek to exploit the information age to increase the velocity of maneuver. Speed must be the essential ingredient of a future landpower force. Speed will be achieved by creating a highly mobile force unimpeded by terrain and unburdened by an agility sapping logistical yoke. To achieve the speed of maneuver necessary to wage 21st Century knowledge-based warfare will require a new concept of mechanized warfare that will free forces of maneuver inhibiting restrictions. The exploitation of knowledge via increased air and ground mobility will result in unprecedented tactical and operational maneuverability.

Such "air mechanized" battle units would be mechanized combined arms echelons of maneuver capable of air assault to operational depths to attack regimental size units and defend against division sized attacks. These units and the personnel and systems they contain will combine extreme speed with superior knowledge to provide precise maneuverability that takes optimum advantage of deadly accurate firepower. The employment of more maneuverable air mechanized battle forces in advance of potent Army XXI forces would create the capacity for 21st Century strategic blitzkrieg. Once again, offensive forces would dominate warfare.

Intertwining To The Year 2025 And Beyond.

The process for intertwining military art and technology for the AAN is depicted in Figure 1. This process is comprehensive, highly coordinated, and relies on significant levels of cooperation among its participants. It

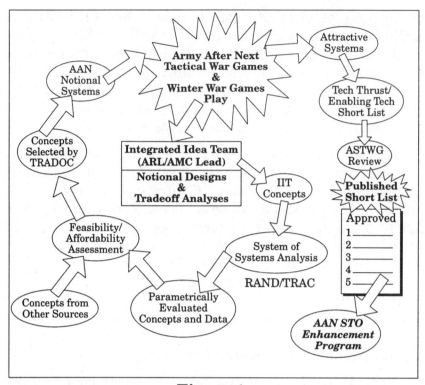

Figure 1.
Science and technology support to the Army After Next development process.

starts with the annual AAN strategic and tactical war games that explore and assess novel concepts of operations and capabilities and then pass through a number of coordinated technology activities and eventually feed back into the AAN war games. This nonlinear process continues until the AAN military art innovations and proposed supporting technologies and systems converge to a feasible, affordable, and militarily significant set of AAN capabilities.

One important output of each yearly cycle of this process is a TRADOC-approved short list of critical AAN enabling technologies that is used to establish new AAN Science and Technology Objectives (STOs) that directly involve private sector participation. This is designed to cultivate a growing private sector involvement in advancing technologies in support of challenging AAN capabilities.

Very early in the AAN study process, the Army recognized that team building among the military art and technology experts was crucial to the overall success of the AAN effort. This observation led to the concept of Integrated Idea Teams (IITs). The objective of these teams is to assess, from a technological perspective, the concepts, capabilities, and notional systems, including tradeoffs, that support AAN operational characteristics and ideas developed through AAN war games. IITs are managed by the Army Materiel Command (AMC) through the Army Research Laboratory (ARL) and are composed of technical experts from Army laboratories, National Laboratories, the private sector, the Defense Advanced Research Projects Agency (DARPA) and the other Services, and academia, as well as those more involved in the military art side of the AAN.

Once the IIT has developed such concepts, these notional system concept designs are then played in force-on-force/system-of-systems high resolution modeling and simulation exercises conducted in collaboration with Rand Corporation, the TRADOC Analysis Center (TRAC), TRADOC, the IIT, and Office of the Assistant Secretary of the Army for Research, Development and Acquisition (OASARDA). The purpose of this is to assess the military significance of these systems within a larger set of warfighting systems and to determine system performance parameters that make a difference on the battlefield. This effort recognizes that maximizing individual system performance does not necessarily result in a more capable and affordable system.

The final step in this process is to assess the feasibility and affordability of selected concepts through a team of experts from the military laboratories, national laboratories, the private sector, and academia. The objective of this effort is to evaluate the IIT notional system designs, in concert with the above force-on-force results, with respect to feasibility (laws of physics, maturity of concept, and schedule) and affordability (development cost, production cost, operations and support costs, and leveraging with the private sector and the other Services and agencies). This effort also provides positive feedback to the IIT on their notional system concept designs. These assessments are then forwarded to TRADOC for review and assessment, and the results are used to decide on the role of these notional system concept designs in the next round of the AAN war games.

An example of an emerging insight from the AAN war gaming that was fleshed out through the IIT process is the concept of air mechanization, which was mentioned earlier. To achieve the requisite speed and agility, 21st Century air mechanization will have to derive from new combinations of air and ground vehicles. A plausible option to provide the tactical and operational maneuverability required for the 21st Century is to include an advanced airframe designed to be both a lifting and fighting vehicle. It would be able to lift, conformably, members of a family of light advanced ground vehicles with long-range, lightweight, highly accurate armaments. The advanced airframe would connect quickly to an advanced ground vehicle while its crew remains inside. The advanced airframe would transport the vehicle anywhere on the battlefield out to a combat radius within hours and deploy it combat ready. In addition to lifting advanced ground vehicles, the advanced airframe would lift or employ a variety of other mission modules.

All advanced ground vehicles would rarely be required to face main battle tanks head-on, which makes it possible to limit their weight by reducing the need for heavy armor. They will survive through a combination of speed, agility, active protection, signature management and control, comprehensive situational understanding, terrain masking, deception, and indirect fire. Greater ground speed on and off roads will be possible because of advanced suspension systems, power trains, and engines. Greater

200

fuel economies will result from significant weight reduction and advanced propulsion system designs.

Thus far, the AAN study has focused on the challenging air mechanization concept involving a high-speed tiltrotor and several versions of a lightweight, highly lethal, mobile companion ground craft. This concept addresses the following: the need to overcome the limitations of ground vehicle speed by transporting the ground craft at high speed via the tiltrotor within theater; the need for a lightweight ground craft to limit the size of the tiltrotor; and the need to overcome the possible absence of an airfield in theater through the self-deployment of the tiltrotor and ground craft combination from CONUS. This system approach to the AAN air mechanization concept has not completed its first cycle through the AAN process depicted in Figure 1. However, the results so far are very encouraging. The first complete assessment will occur sometime in the summer of 1998.

In addition to this process, a complementary set of activities involving the Army Science Board (ASB) and the National Research Council's Board on Army Science and Technology (BAST) are currently under way. The ASB is investigating opportunities to advance strategic deployment capabilities out to the year 2025, while the BAST is constructing an investment roadmap for the Army Basic and Applied Research Programs for the development of technologies that will significantly reduce logistics demand. Finally, OASARDA, in partnership with TRADOC, is planning to initiate a series of technology-based war games that will assist in determining the most productive investment options to support AAN capabilities.

Conclusions

We believe the Army has seized upon a highly compelling vision of its future role in land warfare. It has also carefully thought through a comprehensive process that will determine the key science and technology investments enabling it to achieve this vision. The process the Army has created to navigate into the future is working very well. The future Army and the United States will be the beneficiaries of this cooperative but challenging effort.[1]

ENDNOTE

1. The authors would like to acknowledge the contributions of Dr. Douglas C. Lovelace of the U.S. Army War College and Dr. Tom Killion of the Army Research Laboratory in the preparation of this article.

Chapter Twelve

THE INDIRECT APPROACH: HOW U.S. MILITARY FORCES CAN AVOID THE PITFALLS OF FUTURE URBAN WARFARE

Major General Robert H. Scales, Jr.

Reproduced with Permission Granted by:
October 1998 Issue
ARMED FORCES JOURNAL
INTERNATIONAL
Volume 136, Number 3

THE INDIRECT APPROACH: HOW U.S. MILITARY FORCES CAN AVOID THE PITFALLS OF FUTURE URBAN WARFARE

Author's Introductory Note

The following article was published within the October 1998 issue of *Armed Forces Journal International*. Sixteen months later, while the Russian Army was aggressively destroying the city of Grozny, the editorial staff of *AFJI* awarded the following accolade within their Journal's **Darts and Laurels** Section.[1]

A laurel to the Russian general staff—for adapting. While the 1999-2000 battle for Grozny is a detestable military action, its initial execution was a far cry from the 1996 debacle in the same location. Until mid-December, when Russian forces were mauled during a probe into the city under light armor cover, military analysts were generally impressed by Russian field commander's absorption of lessons learned from the 1996 campaign. Avoiding the close-in engagements which had proven so disastrous during the earlier, failed attempt to seize Grozny, Russian commanders waged a long-range campaign against the city in tandem with an up-close courtship of the media. As one observer noted, the initial, successful campaign plan paralleled the thrust of an urban warfare article by Major General Robert H. Scales Jr., Commandant of the U.S. Army War College, published in the October 1998 issue of *AFJI*.

---

1. February 2000 Issue, Armed Forces Journal International, Volume 137, Number 7, page 64.

THE INDIRECT APPROACH:
HOW U.S. MILITARY FORCES CAN AVOID THE PITFALLS OF FUTURE URBAN WARFARE

Urban warfare, fighting in cities, war in "complex terrain." To the casual observer, the words seem detached, almost pristine. However, the words are starkingly real to military professionals who have seen the images of great destruction and excessive casualties in cities such as Berlin, Stalingrad, Hue, and Beirut. Urban warfare, a subject that many military professionals would prefer to avoid, is still with us. Moreover, it may be the preferred approach of future opponents.

Consider one of the key lessons that emerged from the Spring 1998 Army 2025 wargame conducted at the U.S. Army War College. The enemy (Red Force) conducted a lightning assault to seize and control a web of complex terrain (a large urban area). This enabled it to decapitate the political leadership and control critical lodgment areas. Designed to dismember coalition efforts and collapse American resolve, the Red Force dispersed its army within the cities and prepared to wage an attrition-based campaign. Since the National Command Authority was initially reluctant to turn to the military element of power, the friendly Blue Force was unable to prevent Red from occupying the urban areas. However, once Red moved into the urban areas, the political fallout to regain control of the lodgment area and reestablish a legitimate government left Blue with little choice but to wage an urban warfare campaign.

Although successful, the cost was excessive in terms of battle casualties and time. In retrospect, the Blue approach was exactly the opposite from what should have been taken.

Why? Because by playing into the hands of the enemy, Blue illustrated one of the key issues for 21st Century warfare. How can the force of the future achieve success in complex terrain?

A recent revival of interest in urban warfare has yielded a rich outpouring of intellectual energy and fiscal investment in an effort to exploit interest into a relatively unfamiliar form of warfare. As is often the case in the American inquiry style, there has been too quick a leap beyond the more conceptual aspects of war in urban terrain and into the weapons and tactics necessary to fight street-to-street and door-to-door. I suggest a measured approach to the study of urban warfare. Its premise is that the time-tested tenets of warfare must be applied as rigorously and with the same fidelity in urban warfare as they are applied to other forms of warfare.

NEGATING AMERICAN MILITARY STRENGTHS

In the next century, a future enemy might look to his urban masses as a possible refuge from overwhelming American military power. Technological precision and, more importantly, the will to carry out a strategic plan, may enable him to pursue at least two possible options that might lead to a favorable strategic outcome. Each would seek to nullify American technological advantages of speed and knowledge, while simultaneously pursuing a strategic end state that focuses on the attainment of limited objectives while avoiding defeat.

The first option combines the diplomatic, political, and military elements of power into an operational concept that seeks to delay and disrupt our arrival into a strategic theater. Initially, an aggressor moves swiftly to seize military objectives in a neighboring country. Then, through skillful diplomatic efforts and political maneuvering, the enemy disrupts coalition-forming efforts while simultaneously offering a peace settlement. Central to the enemy's concept is the occupation of complex urban terrain

207

that enables him to control key lodgment areas and national centers of gravity.

If the first option fails, the enemy can burrow his force in the urban terrain and prepare for combat operations. This places the U.S. leadership on the horns of a dilemma. An urban assault largely neutralizes American high-tech speed and mobility advantages. With the added risk of excessive casualties and prolonged campaign timelines, many would question a decision to undertake such an operation.

Urban fighting has always been one of the most destructive forms of warfare. During World War II, the Russian army sustained over 300,000 casualties in their epic struggle for Berlin. American casualties were equally excessive: over 1,000 killed in action to regain Manila and more than 3,000 in the battle for Aachen, Germany. In the Vietnam War, the casualty rates for U.S. Marines who fought in Hue exceeded those from Okinawa's bloody amphibious assault. More recently, the ill-fated Russian attempt to seize Chechnya resulted in the deaths of thousands of soldiers and non-combatants (August AFJI).

But urban warfare doesn't happen all that often. Both sides realize the destructive effects that street fighting may cause. Only a desperate enemy, defending at great disadvantage, willing to sacrifice initiatives, his cities, and a large portion of his military force, has taken to defending cities. A casual glance at the last 500 years of major war history shows that as more of the world blankets itself in urban sprawl, the incidents of actual street fighting have declined.

THE URBAN ENVIRONMENT

A large urban center is multi-dimensional. Soldiers must contend with subterranean and high-rise threats. Every building could be a nest of fortified enemy positions that would have to be dug out, one by one. Moreover, an experienced enemy could easily create connecting positions between buildings.

With limited maneuver space, the urban environment precludes mobility operations and largely negates the effects of weapons, while minimizing engagement ranges. The proximity of buildings plays havoc with communications, further adding to command and control difficulties. Finally, the psychological effects of combat on soldiers are magnified. While the array of threats from multiple dimensions has a debilitating effect on soldiers, it further hastens the disintegration process that haunts all military units locked in close-combat operations.

The proliferating sprawl of urban centers and populations make the challenge of future city fighting even more pronounced. Some estimates indicate that between 60 to 70 percent of the world's population will reside in urban areas by the year 2025. If current global demographic trends continue into the next millenium, we will see the growth of huge urban masses, many exceeding ten million inhabitants. The enormous problems of infrastructure and the demand for social services that threaten to swamp governing authorities in the urban centers of emerging states will most likely worsen. Moreover, the proximity of the disenfranchised to the ruling elite provides the spark for further unrest and sporadic violence.

The future urban center will contain a mixed population, ranging from the rich elite to the poor and disenfranchised. Day-to-day existence for most of the urban poor will be balanced tenuously on the edge of collapse. With social conditions ripe for exploitation, the smallest tilt of unfavorable circumstance might be enough to instigate starvation, disease, social foment, cultural unrest, or other forms of urban violence.

Military leaders who believe that future warfare will not encompass this unpleasant environment are deluding themselves. A little more than one-third of all deployments by U.S. forces over the past 20 years have occurred in complex terrain. As urban areas continue to expand, they will increasingly encompass regions of vital interest to the United States. Representing geo-strategic centers of gravity, these urban areas will contain all the vital functions of government, commerce, communication, and transportation activity.

While some future urban operations may be limited in scope and capable of being controlled by special operations forces and other operatives, others may take place in strategic key terrain of vital interest. Such an operation would require a major American investment of combat forces.

A GREAT EQUALIZER

The dynamics of knowledge and speed that are ideal for open warfare take on an additional dimension when an enemy chooses to occupy key urban areas. An enemy occupies cities to slow us down and avoid our strengths. Rather than suffer the brunt of American military power, where speed and precision technology can be brought to bear, he understands that his intent must be not to seek a clear victory but to avoid losing. The enemy's only ally in these circumstances is time. If he can delay, disrupt, and diffuse our effort to achieve a quick decision, he might be able to force a campaign of attrition in which disproportionate casualties could induce us to grow weary of the conflict. While he surrenders the tactical initiative, the close terrain offers protection from firepower and surveillance and allows further time to prepare a defense.

In open warfare, time is a disadvantage as the need to achieve a rapid victory pushes commanders to attain decisive results. In urban warfare, just the opposite is true. A premature rush into the city works to our disadvantage and plays to the strength of the defender.

History is full of examples of armies that tried and failed to seize a city by *coup de main*. The Israeli army performed brilliantly in executing a lightning counterstroke across the Suez Canal during the 1973 Yom Kippur War. However, once Israel's armored columns entered the streets of Suez, the Egyptians were able to inflict a high number of casualties while stopping the Israelis' progress. The recent Russian experience in Chechnya is equally illustrative. There, a semi-trained and poorly-equipped force successfully waged a war of attrition that eventually wore down the larger, technologically superior Russian army.

While the different technology and tactical skills of armies are a factor, defensive urban warfare is a great equalizer for an under-modernized force. A vast body of historical evidence reminds us that urban warfare is a great casualty producer. Thus, in urban warfare, we must avoid the enemy enticement that lures our forces into such an environment and use time to our advantage.

COUNTERING THE URBAN OPTION

If we are patient, time will place our opponent at a disadvantage. The time advantage reversal occurs due to the enemy's inability to continue to provide for the populace. This will eventually lead to the displacement of the government leadership or hostile action on the part of the populace.

Picture for a moment a conflict against a future enemy state similar to some of our more recent post-Cold War adversaries. After a lightning campaign lasting only days, the mobile formations of our future foe are decisively beaten in open warfare. To avoid total defeat, the enemy rushes his remaining forces into his capital city, a city of sprawling dimensions with millions of people that house his political, cultural, and financial centers of gravity.

As soon as the enemy loses on the open ground and elects to occupy complex terrain, a fundamental shift of battlefield dynamics occurs. He loses the initiative. Time is now solely on the side of the intervening coalition.

211

Without the capacity to maneuver, the enemy cannot escape. Attacking would only result in his destruction. Thus, he arrays his forces throughout the capital to avoid creating lucrative targets for American precision weapons. He impresses the local citizenry into national service and appeals to the world to watch the impending slaughter of non-combatants.

Assuming that Americans are leading a coalition effort, how should the coalition respond? The best option is to preempt the enemy from using complex terrain in the first place. Recognizably, a preemptive approach requires the political entity to build strong domestic and international support, along with developing solid public underpinnings. Moreover, preemptive measures could come in a variety of forms. In the pre-hostilities phase, political and diplomatic means could be used to discourage future aggressive activity. The coalition could also selectively implement force deployment options, such as increasing the presence of naval or air forces and staging pre-positioned equipment. Once hostilities begin, we could force the enemy to fight his way into the urban areas by isolating his army, blocking the key avenues of approach, and augmenting host-nation forces that occupy friendly cities.

If, despite our best efforts, the enemy is able to fall back on a major city, we must be mindful of the limiting factors of using military power. Americans do not expect their military to wage war in an unconstrained manner. It is difficult to imagine fighting another World War II campaign like Berlin or Dresden. In Berlin, between February and May 1945, a third of the total tonnage of bombs was dropped on the beleaguered city, resulting in the deaths of more than 100,000 people. In our struggle to seize Aachen, the city was virtually destroyed.

With many of the major global cities experiencing a host of infrastructure and overcrowding shortcomings, the likely damage from unconstrained urban warfare would require a total rebuilding effort. Such warfare could cause the total dismemberment of basic services and the deaths of thousands of innocent people, along with great collateral damage to homes, hospitals, and other structures, creating a new mass of refugees. Rampant disease and starvation would quickly overcome those lucky enough to survive bombs and missiles.

As the moral beacon for international law, global democracy, and respect for human rights, the United States can ill-afford to undertake such costly operations. In all likelihood, the American people would not tolerate the casualties that an urban assault would produce, nor would they tolerate the civilian casualties or extensive damage to the captive city. The trend to exercise constraint is clear. American-led coalitions and military operations must find a better solution than physically destroying a city in order to rescue it from a hostile force.

Another limiting factor is the desire for a short conflict. One of the enduring legacies of the Gulf War was the expectation for quick victory with few casualties. While the American people have reluctantly tolerated high numbers of casualties and prolonged military campaigns in the past, events in Somalia and Bosnia indicate that the American public has little stomach for excessive casualties in future wars.

In our example, another viable option exists. If preemptive measures fail, rather than initiating a time-consuming, costly attack in complex terrain, I suggest that an indirect approach would accomplish the strategic end at a much lower cost in terms of human life and physical destruction. Implementing an indirect approach leverages the intrinsic instability of the urban mass to our own advantage. By avoiding a direct assault on an entrenched force, we do not engage the enemy on his terms. The indirect approach enables us to maintain the initiative and employ our technologically superior forces to their fullest potential, leaving the enemy with little option.

This option encompasses three fundamental concepts: using an indirect approach, using time to our advantage, and letting the city collapse on itself.

THE INDIRECT APPROACH

In his landmark book on strategy, Liddell Hart contended that in most successful campaigns, the dislocation of the enemy's psychological and physical balance was brought about through use of the indirect approach. This also applies to urban warfare.

Instead of conducting a direct assault and massive strike, coalition forces could establish a loose cordon around the city and control of the surrounding countryside. The cordon would eventually result in complete isolation of the city from the outside world. All avenues, including air, sea, and land arteries, would be blocked. Moreover, the coalition would seek to control sources of food, power, water, and sanitation services. Any vital natural resources would be controlled. Finally, using technological means, all internal information sources and commercial, financial, and governmental nodes would be suppressed, and only information emanating from the coalition would reach the city's population.

Throughout the cordon operation, coalition forces would demonstrate their absolute mastery of the situation, using knowledge and speed to seize, control, and strike selected decisive points within the city. High-altitude unmanned aerial vehicles orbiting miles above the city could maintain unlimited surveillance with a minimum of manpower. Ground-mounted cameras could observe areas susceptible to infiltration. Unless the enemy attacked, coalition forces would not engage in close combat, instead using greater standoff advantages and technology to strike selected point targets, key leadership, and weapons of mass destruction.

As history reminds us, a continued massive use of fire power often has the opposite effect from what is intended.

214

Thus, the coalition would not attempt to achieve complete destruction of the enemy force, but only to destroy those targets that have the greatest impact on the government, the army, and the population. The purpose is two-fold: to demonstrate the futility of further resistance, and to create conditions that will lead to collapsing the enemy's will to continue the struggle.

USING TIME TO OUR ADVANTAGE

Through the use of psychological operations and control of the media, the coalition could create an environment in which the enemy army becomes an unwelcome force. The underlying purpose is to shape the perception that the enemy is a hostile occupying force. This perception eventually turns the population against the enemy. In this regard, the coalition could establish mechanisms to gauge the prevailing moods of the population.

LET THE CITY COLLAPSE ON ITSELF

As the coalition achieves control of the surrounding countryside, it could collect resources to support the establishment of sanctuaries or safe havens around the city. Humanitarian organizations, both governmental and non-governmental, would be encouraged to construct protected camps. The city's population would be encouraged to leave, and coalition forces would freely allow refugees passage through the cordon to the relative security and safety of the camps.

For those who stay, the isolation of the city, in time, would create a refugee problem for the enemy. With the steady depletion of resources, the remaining population would eventually see the government as an impotent entity that can't provide basic services or security for the people. Inevitably, the military forces and their leaders would be seen as the real enemy, particularly among the dispossessed within the city.

Although this approach has its advantages, this is not to suggest that it would always work. The following are key considerations before this approach is undertaken. How much popular support does the enemy have? How willing is the enemy's population to accept suffering? To what extent is the city self-sustaining and for how long? Is there some sanctuary nearby that allows forces to rest and recuperate in safety? To what extent are we relying on a coalition and how strong is the coalition? How coherent were the enemy's military forces when they occupied the city? How close was the city to collapse before the initiation of military operations?

Future conditions will force us to fight in complex terrain. We can no longer fight the destructive campaigns of World War II. The indirect approach enables us to use knowledge and speed to their fullest potential to achieve our strategic ends with the least cost in human life and destruction of physical property.

Chapter Thirteen

RUSSIA'S CLASH IN CHECHNYA: IMPLICATIONS FOR FUTURE WAR

Major General Robert H. Scales, Jr.

Reproduced with Permission Granted by:
NATIONAL SECURITY STUDIES QUARTERLY
Volume 6, Issue 2
Spring 2000

RUSSIA'S CLASH IN CHECHNYA: IMPLICATIONS FOR FUTURE WAR

War does not belong in the realm of arts and sciences;
rather it is part of man's social existence. War is a clash between major
interests, which is resolved by bloodshed.[1]

Clausewitz

Historians recorded the dawn of the twentieth century as a time when the Russian military found itself making an end to a messy siege against a determined enemy on the periphery of its crumbling empire. This military task was made all the more challenging by the social and technological upheavals of the times. As the conflict escalated, Russian military leaders found themselves powerless to overcome their country's traditional political conservatism and economic penury. Fighting during an era of revolutionary change in military science, Russia's military was not able to take full advantage of the opportunities new technologies promised to bring to the battlefield. World opinion generally condemned their military efforts without seeking to understand how vital a Russian victory was to the short-term political health of the Russian ruling elite and the long-term future stability of the region.

Another century has passed, the geographic locations have changed, but the above description of Russia's 1904 Port Arthur siege could also be used to outline the recent Russian siege of Grozny. Exactly nine decades stand between the outbreak of the Russo-Japanese War and the December 1994 attack against the Chechen capital. However, many political-military conditions and observations remain just as relevant today as they were a century ago.

Few western military analysts in 1904 realized the outbreak of the Russo-Japanese War and the battlefield tactics used in Manchuria would become a frightful metaphor for the horror of trench warfare to follow in less than a decade. It has always been difficult to anticipate and comprehend the cycles and pace of change in warfare because, unlike endeavors in finance, medicine, or law, active experience in war is, fortunately, episodic. During periods of relative quiescence, however, it is imperative for soldiers and statesmen to gain vicarious insights through laboratory analysis of past experience, and, whenever discontinuity or brief incidents of war erupt, avoid the temptation to view them as historical anomalies.

THE AFTERMATH: A PRISM THAT REFRACTS VALUABLE INSIGHTS

Even though shots are still being fired in Chechnya's rugged southern mountains, it is not too soon to begin reflecting upon the long-range implications of this tragic war. Across the western world, questions now abound regarding the military implications of this deadly and costly conflict. The aftermath of the war may well provide us with a revealing window of opportunity to glimpse a few guideposts that portend the direction, pace of change, and perhaps even the nature of future warfare.

Russia's first Chechen war was a disaster that almost led to the full secession of Chechnya. The 1994-1996 conflict was degrading for a Russian military already brought low by the Afghan War and the humiliating loss of social prestige and ensuing discomfort that followed the withdrawal from the Soviet Army's East European garrisons. The failure of the first Chechen war revealed to Russia's military leadership profound strategic, operational, and tactical defects. The Russian military rightfully concluded that their civilian leaders never understood the nature of this new style of cultural war. Likewise, they realized that they had badly underestimated the fighting resolve of the Chechen rebels. They were particularly frustrated by a civilian administration that seemed totally incapable of establishing a coherent, consistent policy towards the war.

The Russians also recognized their own unique military shortcomings. Unity of command was never established between the disparate assortment of deployed troops. Senior commanders continued to employ tactics more appropriate for open, mechanized warfare than strict fighting against tenacious guerilla-like bands of Chechens who were operating within restrictive terrain. Commanders in the field never had enough troops for the task, nor were the few units at their disposal sufficiently well trained to fight on difficult urban and mountain battlefields. Undisciplined solders and ineffective leaders eventually led to episodes of corruption, brutality, and *Dedovshchina* (hazing). In the end, Russia's ill-prepared force was unable to take Grozny by storm, nor could their poorly disciplined armed forces win the hearts of the Chechen population.

The first Chechen war never gained popular support in Russia. To most Russians, it appeared the Chechens were winning both the propaganda war at home and the information war abroad. To those outside the battle area, it seemed as if Russian soldiers had become nothing more than expendable commodities thrown mindlessly into a senseless war of attrition. After two expensive years of combat, Russia was forced to negotiate a settlement with Chechen leaders in August 1996.

For the next few years, Chechnya remained a hotbed of unrest with cross-border raids, kidnappings, destruction of neighboring provinces, and efforts to organize a kind of Pan-Islamic movement that promoted the secession of neighboring provinces from Russia. Eventually, Moscow's military leaders resolved to take action. By 1998, they devised and started to rehearse operational plans for a second Chechen war—one they intended to win.

SETTING THE CONDITIONS FOR SUCCESS

Since the time of the Czars, Russia's Army has practiced a method of change and adaptation that reflects the structured, autocratic, and hierarchical nature of the Russian society. In contrast to western militaries, reform within Russia's military occurs more slowly, usually in fits and starts and always under the direction and central authority of the General Staff.[2] In wars of this century, Russian field commanders have learned to adhere to strict regulations and tactical "norms" that dictate behavior in combat to a level of specificity unheard of in the West.[3] The result is a rigid method of warfare that leaves little to chance, uncertainty, inspiration, or serendipity.[4]

The path of change after the first Chechen war followed this Russian pattern with remarkable fidelity. From the beginning, the General Staff recognized the conflict could not be resumed without first securing political and popular support within the homeland. Fortunately for the Russian side, the Chechens assisted by conducting an ill-conceived domestic terror campaign of bombings and border raids that served only to turn popular opinion in Russia squarely against them.

Senior Russian leaders quickly seized the information warfare initiative and aggressively organized a comprehensive effort to gain popular support. Grisly television footage was aired showing Chechen execution of prisoners. The September 1999 unsolved bombings in Moscow presented Russian leaders with an unexpected opportunity to blame the Chechen rebels without any proof of complicity. Additionally, Russia was able to conduct a relatively successful information blockade around the city of Grozny. This "cyberspace curtain" worked to the advantage of Russia's information warriors. Simultaneously, they encouraged helpless civilians to leave the city, and they attempted to win the hearts of the local Chechen population by creating refugee relief centers outside Grozny and in neighboring provinces. Wherever possible, Russian commanders attempted to coopt the area's local elite and tribal elders with the goal of leveraging local support for Russia against the rebel's defensive effort.

DEVELOPING A CAMPAIGN PLAN AND TAILORING IT FOR THE SITUATION

Urban warfare historically has been both time and people intensive, and therefore terribly lethal. During the Second World War, for example, the Russian Army sustained over 300,000 casualties taking Berlin. Stalingrad cost the Russians even more. However, the Russians learned from watching the West that the arrival of democracy takes away from the military the traditional authority to write blank checks on the lives of their soldiers, particularly if they intend to prosecute the war by maintaining popular support at home. To accommodate the realities of this new "democratic" way of war, the Russian Army customized their fighting tactics for mountain and urban fighting by increasing the expenditures of firepower as a means of decreasing expenditures of manpower. They resolved to avoid door-to-door street fighting if at all possible. Initially, the substitution seemed to work.

The Russians reorganized combat forces to overcome their previous unity of command problems. The General Staff clearly demonstrated their ability to learn and apply several key principles of urban warfare based upon their terrible 1994-1996 experience. They created new command and control structures to streamline cooperation between the regular army and the *Vnutrennye Voiska* (VVMVD), the Ministry of Interior's Internal troops. Since the VVMVD is a less capable force, the General Staff ultimately imposed unity of command under its consolidated leadership.

From experience, Russian commanders realized that, even in a firepower-intensive style of urban warfare, numbers of soldiers guaranteed overwhelming force. This time the General Staff sent a total of 93,000 troops—three times the number used during the first Chechen war. Many assorted police formations were committed to conduct "mopping-up" operations once the back of Chechen resistance was broken in the cities. The army grew into a patchwork of military units consisting of a number of small, elite "temporary operational groups" consisting principally of airborne, air assault and special operations units, and the Naval Infantry.

From the beginning the General Staff determined that Grozny could only be taken by first securing, then dominating the Chechen countryside. Instead of a medieval-style siege, the plan was to establish a sort of loose cordon around the city and then begin a series of cautious probes preceded by ample doses of bombs, rockets, and shells. Once control of this sort was established, the Chechens would lose the initiative, and battlefield advantage would shift to the Russians. If senior military leaders could convince their political bosses of the need for patience, time would eventually guarantee victory.

ANALYSIS OF THE RUSSIAN ART OF WAR

As so often happens, politics and the enemy interfere with careful planning. In the beginning, the Russian leadership failed to accurately assess the political resolve of the Chechen rebels. Eventually, political impatience at home caused them to lose the advantage of time and patience. Russia's senior civilian and military leaders failed to maintain the city of Grozny merely as a military objective. When it became apparent to Russia's political leaders that their future survival depended upon a rapid victory, Grozny quickly evolved into a critical political center of gravity. Suddenly the advantage of time shifted back to the defenders.

The western press made much of Russian shortcomings during the second Chechen war. To be sure, in typical Russian fashion, it was a messy and tragically brutal affair. But the Russians did achieve their military objectives, at least for the near term. The Russian General Staff still appears to retain its ability to analyze failure, determine what needs to be done and subsequently dictate corrective actions to the field. While the brain of the army shows signs of life, the Chechen war also seems to tell us that the body of the Russian Army remains on the sick list. Field Commanders simply lacked the resources, both human and materiel, to effectively execute the intent of the General Staff. Poorly trained and led solders will inevitably make a mess of the best-laid plans.

Throughout both Chechen conflicts, the Russians still seemed to be continually surprised by the steadfastness, guile, stoicism, and tenacity of the Chechen fighters. Without question, the Chechens taught the Russians a lesson the United States painfully learned from the North Vietnamese. Given time and a will to win, a determined enemy learns to survive the onslaught from a firepower intensive force. Soldiers become inured to the pyrotechnics and blast of firepower weapons. They learn to disperse and go-to-ground in order to present the smallest and least lucrative targets. Eventually, after the shock wears off, they learn to not only survive, but to remain effective in close combat, even under the most severe bombardment. The Russians in Chechnya relived our own experience in Hue.

The field army's difficulty realizing the intent of the General Staff was most evident by its inability to maintain control of the countryside while attempting to isolate and contain the Chechens inside Grozny. On several occasions the Russians had to return to open warfare in order to push the Chechens back inside their urban lair. The city's defenders were not cut off from their free access to supply bases in the southern mountains until the very end of the conflict.

The Russian plan to replace manpower with firepower was proper for the circumstances. However, as the battle progressed, the Russians found themselves obliged to drop an ever-increasing tonnage of shells and bombs into the city in order to kill Chechens while preserving the lives of their own soldiers. This firepower challenge was exacerbated by the poor quality of materiel and training within the Russian fire support system. Coordination between soldiers in contact with supporting artillery was poorly executed. Often close-in fires seemed to be delivered indiscriminately. Hundreds of rockets, mortars, and artillery rounds were dumped into portions of the city seemingly without purpose or effect. Frustration, revenge, and the desire to cause terror took over as the principal motives for delivering firepower.

The crude Russian firepower system remained woefully imprecise, and their approach continued to display the old-fashioned Soviet preference for mass over quality. The lack of both technical and tactical discretion was clearly evident. Had they been available, a few laser or Global Positioning System (GPS) guided munitions would have been much more effective as a method of striking point targets within the city. While operationally well-grounded, the plan nevertheless failed in large measure because the lack of precision weapons, precision surveillance, and proper battlefield coordination increasingly left the Russians with no other option but to escalate the tonnage of firepower in order to meet the intent of the General Staff. Eventually this deadly escalation left them with no choice but to destroy Grozny and many of its innocents in order to save it.

Russian small unit tactics improved considerably from the first Chechen war. Mounted troops no longer sought to rush the center of the city only to be ambushed and destroyed within smoking, bloody columns stretching down Grozny's inner thoroughfares. Instead commanders followed bombardments by cautiously infiltrating the city, block by block, leading with their best soldiers, using smaller formations with usually either airborne or special forces units. Green conscripts were kept out of the initial movements to contact as much as possible in order to reduce battlefield losses.

But the Chechens learned quickly. After enduring Russia's firepower onslaught, they cautiously sought to snipe the lead formations in order to slow their advance. Simultaneously, they reserved their limited resources for major engagements, usually ambushes at night, against the less well-trained and ill-prepared conscripts in rear areas. Eventually the Russian tactics of leading with fewer and better quality infantry paid off, but the Chechens insured that the cost of victory was very high indeed.

THINKING-IN-TIME: A FEW NUGGETS WITH STRATEGIC IMPLICATIONS

Grozny has been turned into an urban wasteland. Russia's leadership now pretends that the barren, desert-like landscape of Chechnya signals a victory. But 90,000-plus Russian troops will not be able to prevent cross-border retaliation raids, and they most certainly will experience continued guerrilla warfare in the area. Since Russia will not be able to effect either political or economic resolution to the fundamental problems in the North Caucasus region, it should not expect peace anytime soon. More importantly, the potential of a protracted, post-imperial war on its periphery still remains Russia's worst nightmare, just as it did almost one hundred years ago when Japanese forces marched into central Manchuria.

The aftermath of Chechnya seems to reinforce a few insights on the changing nature of war garnered from other post-Cold War battlefields. The Russians re-learned a lesson NATO first taught them in Kosovo: a firepower intensive style of war can reduce casualties. But the cost in destruction and duration of the conflict will be too high unless the firepower is delivered with precision and followed with rapid occupation of the enemy's territory. Ground forces, using great caution, must exploit the effects of firepower, particularly when fighting in difficult terrain such as cities or against an enemy with the will to resist and adapt. Increasingly, as the Russians learned, fewer soldiers must be exposed to contact in order to avoid excessive casualties, and these soldiers should be of exceptional quality, well led, and well equipped. The precise application of firepower, maneuver, and cautious close combat offered the Russians the only tactical scheme by which they could win relatively quickly and with acceptable costs. This is the key lesson of limited warfare: a commitment to limited ends demands the judicious use of limited means. The Russians, unfortunately, lacked the technical precision and tactical means to effectively implement this new precision age paradigm of air and land warfare.

After more than a decade of experience, we are witnessing a geo-strategic shift in the motives for conflict. The Chechen war conforms to a developing pattern that started to emerge several years ago as evidenced by Afghanistan, Lebanon, Bosnia, Somalia, Kosovo, and other conflicts along the periphery of Eurasia. We should anticipate the world beyond 2010 to be an era of rekindled conflict where breakaway regimes will frequently define themselves by their cultural-ethnic identities. Many of these regimes will be radically fundamental in nature and religiously motivated. And many will find warfare as the surest means for defending their culture from outside influences or for imposing their culture on less cultured neighbors.

Explosions of long-simmering conflict, once held in check during the Cold War, will be free to start again. Some of these recently ignited conflicts have been smoldering for generations and in some cases, such as Chechnya, for centuries. As this trend continues, developed democracies and their allies should anticipate future wars that will be conducted within what the Russians habitually refer to as "under-cultured theaters of operation." Most of these clashes between forces will be intractable or unruly. The shooting portion of the conflict may very well end with no decisive advantage to either opponent. Since this type of war will be difficult to manage, the best an intervening power can hope for may well be a truce, stalemate, or some minimum level of sustained violence acceptable to the sensitivities of the world's advanced democracies. The only predictable aspects of this type of conflict, if it is allowed to expand into open warfare, will be its bloody nature, protracted duration, and inconclusive ending.

The recent Chechen saga helps us derive a number of insights regarding Russia's application of military power. To be sure, the war in Chechnya will have a number of implications for Russia and its military forces. As Russia's military leaders begin their inevitable process of assessment and change, we must observe carefully to determine how their Chechnya experience will alter their approach and prosecution of warfare in the future.

The legacies from Chechnya could directly influence Russia's potential evolution into a future regional military competitor. Currently, the average Russian citizen on the street has a heightened regard for Russia's military force, and Russian military leaders will most likely enjoy a greater voice within their government's policy making process. There seems to be an established realization among today's political elite that the future use of military force may be necessary to maintain stability within the country's borders, and likewise, to guarantee the political longevity of the political regime now in power. It would not be surprising to see additional conflicts conducted in order to secure the periphery of Russia's remaining empire.

Senior Russian military leaders, moreover, must now realize the need for additional reform. The timing may be right for them to win both political support and financial resources from the country's political leadership. Military leaders, most certainly, have a greater appreciation for well-trained and more effectively led troops. The Chechnya experience, in retrospect, may be the impetus to build a smaller, more professional, long-serving army. Change within Russia's military will be two fold: heal the body and sharpen the mind. The General Staff will orchestrate their traditional path for reform after they have completed their dialectical assessment of the conflict. And perhaps most importantly, it will not be surprising to see a major commitment from the Russian military to join the unfolding precision revolution.[5]

Finally, from a western perspective, Chechnya tells us the Russians have now convincingly learned a tenet of democratic warfare that will increasingly influence how we in the West prosecute real, shooting wars. In every conflict since the end of the Second World War, we have re-learned the maxim that a political commitment to limited ends will demand strict limits on the means that we are allowed to commit to achieve those ends. For more than five decades, developed militaries have been in search of a method of war that will reduce friendly casualties by increasing the expenditure of precision firepower delivered against opponents. Unless its very existence is at stake, a modern state no longer publicly tolerates the massive slaughter of its soldiers. The Russians are the latest modern state to have learned this lesson. The cost of learning has been too high.

ENDNOTES

1. Carl Von Clausewitz, *On War*, edited and translated by Michael Howard and Peter Paret (Princeton: Princeton University Press, 1976), 149.

2. There is an excellent discussion regarding the Russian General Staff's "Top-Down" planning process published by J. Erickson within the article, "Soviet C^3: Trends, Techniques, and Technology," *Defense Analysis* 7, No.2/ 3 (1991): 263-276. Erickson also references the 1987 benchmark research by James T Westwood, "Evolution and Change in c^{3}s Requirements and Criteria: Soviet *Perestroika*, U.S. Responsiveness," 10-12. 58th Military Operations Research Society Symposium, U.S. Naval Academy (1990).

3. Hemsley has published a detailed analysis and explanation of the Soviet approach to intensive study of past wars and the process they use to develop tactical norms within their troop control procedures. See John Hemsley, *Soviet Troop Control: The Role of Command Technology in the Soviet Military System* (Oxford: Brassey's Publishers Limited, 1982), 89-115.

4. Robert H. Scales, Jr., *Firepower in Limited War* (Novato: Presidio Press, 1995), 166-167.

5. For an outstanding analysis of Russian military reform, read Christopher Donnelley, "Crisis and Reform in the Russian Military," in Williamson Murray, ed., *The Emerging Strategic Environment: Challenges of theTwenty-first Century* (Westport: Praeger Publishers, 1999), 60-85.

Chapter Fourteen

TRUST, NOT TECHNOLOGY, SUSTAINS COALITIONS

Major General Robert H. Scales, Jr.

Reproduced with Permission Granted by:
Winter 1998-1999 Issue
PARAMETERS
Volume 28, Number 4

TRUST, NOT TECHNOLOGY, SUSTAINS COALITIONS

> History testifies to the ineptitude of coalitions in waging war. Allied failures have been so numerous and their inexcusable blunders so common that professional soldiers had long discounted the possibility of effective allied action unless available resources were so great as to assure victory by inundation. Even Napoleon's reputation as a brilliant military leader suffered when students . . . came to realize that he always fought against coalitions—and therefore against divided counsels and diverse political, economic, and military interests.
>
> Dwight D. Eisenhower, *Crusade in Europe*[1]

As Supreme Commander of the Allied Expeditionary Force in Europe during World War II, General Dwight Eisenhower led one of the most successful coalitions in history. By insisting on an integrated staff and demanding an atmosphere of fairness and mutual respect, Eisenhower transcended personalities and many political challenges to his decisions. His success was in large measure attributable to the cohesive—if sometimes contentious—environment at Supreme Headquarters Allied Forces Europe.

Strategists predict that instability and conflict will characterize the 21st century, due to cultural unrest and regional wars engulfing bordering states or consuming states from within.[2] Over the past decade Western democracies and others, mindful of the need to contain the spread of violence, have demonstrated increased willingness to use military force to defuse internal or regional political conflicts or to respond to humanitarian crises.

But smaller and more expensive militaries as well as pressing social needs confront decisionmakers with the need to find ways to contain the cost of such military undertakings. For the foreseeable future the United States will remain reluctant to intervene unilaterally in most crises; as a consequence, the need for coalition partners will shape American strategy.

In all its modern wars the United States has fought as a member of a coalition.[3] Thus, it is likely that U.S. military leaders throughout their careers will confront the challenge of organizing and leading coalitions. Any officer knows intuitively, if not from experience, that interoperability of equipment and compatibility of doctrine and operational procedures pose significant challenges in any coalition. Many also are aware of the costs of rationalizing procurement, doctrine, and training within the NATO alliance; few, however, could even speculate on how to reach NATO's levels of interoperability within a coalition.

Eisenhower's success is instructive here: the compatibility of leaders and staffs in a coalition is more important than compatibility in doctrine or materiel. This article considers technological capabilities, requirements for coalition interoperability, and the need to revive a concept with a long history—the liaison officer as "directed telescope"—to form and manage coalitions.

Communicating In Coalitions

Coalition operations need two simultaneous methods of communication. The first presumes the technical connectivity required within coalitions to perform assigned missions. The U.S. military needs to develope sufficient compatibility in data and information to provide a reasonable level of technical interoperability with prospective coalition partners.

The second method relies on personal and professional relationships with counterparts in other nations. It recognizes the potential impediments of language, cultural differences, and national perspectives when operating in a coalition. Compensating for such impediments requires long-term investments in training select officers to function autonomously under great stress within a multinational environment. Sensitive to national or subnational issues and skilled in building trust based on personal relationships, such officers would help regional commanders-in-chief "see" the complexities of strategic and operational environments.

Alliances and Coalitions

While there are similarities between alliances and coalitions, politically and structurally they are markedly different. Created for collective defense or to cope with a long-term threat, alliances usually rest on formal agreements among nations with mutual interests and (often) cultural ties. Sometimes referred to as "latent" war communities, alliances require a formal structure, agreed-upon rules, and protocols to manage the routine and structure the rest.

For many years Washington's Farewell Address shaped U.S. perspectives on alliances: "Tis our true policy to steer clear of permanent alliances with any portion of the foreign world."[4] By the end of World War II, however, the threat of Soviet aggression proved more compelling than 150 years of tradition. The role of the United States in developing NATO as a barrier to Soviet aggression,[5] and the Organization of American States to improve relations in the Western Hemisphere, needs no review. But alliances remain viable only so long as the reason for their founding endures. The Southeast Asia Treaty Organization (SEATO) dissolved long before the Soviet Union did, and in 1986 the United States suspended security obligations incurred with New Zealand under the ANZUS Treaty (Australia, New Zealand, and the United States).

In contrast, coalitions are transitory, emerging in response to specific threats and dissolving once coalition goals have been met. Politically fragile in nature, they develop out of necessity, sometimes uniting nations without a history of harmonious relations. Since the end of the Cold War, "coalitions of the willing" have been an increasing factor within NATO in dealing with crises affecting the vital interests of only a part of the Alliance. Italy's leading role in the 1997 intervention in Albania may be a harbinger of NATO's future in this respect.[6]

National military capabilities either increase or reduce the coalition's fighting power by their value relative to other coalition members and the capabilities of the adversary. For coalitions facing major operations, member nations with large armies are important. Coalitions formed from roughly equal militaries sharing qualitative characteristics offer versatility. And some coalitions will include members whose participation is symbolic. These states contribute little in military capability; they serve primarily to increase the number of flags at the command post and add international legitimacy.

Technology in Coalitions

Technology is a two-edged sword in coalition operations. Global communications systems enhance connectivity among coalition members; emerging military technology allows unprecedented surveillance. Moreover, information technologies have the potential to accelerate deployments and permit decisive operations.

The downside is that rapid and costly changes in technology also create barriers to effective integration of coalition forces. Thoughtful observers have already noted that in a replay of the 1990-91 Gulf War, there could be three and possibly four distinct levels of technology within the coalition. The United States could be well in advance of the second-tier militaries, such as the United Kingdom, Germany, and France, with the rest of pre-enlargement NATO forces at a third level. The fourth level could include recent NATO accessions and the armed forces of other states. Moreover, while the U.S. military might eventually be able to preempt adversary planning, those same adversaries could limit or negate our ability to achieve surprise by accessing similar technology. Finally, until logistic capabilities improve ways and means for operating in bare-base environments, Army theater requirements and Title 10 responsibilities will pose substantial strategic and operational challenges in either multilateral or unilateral environments.

Attaining technological interoperability will be difficult for coalitions in any case. Each Gulf War participant arrived with its own level of technical sophistication. In some cases participants had advanced systems that were not compatible within the coalition. In others, military units needed substantial assistance to communicate with coalition partners. For example, it required approximately 70 soldiers, 27 tons of equipment, and 80 days of training and coordination to create communication interoperability for an average brigade from the Middle Eastern nations.[7] The sheer number of potential coalition partners and the cost of acquiring common or interoperable equipment may make it impossible to guarantee interoperability in similarly constituted coalitions over the next 5 to 10 years.[8]

To further complicate matters, the rate of change in communications, automation, and other technologies is such that equipment is often obsolete before military organizations can establish and maintain interoperability for coalition operations. In the meantime, availability of off-the-shelf technology may allow potential adversaries to procure the latest equipment even as potential coalition members struggle with obsolete equipment. Technology offers no panacea for conducting coalition operations, regardless of who the members are.

Liaison Officers Can Help

The practice of using liaison officers as "directed telescopes" to facilitate command and control is almost as old as war itself. Beginning in antiquity and continuing into the modern era, ground commanders have relied on carefully selected subordinates to serve as their eyes and ears. These trusted agents, often with direct access to the deliberations that produced the "commander's intent," have provided invaluable information to the commander's immediate staff and others. And during the heat of battle, they assisted commanders by communicating orders and controlling units.[9]

A number of great captains developed communications and information gathering systems that resemble the directed telescope concept of the 19th and 20th centuries. Alexander the Great detailed junior officers as couriers to help control widely separated columns. Caesar's staff included aides who served as observers and couriers for high-priority missions. Napoleon relied on liaison officers to provide vital battlefield information and to clarify his intent to subordinates, while Grant used liaison officers to help form impressions of the morale and spirit of his Army.[10]

Field Marshal Montgomery was perhaps the most creative user of such liaison officers in World War II. He selected and integrated into his personal staff a small group of young combat veterans. With the Field Marshal's authority to go anywhere and see anything, these liaison officers traveled extensively, gathering and reporting information via radio. Many returned at night to Montgomery's command post to provide firsthand accounts of their insights. The responsibilities of Montgomery's officers extended beyond gathering information. They could interrupt normal signal traffic with their reports, and they routinely interacted with senior generals and politicians. Moreover, Montgomery authorized them to ask pointed questions of senior officers who appeared incapable of executing their prescribed tasks.[11] This system allowed him to keep the pulse of British, American, Canadian, and Polish formations under his command.[12] Churchill delighted in hearing the nightly reports from Montgomery's "directed telescopes"; he considered the system invaluable in the command of Montgomery's forces.[13] The question for us today is whether the average Army captain or major could perform such tasks in a coalition environment. Are we preparing such officers in our schools and training institutions?

A Geostrategic Scout

One can expect that skilled junior officers will continue to serve as liaison officers to allied tactical formations much as they have in the past. But what of the strategic level, where geopolitical issues and conflicting national interests truly complicate coalitions and alliances? Until 1990 many U.S. Army officers had experience in NATO, as well as in the culture, economy, politics, and forces of other countries around the world. This familiarity came about largely through the Army's Foreign Area Officer (FAO) program. Prepared by study and assignment, such officers served as high-level liaison officers in good times and bad. Unfortunately, the Army has had to curtail that program during the drawdown.

Recent experience indicates a clear requirement for a cadre of officers whose skills and capabilities would transcend the norms of the FAO program. In an era of short-notice deployments, the Army and the other services need to examine the requirement for sophisticated liaison personnel—officers, noncommissioned officers, and civilians—in the active and reserve components. Such individuals would perform the tasks of the foreign area specialist and more. As in the FAO program, their skills would include language as well as cultural and historical understanding of one or more countries in a region. But they would set their sights much higher to include regional geostrategic and geopolitical matters; knowledge of key regional alliances; awareness of new and emerging technologies affecting the ability of the United States to lead or sustain a coalition; U.S. capabilities in strategic communications, logistics, transportation, and sustainment; the interagency process that determines U.S.

241

involvement in peace support activities; and the international humanitarian support system, including the principal private volunteer and nongovernmental organizations through which most humanitarian and developmental work occurs. This list of capabilities is representative, not inclusive; it defines only part of the challenge facing each regional commander-in-chief every day.

Personnel with the desired attributes would be available to regional commanders-in-chief and commanders of combined and national joint task forces. They would assume the role of advisor to the task force commander in matters as important as those addressed by political advisors to regional or theater commanders. The reported proliferation of political advisors in the Balkans underscores the need for such officers. Traditionally "reserved" for work at the highest headquarters, individuals charged with keeping the task force and other commanders apprised of local political, social, and economic conditions have appeared at many levels in Bosnia. This is a pragmatic solution to an unprecedented requirement. With the FAO concept as the foundation, the Army needs to draw on the Bosnia experience and identify new skills and attributes required at the headquarters of coalition partners in 2025. We can do better than *ad hoc* solutions during crises.

What's the Precedent?

In multinational operations, trust binds the coalition together. "Patience, tolerance, frankness, absolute honesty in all dealings, particularly with all persons of the opposite nationality, and firmness are absolutely essential," Eisenhower wrote to Lord Louis Mountbatten as the latter was preparing to assume command in Southeast Asia.[14] Eisenhower's perspective on coalitions, in large measure shared later by General Norman Schwarzkopf, was that the center of gravity in a coalition is often the coalition itself.

There are a number of historical examples that underline this point.

- Hitler aspired to duplicate Frederick the Great's ability to wear down the great alliance formed against Prussia in the Seven Years War. So his concept for the December 1944 offensive through the Ardennes rested on the assumption that by capturing Antwerp and encircling and destroying British and American forces, the Allied coalition would splinter and result in a peace offer.

- During the Gulf War, Saddam Hussein applied similar reasoning when he attempted to draw Israel into the conflict. Israeli retaliation to the Scud attacks might have unraveled the fragile ties binding the coalition together.

Hitler's offensive met a bitter end in the snows of the Ardennes. Israel's close relationship with the United States enabled Israeli political leaders to exercise restraint, and the anti-Iraq coalition held together, to a considerable degree due to the part played by liaison teams. Trust was a key ingredient in sustaining the 1990-91 coalition.

But trust requires time and a measured appraisal of one another to emerge from personal relationships, particularly those that cross cultures.

- In 1981-83, as the Program Manager, Saudi Arabia National Guard, General John Yeosock earned the trust of the Saudi leadership. Years later, as the United States began deploying forces to the region during Desert Shield, Yeosock was granted access and host nation support by Saudi officials.

- The U.S. Army rediscovered the value of liaison officers in the Gulf War. A group of carefully selected liaison teams established communications between Schwarzkopf and major coalition partners.

The teams in turn reported to the Coalition Coordination and Communications Integration Center, which provided information and clarified orders to coalition members. Later, the center served as a directed telescope for Schwarzkopf.[15] If we intend to achieve a similar degree of success in future coalition efforts, including peace operations, the United States needs to establish programs to educate and train a cadre capable of communicating effectively with coalition partners. The time to begin is now.

Conclusion

Although emerging technology offers promise for applying precision firepower and swift maneuver through enhanced information, it will not eliminate the fog and friction of war. New and improved technologies may enhance the 21st Century commander's ability to communicate with coalition partners, but coalition efforts may still founder on the shoals of technical incompatibilities, language difficulties, cultural asymmetries, and ignorance of key historical and geopolitical issues. The antidote to the fog and friction of coalition warfare is not technology; it lies in trusted subordinates who can deal effectively with coalition counterparts.

NOTES

Lieutenant Colonel Thomas Jordon, Strategic Studies Institute, U.S. Army War College, contributed to this article.

1. Dwight D. Eisenhower, *Crusade in Europe* (New York: Doubleday, 1948), p. 4.

2. Earl H. Tilford, Jr., ed., *World View: The 1998 Strategic Assessment from the Strategic Studies Institute* (Carlisle Barracks, Pa.: U.S. Army War College, Strategic Studies Institute, 26 February 1998).

3. Wayne A. Silkett, "Alliance and Coalition Warfare," *Parameters*, 23 (Summer 1993), 74-85.

4. George Washington, Farewell Address, 17 September 1796, Microsoft Bookshelf 1994.

5. See Alan Ned Sabrosky, ed., *Alliances in U.S. Foreign Policy* (Boulder, Colo.: Westview Press, 1987), pp. 6-9.

6. See Thomas Cooke, "NATO CJTF Doctrine: The Naked Emperor," *Parameters*, 28 (Winter 1998-99).

7. Major General Robert H. Scales, Jr., Chairman's Peace Operations Seminar, Carlisle Barracks, Pa., 11 June 1998.

8. For an assessment of NATO's ongoing effort to apply the concept of a combined joint task force to 16 (soon 19) separate nations, see Cooke, "NATO CJTF Doctrine: The Naked Emperor."

9. Gary B. Griffin, *The Directed Telescope: A Traditional Element of Effective Command* (Fort Leavenworth, Kans.: U.S. Army Command and General Staff College, July 1991), pp. 1-2.

10. *Ibid.*, pp. 10-12.

11. *Ibid.*, p. 30.

12. Nigel Hamilton, *Monty* (New York: Random House, 1981), p. 148.

13. Griffin, pp. 28-33. See also, Alan Moorhead, *Montgomery* (London: Hamish Hamilton, 1947), pp. 147-49; and Bernard Law Montgomery, *The Memoirs of Field-Marshal The Viscount Montgomery of Alamein* (New York: The World Publishing Company, 1958), p. 476.

14. Alfred D. Chandler, Jr., ed., *The Papers of Dwight David Eisenhower: The War Years III* (Baltimore: The John Hopkins Press, 1970), pp. 1420-24.

15. Robert H. Scales, Jr., *Certain Victory: The U.S. Army in the Gulf War* (Washington: U.S. Army, Office of the Chief of Staff, 1993), pp. 122, 381.

Chapter Fifteen

TRUST, MORE THAN TECHNOLOGY, ENSURES INTEROPERABILITY

Major General Robert H. Scales, Jr.

Reproduced with Permission Granted by:
Autumn 1999 Issue
DEFENCE SYSTEMS INTERNATIONAL
Sterling Publications Ltd.
London, England

TRUST, MORE THAN TECHNOLOGY, ENSURES INTEROPERABILITY

The intangible, human dimensions of trust, not technology, will ensure NATO's future position as the pre-eminent security alliance during the 21st century.

As the 20th century draws to a close and NATO leaders pause to celebrate the alliance's past 50 years of success, it is timely and appropriate to discuss NATO's organisational strategy for the next five decades. Without question, NATO faces a midlife challenge as the alliance crosses the threshold of a new millennium. If NATO hopes to step boldly into the 21st century, it must strengthen its trust building mechanisms while pursuing the quest for technological interoperability. To be sure, this technical interoperability is an important factor and must continue to he a key organisational focus. Fostering the intangible sense of trust, however, is more important than the coordination of tangible technical connections. It is these human relationships, ultimately, that will ensure NATO's continued political and military interoperability.

The primary focus

The organisational blueprint for a viable multinational partnership must be primarily based upon trust and subsequently facilitated by technological interoperability as NATO prepares to resolutely enter the new millennium. The impediments of technological connectivity pale as secondary issues when attempting to communicate and coordinate within a multinational relationship. Trust, not technology or doctrine nor materiel binds and sustains a successful alliance especially during times of crisis. Trust, more than technology, makes its possible to develop organisational consensus while designing a collective

249

solution that may not require the application of standards from the 'lowest common denominator test.'

Building a sense of trust and shared interests is a labour-intensive venture that requires a long-term commitment of human resources. Professional rapport between officers of various nations cannot be purchased, garnered overnight or mandated. Rather, trust must be nurtured and fostered over a period of time among individuals who are sensitive to each other's national or sub-national concerns. Trust, fostered by regular consultation, becomes the adhesive that binds a multinational partnership despite individual national differences. The foundation of trusting relationships must be established earlier rather than later to ensure that it will be available when it may he needed for the complexities of future strategic and operational battlefield environments.

Allied solidarity

While there are similarities between alliances and coalitions, politically and structurally they are markedly different. However, both must achieve unity of effort in order to he successful. This solidarity requires two simultaneous methods of communication. The first presumes a reasonable level of technical interoperability, whereas the second relies on personal and professional relationships with counterparts from other nations.

Overcoming the fog and friction of complex military operations is not a new security challenge and professional relationships were used long before the invention of the microchip. Many great leaders from the past were confronted with complex command and control requirements and they relied extensively on a network of trained liaison officers. In fact, the practice of using liaison officers as 'directed telescopes' to facilitate command and control is almost as old as war itself. Beginning during antiquity and continuing into the modern era, commanders have relied upon carefully selected subordinates to serve as their eyes, ears and military ambassadors. These trusted agents, often with direct access to the deliberations that produced the 'commander's intent,' have provided invaluable information to subordinate commands throughout the theatre of many past military operations.

The chronicles of history document examples where a number of great captains have used trusted liaison officers to establish and maintain effective command, control and communication functions. Alexander the Great detailed junior officers as ambassadors to help control widely separated columns. Caesar's staff included aides who served as observers and couriers for high-priority missions. Napoleon relied on liaison officers to provide vital battlefield information and to clarify his intent. Field Marshal Montgomery was perhaps the most creative user of such liaison officers during World War II. He selected and integrated into his personal staff a small group of officers who routinely interacted with other senior generals and civilian political leaders[1]. I These historical examples raise a central question for us today: are we preparing young officers in our schools and training institutions to effectively function within a composite multinational environment as contemporary directed telescopes?

New and improved technologies will most certainly improve the 21st century commander's ability to communicate with alliance partners, but operations may still founder on the shoals of technical incompatibilities, language difficulties, cultural asymmetries and ignorance of key historical and geopolitical issues. The antidote for this type of fog and fiction is not more technology; it lies in trusted subordinates and liaison officers who can deal effectively with military and civilian counterparts. In an era of short-notice deployments with complex mission requirements, we need to examine the anticipated demands for sophisticated liaison personnel who would perform the tasks of foreign area specialist with ambassador-like responsibilities. Their skills should include not only language proficiency but also an understanding of cultural and historical differences between one or more alliance partners.

The technology solution

The quest for technological interoperability has a number of inherent limitations. But, we can not ignore the need to address this challenge; it must be a part of the overall plan for the future. Increased attention must be given to the accelerating pace of technological change and the different rates of acquisition that will permit NATO members to introduce these advanced capabilities into their inventories. In reality, there is not enough money within any of the defence budgets to attain and sustain technological interoperability among the entire NATO alliance and the states within its developing Partnership for Peace effort. The growing number of nations and the sheer cost of acquiring common or interoperable equipment most certainly makes it impossible to always guarantee system interoperibility.

Further complicating this matter is the rapid rate of change within command, control, communication and information links. In many instances, the technological half-life of these systems is such that military equipment is often obsolete before units can field and train with these systems. In the meantime, availability of off-the-shelf technology may allow potential adversaries the opportunity to procure the most current equipment while alliance members struggle to use obsolete equipment. There is no 'technological silver bullet' and even though technology will always be a supporting dimension of multinational operations, it will never become the panacea chat will overcome the fog and friction of complex military operations.

Enduring strategic solutions

The new century will most certainly bring a new form of future warfare. We should expect the information age to alter the means of future warfare just as decisively as the machine age altered the conduct of war during the 19th and 20th century. There is a historic and symbiotic relationship between advancing technology and the evolving means of warfare.[2] The sense of relative stability, maintained through the balance of power that existed during the Cold War, will be more difficult to achieve during the next 20 years as long-standing, multi-polar tensions erupt and competing hegemons attempt to dominate their respective regions. Conflict will abound as some nations redress historic grievances and others open old wounds that have been festering for centuries.

During the past decade, Western democracies and others, mindful of the social need to contain the spread of violence, have demonstrated increased willingness to use military force to defuse internal or regional political conflicts or to respond to humanitarian crises. In many instances, the need for synchronised NATO military action may be greater than in the past. There are numerous vital political and military outcomes that can only be achieved through the actions of an alliance or coalition. The raison d'être frequently involves more than the need to assemble equal or compatible military partners. Alliances and coalitions have historically provided military commanders with the opportunity to achieve an overwhelming mass of force on the battlefield They also provide the organisational framework for demonstrating political consensus.[3]

In many cases, the political heft of multinational partnerships may be the single most important commodity as the 'war of national resolve' is waged. Moreover, this solidarity may be the only way to achieve enduring, strategic solutions within a complex web of international security concerns.

The next frontier

NATO has five decades of remarkable achievement and we anticipate this outstanding track record to continue well into the next century. As this multinational partnership seeks to sustain regional peace and security throughout Europe, we should expect complex future security challenges that will require the commitment of military capabilities. Planning these future NATO-sponsored operations will require particular attention to the challenges of technical interoperability. In fact, NATO's current membership action plan encourages aspirant members to pursue interoperability upon accession into NATO. The next two decades, most certainly, will place new demands upon NATO's command and control capabilities and highlight the need for increased system interoperability. This technical connectivity, however, is a secondary issue when examined against the requirement for human factors that promote multinational 'interoperability.' The organisation and efficiency of any alliance or coalition operation will ultimately depend upon a single, intangible characteristic-trust. The foundation for this collaboration must be built upon a sense of mutual respect, tolerance and a commitment to the shared values of democracy. Our senior leaders must foster the military education and staff exchange programmes that will develop a generation of sophisticated liaison officers capable of facilitating the challenging, multinational operations alliance members will face in the next century.

References

1. This idea was developed by MG Scales within an essay recently published in *Parameters*, Winter 1999, Volume 28, Number 4.

2. For additional information regarding this thesis, read "The Dawn of a New Age of Warfare" by MG Scales. *Defence Systems International*, Spring 1999.

3. This concept was first articulated by MG Scales in an essay published in the January 28, 1999 issue of *Newsday*.

Chapter Sixteen

IN WAR, THE U.S. CAN'T GO IT ALONE

Major General Robert H. Scales, Jr.

Reproduced with Permission Granted by:
January 28, 1999 Issue
NEWSDAY NEWSPAPER
235 Pinelawn Road
Melville, New York

IN WAR, THE U.S. CAN'T GO IT ALONE

Are military coalitions political relics of the past or viable instruments of modern political power? Some analysts argue that coalition warfare, like the dinosaur, is traveling a path toward extinction.

These commentators use the growing technological gap between militaries as the primary rationale to suggest that the United States will no longer be able to fight alongside a less technically developed military. Moreover, fighting doctrine, language, and other cultural differences seem to impede rather than bond nations into a coalition that will be able to fight for a common cause.

On the other hand, to envision the United States trying to fight any future war without partners is inconceivable. The United States has fought all its modern wars as a member of a coalition, and we will find coalitions to be militarily viable well into the 21st Century. Furthermore, future coalitions will continue to provide America's leaders with the most reliable means of achieving successful, enduring strategic results.

To be sure, America's political leaders will always reserve the option to apply military force unilaterally when a nation-state or hostile state-like actor has violated our interests or those of our allies. These tactical military actions can be used either to destroy a capability surgically or to administer punishment for an aggressor's offending actions.

The results of precision strikes are immediately perceived, but rarely enduring. They provide us, without question, a temporary national gratification or perhaps a sense of moral victory. At best, they signal to rogue actors our watchful commitment to international security and regional stability.

However, long-lasting strategic effects will only be realized when the convergence of mutual national interests unleashes the international will of a coalition.

There are various vital political and military outcomes that can only be achieved through the actions of a coalition. Its *raison d'etre* frequently involves more than the need to assemble equal or compatible military partners. Coalitions have historically

Reproduced with permission from Martin Kozlowski.

provided military commanders with the opportunity to achieve an overwhelming mass of force on the battlefield. Coalitions also provide the organizational framework for developing and demonstrating political consensus.

War has always been a test of national wills. The conduct of war involves more than the destruction of physical resources. Beyond the boundaries of the battlefield, war must ultimately influence public perception and public opinion. Victory is only achieved when you break the national determination of your opponent and persuade him to accept your final terms and conditions for peace. The political heft of a coalition becomes an invaluable commodity as the "war of national resolve" is waged.

Ultimately, the formation of any coalition hinges upon a single, intangible characteristic—trust. The impediments of national and cultural differences pale as secondary issues when attempting to communicate within a coalition. Trust, not technology nor doctrine or materiel, binds and sustains a successful coalition.

Building this sense of trust and shared interests is a labor-intensive venture that requires a long-term commitment of resources. Professional rapport between officers of various nations cannot be purchased, garnered overnight, or mandated. Rather, trust must be nurtured and fostered over a period of time among individuals who are sensitive to each other's national or subnational concerns.

Trust becomes the adhesive that binds a coalition despite individual national differences. The foundation of trust must be established earlier rather than later to ensure that it will be available when it may be needed for the complexities of strategic and operational battlefield environments.

The information age promises to change the nature of 21st Century warfare just as decisively as the machine age altered the course of war in the 19th Century. But the need to fight within a coalition will prevail as an urgent political and military necessity. We should anticipate not only a seismic shift in the character of technology, but also an increasingly complex web of international security concerns.

Global restraint, maintained through the balance of power that existed during the Cold War, will be more difficult to achieve as long-standing, multi-polar tensions erupt, and competing hegemonies attempt to dominate their regions. Conflicts will abound as some nations redress historic grievances and others open old wounds that have been festering for centuries.

In many instances, the need for military coalitions will be greater than in the past because coalition warfare will be the only way to achieve enduring, strategic solutions.

259

Chapter Seventeen

EUROPE AS A STRATEGIC STAGING BASE FOR 21ST CENTURY STABILIZATION OPERATIONS

Major General Robert H. Scales, Jr.

Strategic Studies Institute
U.S. Army War College
The Future of the American Military Presence
in Europe Conference Proceedings
May 2000

EUROPE AS A STRATEGIC STAGING BASE FOR 21st CENTURY STABILIZATION OPERATIONS

Toward the end of 1995, I was privileged to launch and then participate in, for some 2 and 1/2 years, the Army's so-called Army After Next (AAN) Project, which sought to define the shape and character of landpower beyond the year 2010 and to investigate two of the principal factors that cause styles of war to change—technology and geostrategy. We had some powerful tools to help us hypothesize what conflict might look like out beyond 2010, including both tactical and strategic war games and numerous conferences. AAN war games were conducted at Fort Leavenworth and Carlisle Barracks, and because of the complexity were extremely difficult to do. The Army's great doctrinal revolution had occurred in the late 1970s and early 1980s at the operational level, and that was difficult enough. But now we were attempting to reestablish the tenets of landpower during warfare at the next higher level.

We conducted a series of exercises using force on force in free-play scenarios. It is really challenging to replicate National Training Center exercises in the computer-based simulations of Collins Hall at the Army War College, but we did it four times.

Collaterally, in conducting a historical inquiry into the changing cycles and patterns of war, we observed that war has mutated from wars of religion to wars of kings to wars of nations to wars of ideology, and so forth. Increasingly, it became apparent that the fall of the Soviet empire might foster a new era of wars characterized by ethnic and cultural conflict. Accordingly, we postulated a clash in the year 2020 involving a newly emergent hegemonic power in central Asia seeking to reestablish ethnic and cultural dominance over a small country in southeastern Europe. The hegemonic power aimed to achieve its strategic and operational objectives quickly—that is, to put forces on the victim's ground, disperse them, and then begin a process of cultural transformation in that country before the United States could project forces into the region and initiate an effective response.

We also made a series of visits, an intellectual odyssey if you will, to representatives of all the major armies around the world island. For my part, I spent almost 2 years doing this, enjoying an opportunity to conduct searching discourse with the leaders of most of the armies in eastern and central Asia. Based upon impressions gleaned from my visit and similar visits by other AAN Project team members, we formulated a general outline of what the nature of conflict might be out to the year 2025 and beyond. It tended to confirm our earlier suspicions, based upon historical investigation, that the most likely causes for conflict during that period would be ethnic and cultural in nature.

It seemed to us that such conflicts would arise along those historical borders separating traditionally antagonistic economic, religious, ethnic, national, or cultural groupings. The territories of such disputants are analogous to geological tectonic plates, colliding against and ultimately riding over or sinking under adjacent plates in an eternal friction of heat, strife, and violence. Such collisions have been the occasion of major wars for the last 5,000 years. To borrow Samuel Huntington's famous fault line analogy ("The Clash of Civilizations," *Foreign Affairs*, Summer 1993), it seemed to us that the greatest potential for serious combat during our time frame would occur along these traditional fault lines.

History clearly shows that when the artificial caps that suppress or sublimate ethnic and cultural conflict are removed, the actors revert to this approach and conflict resumes. Thus it seemed to us that the maintenance of security and stability along these fault lines would depend on the ability of political structures to manage the inevitable tensions by means short of war. In any event, we were certain we knew where tensions were most likely to flare into outright hostilities. That is why we chose southeastern Europe as the setting for our first war game. It happens that this particular region marks the intersection of not two but three fault lines—Eastern Orthodox Christianity, Islam, and Western Christianity.

In talking to the potential major actors, it seemed to us that we were seeing an almost spontaneous process of change well under way among many of the armies around the world island. We observed, first of all, a shedding of Cold War baggage and attitudes. I was struck particularly by how quickly armies of the world are relinquishing major weapon systems and readjusting their style of war to a light force milieu. Even in large mass armies, such as those around the Asian rim, we saw a process of streamlining and lightening of the forces. Perhaps surprisingly, another interesting phenomenon we observed was an attempt by the officer corps in many of these armies to forego corruption and doctrinaire ideological stances—thus producing a more mature, professional, and better-educated officer class.

It was also somewhat of a shock to discover how knowledgeable of American operational methods many of these officers are. They also are intensely curious about how Americans fight. More specifically, they are interested in our doctrinal focus on the operational art. These armies in many ways have moved into the era that we faced back in the early 1970s. Much as we did, they moved from a tactical focus to one more directed at operational art and operational maneuver. Strategically, they seem bent on deflecting the ability of major world powers to interfere with their own hegemonic ambitions, principally by defeating incursions from air and sea.

They are also turning their attention to information technologies, but they come at it from a different vantage point than we do. The last trip I made was to China. I had a chance to talk to my counterpart in that country. Many of his questions and comments dealt with information technology, information warfare, and so forth. His take was quite interesting. He said,

> General, the information age is neutral; you have your style of war that is facilitated by information technology. It gives you the ability to see with great clarity and to strike with great speed and precision. But in our style of war, information technology is also helpful because the Internet and cellular communications allow us to do what we do best, which is to fight wars of area control; to capitalize on the endurance of our people; to exploit time and the inherent power of forces on the defensive to disperse, to go to ground, to control wide areas of territory, and still to maintain the ability to mass on demand.[1]

The only English term he used during our conversation was "non-nodal Army," as contained in the following sentence delivered in Chinese:" What we seek to build is a non-nodal army." He was saying that modern distributive communications would permit control of massed armies without the necessity of large, cumbersome, hierarchical control headquarters.

Thus as the tectonic plates begin to collide in the post-2010 time frame, they are going to bring with them the possibility of collisions between different styles of warfare along these critical lines of contact. It seems to us that the war in Kosovo may very well have provided a foretaste of how such warfare might play out in the future.

Beyond the year 2010, though we might not see the rise of a true peer competitor, we may very well see the emergence of what was referred to in our AAN study as a "major competitor," one that uses its inherent strengths to counter our inherent weaknesses. In practically every country I visited, when I asked the question, "What are America's military weaknesses?" the answer that came back was "aversion to casualties and the political need to end the war quickly." Therefore, as one officer told me, "Time is our friend and time is your enemy." Another recalled to me the famous response of Ho Chi Minh in 1964 when a French journalist asked him how he could possibly expect to beat the world's most technologically advanced country: "They will kill many of us, we will kill a few of them, and they will tire first."

Major competitors out beyond the year 2010 will not try to re-create a bipolar world. They won't try to match the United States weapon system for weapon system. They will focus on landpower and the ability to maintain an army in being. Their object will not be to defeat the United States, but rather to avoid losing. Meanwhile time will take its toll, or so the thinking goes, on the American popular will, and victory will accrue to our competitor by default. Remember Vietnam?

Now what does all this have to do with America's future relation with Europe? To go back to the AAN war games played in 1997 and 1998, in every one of those war games the critical element in achieving success was the ability of American forces to arrive early and position themselves so as to prevent the enemy from settling in and establishing control over the areas comprising his operational and strategic objectives. And regardless of the site of actual hostilities—in southeastern Europe, in Northeast Asia, or in the Middle East—Europe remained the critical launch platform.

Though we assumed initially that we would be able to project forces from the continental United States early enough to block the enemy on the ground and thwart his operational design, we later found that expectation to be totally unrealistic. Some form of forward stationing, whether of materiel or forces in being, had to be available at strategic intermediate staging bases in Europe. The forces already in Europe were usually the ones that arrived in the theater of hostilities first and applied the initial preemptive counterstroke. This action was critical because if the enemy succeeded in accomplishing his initial objectives, then friction became a problem, time turned against us, casualties began to mount, resolve began to erode, and a successful outcome became extremely problematic.

It thus seemed to us in the AAN business that Europe would continue to have a vital role to play in the maintenance of global security and stability. It sits astride or near the intersection of three of the most active and dangerous strategic tectonic plates. Thus, whether as a site of conflict or solution for conflict, Europe remains critical on proximity grounds alone. Moreover, it represents a secure intermediate staging base that proved decisive in all our war scenarios.

Does that mean that the nature of our forces in Europe should remain immutable? While our games did not answer that question specifically, they seemed to suggest that tasks like humanitarian support, force projection support, C4ISR, forward intelligence support, and forward logistics basing are becoming increasingly important.[2] The possession of a forward logistics base will become particularly essential. It may therefore be that over the next 15 to 20 years the nature and character of forces in the region will change to reflect these growing support priorities. Whatever the precise nature of the forces in Europe, however, the AAN studies, exercises, and war games led me to conclude that Europe will continue to be a critical arena for the maintenance of global security, and that the United States can most efficiently and effectively contribute to such security by retaining appropriate forces in Europe.

ENDNOTES

1.Conversation with PLA senior leaders at the Nanjing Army Command College, Nanjing, China, August 21, 1998.

2.The acronym C4ISR encompasses command, control, communications, computers, intelligence, surveillance, and reconnaissance.

Chapter Eighteen

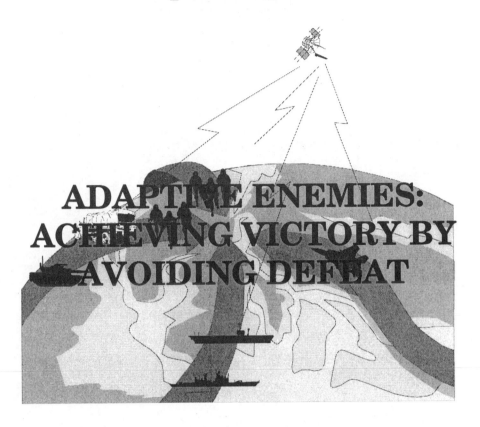

ADAPTIVE ENEMIES: ACHIEVING VICTORY BY AVOIDING DEFEAT

Major General Robert H. Scales, Jr.

Reproduced with Permission Granted by:
JOINT FORCES QUARTERLY
Autumn/Winter 1999-2000
Issue Number 23

Adaptive Enemies: Achieving Victory By Avoiding Defeat

Authors Introductory Note

This article was developed immediately after the war in Kosovo. It is an adaptation of Chapter Four, which was written after a trip to Asia in1998. In the original article that was published by STRATEGIC REVIEW, I suggessted that foreign militaries were beginning to perceive our fixation on a firepower-centered way of war as an exploitable weakness. In fact, some states, armed with experience gained against us in real war, had already begun to evolve a doctrine to counter our superiority in precision. These potential adversaries have concluded that dispersion, deception, patience and a willingness to absorb punishment offers the means to endure precision strike long enough to outlast a technologically superior foe. Subsequent practical experience in Kosovo caused me to modify this argument somewhat, but not much. This essay also introduces my Newton Corollary thesis that suggests the chronicles of military history clearly indicate each dominant military advantage eventually yields to a countervailing response. This battlefield trend is very discernable. Adaptive opponents, moreover, have been learning faster and we must aniticpate a future military challenge that will attempt to defeat our preoccupation with precision strike.

ADAPTIVE ENEMIES: ACHIEVING VICTORY BY AVOIDING DEFEAT

Once the dogs of war are unleashed, and the shooting begins in earnest, conflicts tend to follow unpredictable courses. As Clausewitz warned many times in his military classic,[1] wars are contests between two active, willing opponents both of whom expect to win. Thus an action by one side to gain advantage precipitates a response by the opponent to counter it. Once begun, war with its neatly crafted plans and comforting expectations quickly devolves into a series of stratagems and counter stratagems by both sides as each seeks to retain advantage on the battlefield long enough to gain a decisive end by collapsing the enemy's will to resist.[2]

In spite of its video game image, NATO's war against the Serbs proved to be no exception to the classic Clausewitzian construct. The Serbs sought to overcome a tremendous materiel and techno-logical disadvantage by capitalizing on their own strengths: the ability to gain operational objectives quickly and then disperse in order to avoid the inevitable aerial assault they knew would follow. The Serbs trusted that patience, tenacity, guile and the ability to sequester ground forces throughout the countryside would give them the interval they needed to out wait the resolve of the NATO coalition. This plan, however, did not work. The political will of the NATO coalition proved to be stronger in the end than that of the Serbs. But the skill and

1. Carl Von Clausewitz, *On War*, edited and translated by Michael Howard and Peter Paret, Princeton: Princeton University Press, 1976.

2. This Adaptive Enemy thesis was originally published within the Winter 1999 issue of *Strategic Review*. Major portions of this JFQ essay are reproduced with permission granted by *Strategic Review*.

perseverance of the Serbian army, in the face of an overwhelming onslaught by a thousand or more NATO aircraft armed with precision weapons, present us with a compelling demonstration of a thinking, creative, and adaptive opponent who can foil the best prepared plans of a superior opponent simply by capitalizing on his own inherent strengths while minimizing those of the opposition.

For the last fifty years the militaries of the Western powers, and particularly the United States, have been remarkably consistent in how they have chosen to go to war. We have inherited the remarkable ability to translate technological innovation, industrial capacity and national wealth into effective battlefield advantages because of our enormous defense expenditures during the Cold War. However, in this new era of limited wars, our commitment to limited ends now demands the use of limited means. Therefore, the lives of our soldiers have become our most precious resource and we increasingly seek to develop a method of war that will replace manpower expenditures with an ever multiplying expenditure of firepower.

But as we have seen in Kosovo, our future enemies are watching. They understand our preoccupation with firepower. Therefore, we should not be surprised when we encounter a future opponent who has learned how to nullify our firepower advantage. We have consistently been slow to perceive the growing effectiveness of the opposition in part because of a characteristic Western arrogance that presumes that, to be a challenge, non-Western militaries must either symmetrically challenge us or mimic Western ways of war. As a result, the growing skill among non-Western militaries at countering our firepower centered method of war has remained shrouded in the shadows of unfamiliar military cultures. Thus, U.S. military analysts have missed much of the discourse and experimentation occurring among thinking military institutions outside the West due in part to the cultural schism that divides the world's advanced industrial democracies from the other four-fifths of the planet.

The Serbs were certainly not the first opponent to demonstrate adaptive strategies against our Western way of war. More than five decades ago, the Japanese demonstrated their analytical ability to survive America's firepower intensive attacks during the closing months of the Pacific campaign in World War II. During the battles of 1943 and 1944, the Americans won a series of quick and decisive victories by using the mobility and firepower of their amphibious forces. But the Japanese carefully observed this method of attack and by the end of 1944 they had entirely revamped their defensive plans for the islands that guarded the approaches to their Homeland.

In Okinawa, the Japanese abandoned their failed doctrine of beach defense and buried their force under a vast array of pillboxes, switch lines, and deep bunkers to carry out an extended defensive scheme centered in the southern portion of Okinawa. The Japanese recognized that they could never match American firepower, but they maximized what little firepower they had by using mortars and artillery in sufficient numbers and with enough deadly effect so as not to completely cede the firepower advantage to the Americans. Fighting their way through deep defensive lines, the Marines and Soldiers eventually took the island and destroyed the Japanese Tenth Army—with approximately 70,000 Japanese soldiers and 70,000 Japanese civilians killed. But the U.S. casualty bill for the island fighting was horrendous: 65,631 killed or wounded.

The Chinese Civil War:

Soon thereafter, another effort to redefine and codify an Eastern approach to defeating the Western way of war began in the mountain fastness of Manchuria immediately after the end of the Pacific war. Mao Tse-tung and his marshals developed a body of doctrine adapted from their successful wartime guerrilla campaigns and modified their concepts to fit the demands of a conventional war fought against an enemy superior in technology and materiel.[3] Mao perfected his new way of war against the nationalists during the Chinese Civil War fought between 1946 and 1949. His concepts were simple and centered around three tenets, the first and most important of which was "area control." To be successful Mao's army first needed to survive in the midst of a larger, better-equipped enemy.[4] To ensure survival he divided his army into small units and scattered them across a broad expanse of territory. Controlling and maintaining cohesion among such a disparate and scattered force was and remained his greatest challenge.

Once his force was supportable and stable, Mao proceeded to apply the second tenet, which was to "isolate and compartmentalize" Nationalist forces. The challenge of this phase was to leverage control of the countryside to such a degree that the enemy gradually retreated into urban areas and along major rail and road lines of communications.[5] The final act of the campaign demanded an ability to find the enemy's weakest points in order to collect and mass overwhelming force against each point sequentially, much as one might take apart a string of pearls, one pearl at a time. Mao's new style of conventional war, while effective, demanded an extraordinary degree of discipline and patience to persevere under extreme hardships. It also demanded the ability to transition quickly from an area control force to a force capable of fighting a war of movement.

---

3. Mao Zedong, "On the International Front Against Fascism," *Selected Works of Mao Tse-Tung,* Vol. III, Beijing: Foreign Language Press, 1967; William H. Whitson, *The Chinese High Command: A History of Communist Politics, 1927-1971,* New York: Praeger Press, 1973.

4. Mao Zedong, *Selected Works of Mao Tse-Tung,* Vol. I and Vol. III, Beijing: Foreign Language Press, 1967.

5. Frederick Fu (F.F.) Liu, *A Military History of Modern China: 1924-1949,* Princeton: Princeton University Press, 1956.

From China to Korea:

Within a year of the end of the Chinese Civil War, the Americans severely tested Mao's methods in Korea. During the early days of the Chinese intervention—beginning in October 1950—the People's Liberation Army (PLA) badly misjudged the killing effect of American artillery and tactical air power. Pushed too quickly into maneuver warfare, the Chinese massed in the open, often in daylight, to expand their control over the northern portions of the Korean Peninsula.[6] They extended their narrow lines of communications farther down the mountainous spine of Korea as they advanced.[7] But they soon found their logistic support exposed to the terrible effects of American air power. The Chinese paid a horrific price for their haste. Their spring 1951 offensive sputtered to a halt as U.S. artillery and aerial firepower slaughtered Chinese soldiers in masses, while air interdiction cut their supply lines and forced a retreat back across the Han.

Brutal experiences led quickly to sober lessons relearned from the Chinese Civil War. As a highly skilled complex adaptive system, the Chinese Army quickly adjusted to the actual conditions of this new war. Over the next two years, subsequent Chinese attacks remained limited and controlled. The Chinese high command learned to hold most key logistic facilities north of the Yalu River well out of reach of U.S. air attacks. South of the river the Chinese dispersed and hid their forces while they massed only in the period immediately before launching an attack. PLA soldiers moved at night and chiseled their front lines of resistance deep into hard, granite mountains. American casualties soon mounted, while the Chinese stabilized their

---

6. Bin Yu, "What China Learned from Its Forgotten War in Korea," *Strategic Review*, Summer 1998.

7. Russell Spurr, *Enter the Dragon: China's Undeclared War Against the U.S. in Korea, 1950-51,* New York: Newmarket Press, 1987.

casualties at a rate acceptable to their political leadership. Far more Americans died in combat during this "stability phase" of the war than during the earlier period of fluid warfare. A cost acceptable to the Chinese became too costly to the Americans. The result was an operational and strategic stalemate. To the Chinese, stalemate equaled victory.[8]

From Korea To Vietnam:

Over the next two decades the Vietnamese borrowed extensively from the Chinese experience and found creative ways to lessen the killing effect of firepower, first against the French and then against the Americans. The Vietnamese also proved highly skilled in adapting to the new challenges posed by their Western opponents. The Viet Minh based their tactical and operational approach on Mao's unconventional methods. Their conduct of the battle was remarkably reminiscent of siege operations conducted by the PLA during the Chinese Civil War. In both cases the secret of success proved to be dispersion and careful preparation of the battlefield. The Viet Minh remained scattered in small units whenever possible to offer smaller, and thus less detectable and less lucrative targets, and to allow their troops to live off the land. Fewer supply lines and logistic sites offered even fewer opportunities for interdiction fires.

To win, the Chinese, and eventually the Viet Minh, needed to attack. Successful attacks demanded the ability to mass, at least temporarily. The Viet Minh needed to exercise great care in massing under the enemy's umbrella of protective firepower. Superior intelligence provided sufficient information to select the right time and place. Their ability to collect and orchestrate the movement of tens

8. T.R. Fehrenbach, *This Kind of War*, New York: The Macmillan Company, 1963.

of thousands of soldiers at just the right moment allowed attacking forces to collapse the enemy's defenses before French firepower could regain the advantage. This remarkable ability to "maneuver under fire" perfected against the Nationalist Chinese and the French, reached new levels of refinement during the second Indo-China War against the United States.

General Giap learned quickly to accommodate his strategic plans to the new realities imposed by American firepower. The North Vietnamese relearned the importance of dispersion and patience. They redistributed their forces to keep their most vulnerable units outside the range of American artillery while they moved their logistic system away from battle areas into sanctuaries relatively safe from aerial detection and strikes. Thus, the VC and NVA dusted off and applied many of the same methods that had proven useful in previous Asian wars against Western style armies.

From Vietnam to Afghanistan:

Half a decade later, and half a continent away in Afghanistan, the Soviets learned the same harsh, firsthand lessons of overconfidence when first-world military organizations confront third-world militaries which have the will, tenacity, and skill to remain effective in the field despite complete firepower inferiority. Year after year, the Soviets arrayed themselves for conventional combat and pushed methodically up the Panjir Valley only to be expelled a few months later by a seemingly endless and psychologically debilitating series of methodical and well-placed ambuscades and minor skirmishes. Borrowing a page from the American textbook in Vietnam, the Soviets tried to exploit the firepower, speed, and intimidating potential of armed helicopters. They employed helicopters principally as convoy escorts and to provide fire support. At times, Hind helicopters proved enormously lethal and effective, particularly early in the war, when the Mujahideen were psychologically unprepared. But the

Mujahideen eventually borrowed a page from the Vietnamese textbook. They first learned to employ heavy antiaircraft machine guns and later Stinger shoulder-fired missiles to shoot the gunships down in increasing numbers. The result of military frustration and defeat in Afghanistan presaged the collapse of the Soviet Union.

Israel and the Middle East:

Beginning in 1982, after nearly three decades of failure in open warfare, an alliance of Arab state and non-state actors pushed Israeli mechanized forces out of Beirut. Back streets, tall buildings, and other forms of urban clutter provided the Arabs just enough respite from the firepower intensive methods of the Israelis to wear away Israeli morale both in the field and at home. Unable to bring the full force of their superior maneuverability and shock effect to bear, the Israelis paused just short of their operational objectives. Excessive casualties and the public images of bloody excesses on both sides eventually resulted in an Israeli withdrawal from Beirut. This success in Beirut soon provided Israel's enemies in the region with a new and promising method to offset the Israeli superiority in open mechanized combat. Now a spectrum of low-tech threats, that run the gamut from weapons of mass destruction delivered by crude ballistic missiles, to random acts of terrorism, to children throwing rocks at soldiers, confront an increasingly frustrated Israeli military and public.

One of the more curious ironies of the recent wars in the Middle East has been the fact that Western style militaries have had great success when fighting against non-Western enemies who mimic Western firepower doctrines. The Gulf War is the most recent example of failed efforts by Arab states stretching back through the conflicts in the Middle East to 1948. In 1973, Arab armies enjoyed some measure of success while employing Western methods, but their success was as much due to Israeli overconfidence as to the limited aims the Arabs sought.

Operation Desert Storm:

During the Gulf War, despite an extraordinary level of incompetence at the highest level of the Iraqi leadership, the Iraqi Army displayed considerable capacity to adapt on the battlefield. As the American air campaign began to focus on the destruction of the Iraqi ground forces in the Kuwait Theater of Operations (KTO) in early February, the Iraqis almost immediately began to adapt in order to limit their losses.[9] By constructing berms around their tanks and by scattering them widely across the desert, the Iraqis insured that an aircraft dropping precision-guided bombs would only be able, at best, to destroy a single vehicle with each pass. By burning tires next to operational vehicles they spoofed their tormentors into missing the real targets; and finally by using antiaircraft effectively they kept a substantial portion of coalition aircraft at an altitude where they were unable to do substantial damage.

The best trained Iraqi units endured several weeks of allied air bombardment with unbroken will and their combat capability essentially intact. The most impressive indication of the Iraqi ability to adapt came in the operational movement of a substantial portion of the Republican Guard during the first hours of Desert Storm. Elements of two divisions shifted from a southeastern defensive orientation to defensive positions facing to the southwest along the Wadi al-Batin. In those positions the Tawakalna Republican Guard Division and the 50th and 37th Armored Brigades would be destroyed by the U.S. VII Corps.[10] Nevertheless, sacrifice by these units provided time for the remainder of the Republican Guard to escape. Significantly, the Republican Guard carried out this movement in terrain and weather conditions ideally suited

---

9.   Robert H. Scales, *Certain Victory: The U.S. Army in the Gulf War,* Washington, DC: Office of the Chief of Staff United States Army, 1993.

10. Scales, *op. cit.*

to interdiction and despite the overwhelming superiority of coalition air power.

NATO and Kosovo:

Placed in suitable historical context, the Serbian response to the NATO onslaught is nothing more than another data point along a continuum of progressive, predictable adaptation by technologically dispossessed militaries who are willing to challenge Western militaries armed with superior precision firepower. Like their fellow Asian travelers, the Serbs sought victory by avoiding defeat. In a similar fashion, the Serbs conceded the vertical dimension of the battlespace to NATO. They were content with an approach that only hoped to shoot down a few allied aircraft using ground mounted guns and missiles. This hope was underscored with the expectation that a few dead or captured allied airmen would contribute to the gradual degradation of NATO's resolve. Even if a shoot down was not possible, the Serbian force sought to keep their antiaircraft assets sufficiently viable because they knew ground targets would be difficult to spot from high altitudes.

The surest way for the Serbians to avoid defeat was to keep their army in the field viable — both to act as a defiant symbol of national resolve and to be the legitimate Serbian guarantor of sovereignty over the occupied territory. To maintain an effective "army in being," the Serbs likewise borrowed from successful past precedents. Units quickly went to ground, and dispersed across a broad expanse of territory. They quickly computed the pace at which the allies could find, target, and strike uncovered targets and then devised the means to relocate mobile targets inside the allied sensor-to-shooter envelope. Camouflage, decoys and spoofing techniques proven so effective by Asian armies were repeated with varying degrees of success by the Serbs. As the allies became more proficient at spotting troops, the Serbs sought even greater dispersal and went deeper to ground.

Toward the end of the conflict, significant success from the air came with the appearance of an infant ground presence in Kosovo in the form of the Kosovo Liberation Army. The KLA was not terribly effective in open combat against the better armed Serbs but the presence of large scale KLA units amongst them forced the Serbs to come out of protective cover and mass. The results were predictable and remarkably consistent with past experiences in combat against the Chinese and NVA. Troops moving, massed, and in the open present the most lucrative targets for destruction by fire from the air. Yet the Serbian army was never severely damaged because it was simply too large and well protected to be completely destroyed from the air. Since total destruction was not feasible, as in all battles of attrition, the contest in Kosovo soon devolved into a test of time and will. Ultimate victory would be achieved by the side that could endure the longest without collapsing their national resolve. Once it became evident to Milosevic that NATO's political resolve would not be broken before a threatened ground assault could materialize, he chose, as always, the most expedient path. Seeking to ensure his own political survival, the Serbian leader ceded Kosovo to the Allies.

Implications for the Future:

The example of Kosovo again reinforces the conclusion that non-Western militaries are increasingly internalizing the lessons of recent wars against technologically superior foes. Recent thoughts and writings concerning the operational and tactical problems confronting them in a fight against Western style military organizations suggest some clear warnings for the future.

First, non-Western militaries understand that the West does possess vulnerabilities: an aversion to casualties and excessive collateral damage, a sensitivity to domestic and world opinion, and an apparent lack of commitment to prepare for and fight wars that are measured in years

282

rather than months. They also perceive that Americans, in particular, still remain committed to a style of war focused primarily on the single offensive dimension of precision strike. Moreover, they are already thinking about how to target Western vulnerabilities while capitalizing on their three intrinsic advantages: time, will, and the inherent power of the defensive. Taking a page from Mao and Giap's strategy, our potential future opponents have learned the value of time and patience. From their perspective, swift success is not essential to achieve ultimate victory.

Future adversaries have also discovered the apparent advantages that can be gained when they interfere with an intruding power's intention to end the conflict quickly and at minimum cost. Thus, the logic of their strategy will lead to efforts that impede rather than prevent the intrusion of a Western opponent. In recent wars, non-Western armies have learned to limit the damage and duration of air campaigns by dispersing their forces in the field and by distributing telecommunications, logistics, and transportation infrastructures as widely as possible. Moreover, they understand that sophisticated air defense networks, whose effectiveness depends on airfields, surface to air missile sites, and complicated and vulnerable command and control nodes, have become more of a liability than an asset.

Once conflict on the ground begins, potential opponents understand they must capitalize on their superior mass to offset the lethal firepower and precision technology of Western armies. They will capitalize on the positional advantages of being on the defensive in or near their own territory. As they gain confidence, they will search for opportunities to mass sufficient force to achieve local successes. As in the air campaign, the enemy will seek to frustrate Western ground forces by employing just enough modern weaponry to extend the campaign indefinitely. A few precision cruise missiles against major logistic bases will add to the casualty bill that Western militaries must explain to their civilian populations back home. The object will not be decisive victory, but rather stalemate. More importantly, a stalemate arrangement will inevitably result in the erosion of Western political support for the conflict, especially if it is sustained for any prolonged period of time.

Early Signals of Change:

As non-Western militaries develop concepts for defeating the American firepower-centered method of war, the character and composition of their forces will slowly change. The impulse that existed during the Cold War to mimic Western force structures is rapidly disappearing. Foreign militaries that were once Cold War clones are taking on identities unique to their own culture and societies. The mountains of metal, consisting of expensive yet often second-rate air, sea, and ground machines of war that today serve as potentially lucrative targets in a conflict against modern Western militaries are rapidly disappearing. Non-Western armies, in particular, are getting lighter. The need to survive and remain effective against the threat of overwhelming Western killing power is forcing them to develop means to disperse, hide, or if possible eliminate the vulnerable logistics, transportation, and telecommunications facilities that now characterize the Western way of war.

Evidence of this trend lies in the shopping lists of many wealthier non-Western militaries. Instead of investing in sophisticated aircraft and blue water fleets, most are purchasing or developing cheap weapons of mass destruction and methods of delivering those weapons. Mines, both sea and land, as well as distributed air defense weapons add credence to the conclusion that the intent of these militaries is to use such weapons as a means to keep potential enemies at bay. Most defense expenditures and attention are going toward land forces because armies provide political legitimacy in non-democratic states. They are also the most useful instrument for regional wars of aggression, as well as the surest means for suppressing internal dissent and thwarting troublesome outsiders.

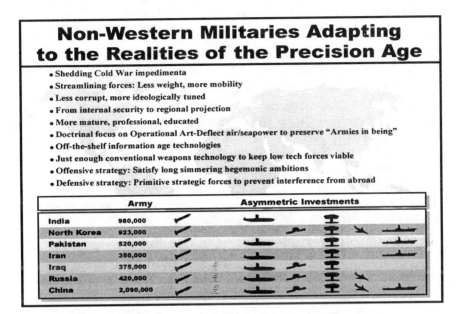

Non-Western Militaries Adapting to the Realities of the Precision Age

- Shedding Cold War impedimenta
- Streamlining forces: Less weight, more mobility
- Less corrupt, more ideologically tuned
- From internal security to regional projection
- More mature, professional, educated
- Doctrinal focus on Operational Art-Deflect air/seapower to preserve "Armies in being"
- Off-the-shelf information age technologies
- Just enough conventional weapons technology to keep low tech forces viable
- Offensive strategy: Satisfy long simmering hegemonic ambitions
- Defensive strategy: Primitive strategic forces to prevent interference from abroad

	Army	Asymmetric Investments
India	980,000	
North Korea	923,000	
Pakistan	520,000	
Iran	350,000	
Iraq	375,000	
Russia	420,000	
China	2,090,000	

The Information Age Is Neutral:

At present there are too many in the U.S. and other Western military organizations who believe that they can best address the appearance of a major competitor in the next century by exploring the technologies of the information age to develop ever more effective means of finding the enemy and killing him from a distance. There are, unfortunately, a number of troubling concerns with this premise. The most obvious is that the information revolution will be neutral in this looming competition; in fact it may favor the competition more than it favors Western militaries because potential enemies will be able to tailor new technologies to their particular style of war without becoming information-dependent. On one hand, the increasing flow of information is quite literally drowning commanders, staffs, and intelligence organizations. This information overload challenge is one of the crucial by-products of the information age—one that we have yet to solve. The evidence is already clear that information technology will not simplify the decision-making process, but in fact makes it more complex. Our future opponents, however, given their expectations and aims, will require much less information to strike effectively—particularly since their aim is not to win a decisive victory. They will be, moreover, less dependent upon the microchip to conduct their method of warfare. A thinking opponent will quickly realize that our intensive reliance on information age technologies becomes a weakness that can become an asymmetric target.

A reading of current military writing from abroad, particularly Asia, reveals that many armies are already placing extraordinary emphasis on information operations and information warfare. At present, American analysts are taking considerable comfort in the observation that few have made serious investment toward either information warfare or precision systems similar to those possessed by Western military organizations. What, however, they fail to see is that Asian armies already understand that advances in information technologies will favor their style of warfare just as much as it does the western style. In particular, the Internet and wireless, non-nodal communications will allow dispersed armies to mass rapidly. As information becomes more secure and information centers more dispersed and less vulnerable, potential opponents will wield more flexible and agile land forces. Moreover, they will be able to divide their forces into smaller and thus less detectable increments. In perhaps one of the strangest potential ironies of the future, Western information technology may well provide non-Western armies solutions to two vexing problems. First, cellular technology and the Internet may allow them to maintain a concert of action for long periods among widely dispersed units. Second, these same technologies will allow them to orchestrate the rapid massing of dispersed units when opportunities arise to transition onto the offensive.

The result may well be a technological foot race that either side could win. As we develop the technologies to find and kill an enemy, our potential opponents will develop the technologies to become even more difficult to find. The prospect becomes even more sobering when one considers the fact that the commercial sector is now in the process of providing future competitors with the tools they need, as our research centers continue to perfect non-nodal, distributed, and netcentric global information technologies for paying customers on a world-wide basis. Moreover, potential U.S. opponents do not have to spend a dime for the development of any of these systems. And again we must remember that such opponents have a very different strategy in mind for the next war. They have only to create a stalemate and inflict sufficient casualties on Western forces to raise political difficulties for the political leaders who decided to intervene —in the words of Neville Chamberlain — in "a quarrel in a far away country between people of whom we know nothing."

Defeating the Adaptive Enemy:

Clausewitz provides us with a harsh and accurate warning about the fundamental nature of war:

> War, however, is not the action of a living force upon a lifeless mass (total nonresistance would be no war at all), but always the collision of two living forces. The ultimate aim of waging war ... must be taken as applying to both sides. Once again, there is interaction. So long as I have not overthrown my opponent I am bound to fear he may overthrow me. Thus, I am not in control: he dictates to me as much as I dictate to him.[11]

It is this fundamental Clausewitzian point that Western, and American military organizations in particular, are in

---

11. Carl Von Clausewitz, *On War*, edited and translated by Michael Howard and Peter Paret, p. 77.

danger of forgetting. Our potential opponents in the next century will have thought long and hard about how to attack our weaknesses.

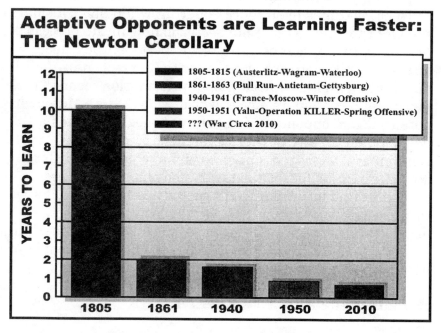

To be sure, firepower can be paralytic in its effect. But paralytic effects by fire are always fleeting. Armies have shown time and again that they can become inured to the paralytic effects of firepower and can even learn creative ways to lessen its destructive effects. Add to this factor the ability of non-Western armies to utilize the advantages of time, mass, will and the power of the defensive, and the single American advantage of superior killing power becomes much less persuasive as an instrument of war than it appears on first consideration.

The corollary to Newton's fundamental law of physics echoes with a sense of urgency: every successful technical or tactical innovation that provides a dominant military advantage eventually yields to a countervailing response that shifts the advantage to the opposing force. America's military dominance in firepower and attrition warfare has been on display for almost five decades. We must anticipate a future military challenge that will attempt to defeat our preoccupation with precision strike. We must use the time we have in the decade ahead to restore balance in our future method of war. Our future arsenal of military capabilities must include a 21st Century sword with two equally compelling edges: precision maneuver as well as precision firepower. Without these two applied in balance and harmony, future conflicts might well devolve into massive wars of attrition. Let's begin now to take on the challenge of a future adaptive enemy and begin now to build a balanced force to defeat him.

INDEX OF SELECTED TERMS

NATO, 38, 236, 237, 238, 249, 252–254, 272–273
  Kosovo and, 281–282

Netherlands, 26

New Look, 25–26

Newton, Isaac, 86, 288

New Zealand, 237

Noriega, 103

North Korea, 57

North Vietnam, air campaign against, 35

North Vietnamese Army (NVA), 50–51, 278

Office of the Assistant Secretary of the Army for Research, Development and Acquisition (OASARDA), 199, 201

Okinawa, 46–47, 116, 208, 274

Operational art, 114

Operation Desert Storm. *See* Gulf War

Operations
  future wars and, 119–124
  limited wars and changes in, 103–106
  split-based, 180

Organization of American States, 237

Pacific Rim, national interests in, 133

Panama, 103

Partnership for Peace effort, 252

Peer competitors, 169

Pentomic reorganization, 163

People's Liberation Army (PLA), 48–49, 53, 276

Persian Gulf War. *See* Gulf War

Planning, shift from threat-based to capabilities-based, 131–132

Political purposes, future wars and, 70–71

Politics, limited wars and domestic, 94

Pork Chop Hill, 79–80, 95

Potential force, 165–166

Powell, Colin L., 131–132

Precision Age. *See* Limited wars

Precision firepower. *See* Firepower

President's National Security Strategy, 132

Programmed force, 165

Program Objective Memorandum (POM), 165

Psychological collapse, 15, 162
  in future wars, 117
  in Gulf War, 140

Rand Corp., 199

Regional hegemons, 127–130

ABOUT THE AUTHOR

Major General Robert H. Scales, Jr., became the 44th Commandant of the U.S. Army War College in August 1997. Before moving to Carlisle Barracks, Pennsylvania, he was the Deputy Chief of Staff for Base Operations and the Deputy Chief of Staff for Doctrine at the Training and Doctrine Command Headquarters, Fort Monroe, Virginia. He is a 1966 graduate from the United States Military Academy and he later received a Masters and Ph.D. in history from Duke University.

Commissioned as a field artillery officer, General Scales served in numerous command and staff positions throughout the Army. His commands include four artillery batteries, two in Germany and two in Vietnam; an artillery battalion in Korea and the U.S. Army Field Artillery Training Center, Fort Sill, Oklahoma. He also served as the Assistant Division Commander, 2d Infantry Division, Eighth U.S. Army.

His decorations include the Distinguished Service Medal, Silver Star, Legion of Merit with four Oak Leaf Clusters, the Bronze Star Medal, Meritorious Service Medal with four Oak Leaf Clusters and the Air Medal. He wears the Senior Parachutist Badge, the Army Staff Badge and the Ranger Tab.

General Scales is the principal author of *Certain Victory*, the 1993 official Army account of the Gulf War. His latest book, *Firepower in Limited War*, is a 1994 publication that outlines the history of fire support in post-World War II conflicts. During the past four years, General Scales has published numerous articles within several European and American defense journals. In November 2000 he retired from active duty.